The Revised

Knit, Cut and Sew:

Book 2

PAM TURBETT

BY THE SAME AUTHOR

"Cut and Sew: Working with Machine-Knitted Fabrics" published by Batsford, 1985
"The Techniques of Cut and Sew" published by Batsford, 1988
"Knit, Cut and Sew: the Basics" published by Pam Turbett: 1st. edit. 1989, 2nd. edit. 1990
"The Revised Knit, Cut and Sew: Book 1" published by Pam Turbett, 1993

COPYRIGHT PAM TURBETT, July 1994
All rights reserved. No part of this publication may be reproduced in any form or by any other means without permission from the author.

PUBLISHED, 1994, by PAM TURBETT, 17 Forest Rise, Liss Forest, Hants. GU33 7AU.
British Library Cataloguing in Publication Data
A catalogue record for this book is available from the British Library

ISBN 0 9514487 3 0

Designed and produced by Pam Turbett
All illustrations by Pam Turbett except where otherwise credited

Printed and bound in Great Britain by Biddles Ltd., Guildford and King's Lynn

CONTENTS

	Page
ACKNOWLEDGMENTS	4
INTRODUCTION	4
Chapter 1 UPDATING 'BOOK 1'	5-7
Chapter 2 PATTERN ALTERATIONS: (Large busts. Rounded shoulders)	8-12
Chapter 3 DARTS	13-15
Chapter 4 PIPING	16-19
Chapter 5 COLLARS AND NECKLINES	20-30
Chapter 6 SLEEVES	31-43
Chapter 7 SHOULDER PADS	44-48
Chapter 8 POCKETS	49-59
Chapter 9 BUTTONS AND BUTTONHOLES	60-70
Chapter 10 ZIPS	71-77
Chapter 11 SKIRTS (Fitting and applying waistbands)	78-85
Chapter 12 BINDINGS	86-91
Chapter 13 LININGS	92-96
Chapter 14 PATCHWORK AND QUILTING	97-102
Chapter 15 APPLIQUÉ ON KNITTED FABRICS	103-106
Chapter 16 MAKING A SIMPLE, CUT-AND-SEW TAILORED SKIRT	107-108
Appendix 1. Recommended Reading	109
Appendix 2 Suppliers	110
INDEX	111-112

ABBREVIATIONS are used in the diagrams, as follows:

```
R.S. = Right Side      W.S. = Wrong Side      tog. = together
C.F. = Centre Front    C.B. = Centre Back
```

ACKNOWLEDGMENTS

I owe my very grateful thanks, yet again, to all the individuals and organisations listed in my previous books; their contribution to what expertise I have in this field. has been invaluable. I would like to thank the following for more recent information, support and assistance:
Mr. and Mrs. Bull of Harlequin, Manningtree, Essex.
The Handler Textile Corporation of America
The Leicester Thread and Trimming Manufacturers Ltd.,
H. Morgan Hicks, Designer of Knitted Fabrics, Art Inst. of Seattle, U.S.A.
Peggy La Riviere of London

Also Jane Bousefield and Judy Clayton, the most recent of the many ladies who have so kindly knitted fabrics for me - and my wonderful husband without whose generous help and co-operation I would have achieved nothing!

INTRODUCTION

This book is meant to be used in conjunction with (and to follow on from) "The Revised Knit, Cut and Sew; Book 1" (which has the same cover, but in red!) It specifically replaces my earlier book, "The Techniques of Cut and Sew" (Batsford Publishing, 1988) which has long been out of print, and it contains much of the material from that book.

Inevitably, the basic materials change and so do my teaching methods, so I have included an 'updating' chapter which refers back to "The Revised Knit, Cut and Sew: Book 1". I have also included four new items for which I am constantly asked
1. A chapter devoted to clear instructions for altering dressmaking patterns to allow for two of the most common figure problems: i.e. rounded shoulders and a heavy bust.
2. Instructions for making bound buttonholes.
3. A chapter on lining knitted garments, whether made by knitwear techniques or by the cut-and-sew methods which I teach.
4. Instructions for a simple, tailored and lined skirt cut in three panels.

'BOOK 1' was devoted to all the preliminary 'things you need to know' when commencing to make a cut-and-sew garment, from buying a dressmaking pattern and knitting the fabric to making a variety of neatly finished seams and coping with the intricacies of modern sewing-machines and overlockers.

'BOOK 2' explains how to cope with the actual sewing processes which crop up later, during the garment assembly. I have aimed to explain, and illustrate carefully, techniques such as making darts, inserting sleeves, putting on collars, coping with shoulder pads, making pockets, and sewing in zips, etc., always with particular reference to the problems likely to be encountered when using such a volatile medium as domestically machine-knitted fabrics.

'BOOK 1' AND 'BOOK 2', *used together*, provide practically all the necessary information to enable the reader to make a wide variety of high-quality, cut-and-sew clothes from fabrics knitted on domestic knitting-machines.

If you use a knitting-machine and can also sew, there is almost no limit to the beautiful and totally individual clothes you can make - believe me!

Pam Turbett. July 1994.

CHAPTER 1

UPDATING 'BOOK 1'

Since the years when I wrote my two first books on Cut-and-Sew techniques, for Batsford, I have made many more clothes in knitted fabrics, visited countless machine-knitting clubs, met a vast variety of knitters and dressmakers, taught workshop classes, and discussed problems with students, teachers, designers, retailers and manufacturers, both here in the United Kingdom and in the United States.

Some of my own theories have been modified and my way of teaching the techniques has undoubtedly altered. Even during the comparatively short interval between writing this book and the publication of "The Revised Knit, Cut and Sew: Book 1" in February 1993, there have been changes and developments. In addition, my students are constantly presenting me with new and useful ideas so I am well aware that the learning process never stops!

So here are some amendments to 'Book 1' which you should note.

Chapter 1, Equipment for Cut and Sew

Page 6
The Passap Topjet Vario professional-type steam-iron system still seems to be the best buy despite its initial cost, but, to avoid damage and to keep it running smoothly, *do remember to change the crystals in the filter as soon as they turn colour.* Packets of the appropriate filter crystals can be obtained through Bernina or Passap agents and it is worth keeping a packet in reserve. If you use bottled distilled water, or even water which has already been through a kitchen filter-jug, you will considerably prolong the life of the crystals.

Page 9
"Pam's Ham" is a kit for making a tailor's ham - all you otherwise need is the fine dry sawdust for filling it. The kit is obtainable by mail order from me; see Suppliers List on p110.

Page 11
Rotary cutters. I particularly like the 'Fiskars' version which has a very comfortable and well-balanced handle. Rotary cutters are growing more popular, especially for cut-and-sew, because they cut knitted fabrics so neatly and the fabric remains flat. The self-healing cutting-mats (vital because they prevent damage to your table-top) are still expensive but it may be worth investigating the ones sold by retailers of picture-framing equipment.

Page 12
Equipment for Marking. Typist's correcting fluid! Making a truly visible mark to indicate notches, dots, etc. has always been a problem when using dark-coloured knits until one of my students, Cicely Robinson, came up with this brilliant notion. I find that the Pentel Micro-Correct pen is superb for marking as the fine ball-point gives great accuracy. *It does not, wash away with cold water* so be careful where you use it. Most marks are within the seam allowances where they are usually hidden.

Chapter 2, Other fabrics and "Notions"

Page 16. Vilene Fusible Interfacings.

VILENE, whilst still retaining those fusible interfacings listed in Book 1, are now producing several variations of which the following are recommended.

'H410 Stitch Reinforced' is specially designed for tailoring; here the usual Vilene felt-like, non-woven interfacing fabric actually contains lengthwise threads at 6mm (1/8in) intervals which give considerably increased vertical stability and strength. Oddly it is described as being 'non-stretch' when in fact it has quite considerable ability to stretch widthwise. Available in white and charcoal.

'Vilene 280' is a very lightweight, high bulk Vilene Fleece, described as "excellent thermal insulation, breathable, easy to use, stays soft and keeps its shape even after dry-clean and repeated washing". It is *not* fusible so has to be sewn in, but is approximately 1cm(3/8in) thick (a lot bulkier than Quiltex) and most knits cling to it very obligingly. Use it for making quilted garments from knitted fabric. Do the machine-quilting from the right side, making lines of stitching to fit in with the stitch-pattern of the knit.

'Vilene H640' is a thinner volume fleece (4mm thick) which *is* fusible - and -

'Vilene H630' is the same but even thinner.

These are, at the time of writing, still very new and I do not have precise instructions for application but a damp cloth with a medium, dry iron for 15 seconds is indicated.

Page 16. Fusible Woven Interfacings (these are *not* made by Vilene)

I am using fusible woven interfacings more often now, especially for jackets and coats which are to be lined and for which no stretch factor is necessary. Remember that these remove all stretch from the knit except on the bias grain. See Appendix 2 for addresses of suppliers.

'Ultrafine', is a very fine cotton muslin, 90cm(36in) wide, black or white, washable at 60°C and dry-cleanable, works well in softly tailored jackets and is lighter and more drapeable than the rather crisp 'Stayflex'.

'Supersoft' is also an excellent interfacing for tailored coats and jackets; this is a cotton and viscose mixture, 90cm(36in) wide, usually in beige only. Washable at 40°C and dry-cleanable, it gives a really softly draping effect.

Page 17.

Sleeve heads, made by Vilene. If unable to obtain these, try cutting them from Vilene 280 High Bulk Fleece (mentioned on p.92 of *this* book). Simply follow the shape of the top of the Sleeve pattern.

Page 18.

The new *Vilene 'Stitch Reinforced Edge Tape'* is a useful alternative to tape or ribbon for stabilising seams. It is reinforced with lengthwise threads (similar to H410 interfacing) and is fusible. It is actually 2cm wide but is more convenient to use when cut in half lengthwise. Easy to use on the straight shoulder seams but a little more difficult when trying to bend it around the curve of an armhole seam. Also recommended for stabilising lapel break lines, front edges and hems.

Chapter 3, Planning the Cut and Sew Garment

Pages 19 and 29

Item number 5 in the 'programme': "Knit a tension swatch". More recent experience has shown me that the swatch *should be 200 rows long* rather than the 100 rows I stipulated then. This provides a more accurate calculation for the number of rows needed to produce a required length.

Chapter 5, The Fabric: Designing, Knitting and Preparing it

Page 30 - Pressing the Fabric - *o.k. I give in!*

They always say that the ability to change your mind does at least prove that you *have* a mind! Due to my dressmaking background, I have always previously stressed very strongly that the knitted fabric must be thoroughly steam-pressed with the full weight of the iron firmly down on it. This was partly to ensure that no further change in the knit would occur when the seams were pressed. However, I have recently had several students coming to my garment-making workshops with beautifully textured knits, containing acrylic fibres, which they have been very reluctant to 'kill' and flatten, so I have had to re-think this problem rather carefully.

In the end we have managed to compromise very successfully with a 'steaming only' technique - i.e. the iron does not touch the fabric, but, by 'hovering' it closely above and blowing out plenty of steam, the fabric becomes warm and slightly damp. This improves the appearance of the knitted fabric initially and enables it to be patted into shape by gentle finger pressure. When seams are sewn the seam allowances can also be persuaded into position by steaming again, and by applying gentle finger pressure.

I have recently had an opportunity to use the "Steam-It" system (Model 1500). This comprises a metal container into which 1 litre of tap water is poured; the resulting steam rises through a plastic hose and is applied to the knitted fabric through a nozzle; the whole thing looks a bit like a vacuum cleaner but it is amazingly effective for removing creases. There is no flat, heavy surface and the nozzle should not be pressed downwards on the fabric, but knits can be made hot and damp and can then be rendered smooth and even by gently stroking with the hand. This helps to bond the fibres together so that fraying is unlikely. This system actually produces much more even 'flattening' than a normal steam-iron because the knit is not being pushed around and stretched by the weight of the iron. See Suppliers list on p.110

However, a problem still exists if a fusible interfacing is to be used. The pressure required in order to iron it on, with a damp cloth or even with a dry cloth or tissue paper, will flatten the fabric anyway. If you desperately want to retain a really crunchy texture you must either use no interfacing, or use a sew-in interfacing. Alternatively, if the 'lapped' seam technique is used, where the seam allowances are top-stitched in place, pressing seams becomes unnecessary. But remember that the knit should always be at least steamed, otherwise fraying can be a real problem!

Chapter 11:   Finishing Garment edges

Page 65 - Binding 9 (with suede or soft leather)

Use the Hongkong Binding method described on p.45, illustrated on p.46 of Book 1. This works well and looks very effective (and expensive!) when used as a binding edge for unlined wool coats - as one of my students has recently proved! If you buy whole skins, measure and cut the strips very evenly and accurately, using a rotary cutter against a steel or perspex rule.

CHAPTER 2

PATTERN ALTERATIONS
FOR LARGE BUSTS AND ROUNDED SHOULDERS

Pattern adjustments for larger-than-standard waists and hips are comparatively easy to deal with, simply by adding extra width on the vertical seams wherever a larger circumference is needed. However, there are two other problem areas which are rather more difficult to deal with and which crop up very frequently when students in garment-making workshops are checking their paper patterns against their own measurements. These can be described, politely or not, according to your point of view, as *'Well-Endowed Bosoms' and 'Dowagers Humps'*!

Here are some directions for making these adjustments. It is a good idea to try out these alterations on the body by cutting out your revised pattern first from paper, Vilene or old sheeting and making a *toile*. Check, and adjust if required, before risking your knitted fabric.

Adjusting paper patterns for large busts
The 'well-endowed' can be identified as being those who wear a 'C' cup bra' (or larger).
In terms of the bra' industry, an 'A' cup bra' is for a 'small' bust and a 'B' cup bra' is for a 'normal' bust. Dressmaking sizing is based on 'normal' people (actually, I very rarely come across a completely 'normal' figure and when I do, the owner is usually under 30!). Therefore, anyone wearing a C (or larger) cup bra' will need to adjust their paper patterns to allow for both the extra circumference and the extra length required at bust level on the Front section. This is usually achieved by making a dart (or darts), pointing towards the bust point, or by enlarging a dart which is already there. Failure to do this will result in tightness and badly fitting armholes at the Front.

For patterns which already have a bust dart,
1. Hold the Front paper pattern against your figure; check that the shoulder seamline is aligned with your own shoulder-line and that the centre-front line is correctly positioned down the centre of the body.

2. Mark on the pattern, with a felt-tipped pen, the exact position of your own bust point. Label it BP.

3. Re-align the dart, if necessary, so that it points towards the newly-marked bust point. Remember that the dart looks better if it slopes *up*wards towards the bust rather than downwards

4. **Fig. 1.** Cut the pattern from the side, up the centre of the dart between C and D, and on to the bust point (BP). From there cut straight up to a point halfway along the shoulder seamline A-B.

5. **Fig. 2.** Place the pattern on another sheet of paper; open up the cuts so that the gap between the two corners at BP is as follows:
1.3cm(1/2in) for a C-cup bra'; 2cm(3/4in) for a D-cup bra'; 3.2cm(1 1/4in) for a DD-cup bra'.
For larger cup sizes increase the gap proportionately. Stick the paper pattern down on the sheet of paper. Be very accurate about that gap!

6. **Fig.3**. Re-draw the dart so that it aims directly towards BP but ends at least 3cm(1 1/4in) short of it. The two lines which form the dart must be exactly the same length, so point D has

to be moved outwards which gives you an extension on the side seam, and the extra width required. The angle of the line D-E depends upon the amount, if any, of extra width needed at the waistline.

7.   Fig.4. The shoulder-line A-B now has a kink in it; re-draw it as a straight line.

8.   Fig.4 again. You now have extra width but not extra length. Check the fitting of your toile and add extra length at Centre Front (F) if necessary, sloping it back to point E at the side.

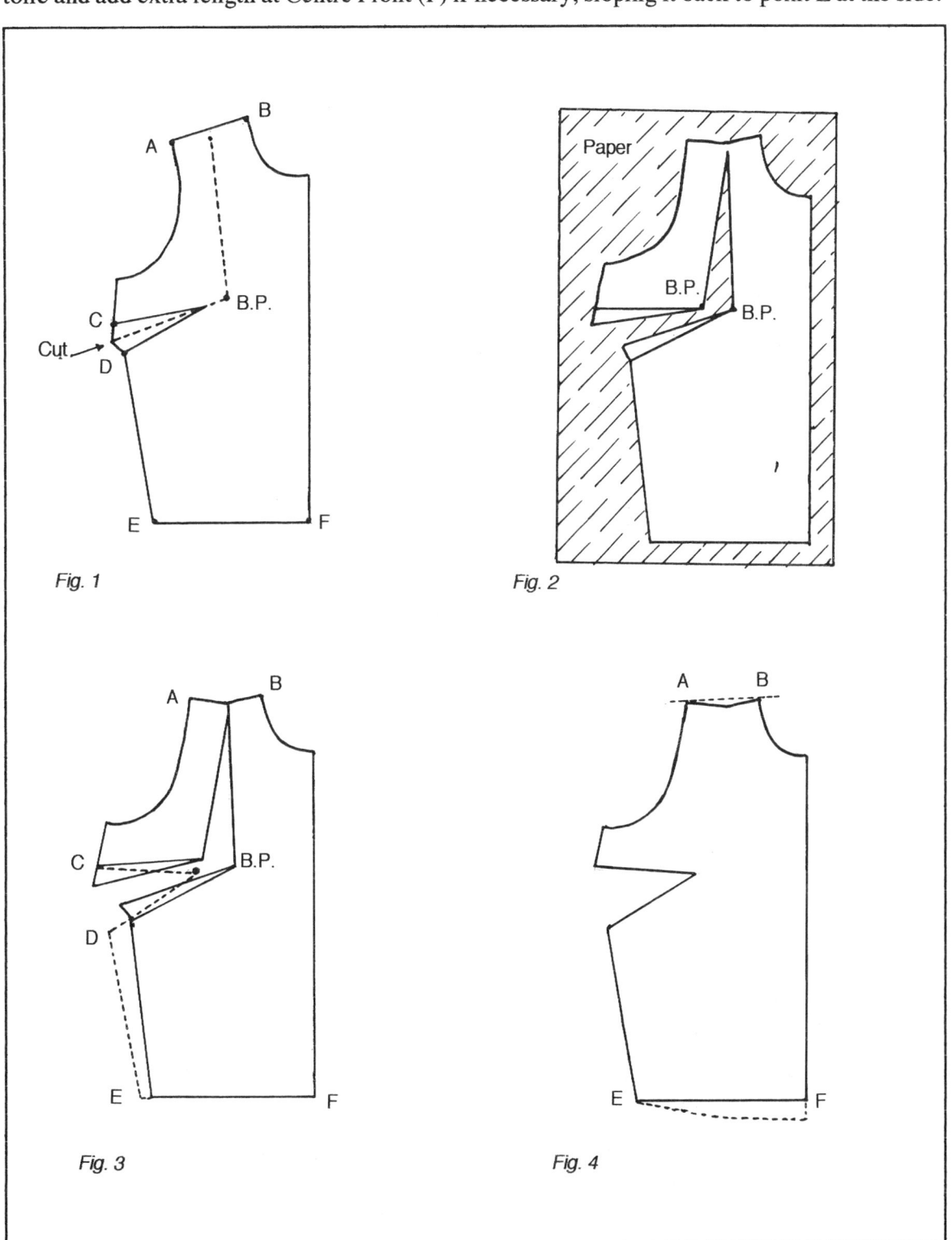

Fig. 1

Fig. 2

Fig. 3

Fig. 4

Page 10

For patterns which have no bust dart
Space for a dart has to be made. This looks complicated but it is a process which is well worth the learning; if you follow the instructions one step at a time you will actually find it quite easy! You will need a sheet of paper a little larger than the paper pattern for the upper Front

1. Check and mark your own bust point on the paper pattern as in para.1 on p.8. Label it BP.

2. **Fig.5.** With the paper flat on a table, rule four straight lines which all meet at B.P.
    A-B.P. from the curve of the armhole.
    B-B.P. slanting upwards from the side.
    C-B.P. from the waistline, parallel with the Centre Front line.
    D-B.P. at right-angles from the Centre Front line.

3. Make three cuts from B, C and D, to B.P.

4. Make one cut from B.P. to A, *only as far as the armhole seamline.*

5. **Fig.6.** Take a sheet of plain paper, a little larger than the garment Front pattern. Roughly halfway across the width, rule two vertical parallel lines. The distance between the lines is *1.3cm(1/2in) for a C-cup bra'; 2cm(3/4in) for a D-cup bra'; 3.2cm(1 1/4in) for a DD-cup bra'.* For larger cup sizes increase the gap proportionately. Label these lines W and X, as shown.

6. Rule a third vertical line, parallel to line X, and label it Y. The distance between lines X and Y is the same as B.P.-D on your paper pattern.

7. Roughly halfway down the plain paper, rule a horizontal line at right angles to lines W,X and Y. Mark point B.P. exactly where this line crosses line X.

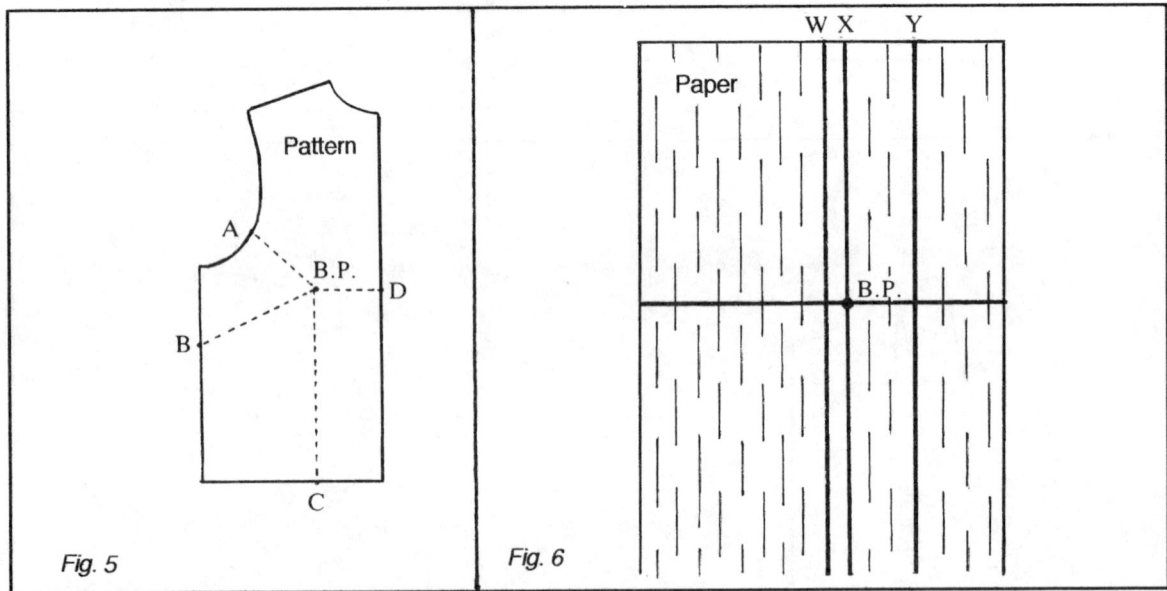

Fig. 5

Fig. 6

8. **Fig.7.** Place the top half of the paper pattern on the plain paper, aligning the B.P. points and keeping the Centre Front line straight on line Y. Spread the cut A-B.P. open until the B.P. mark on the lower armhole section touches line W. Tape these in place. A small crease will form in the armhole seam allowance.

9. Place the two lower pattern pieces on the plain paper, as shown in Fig.7; the *left* side of the line C-B.P. should align with line W; the *right* side of line C-B.P. should align with line X, but should be lowered so that the waistline is straight. The two lines B-BP must meet at BP, on line W; the space between these two lines is now the dart which will be sewn up when

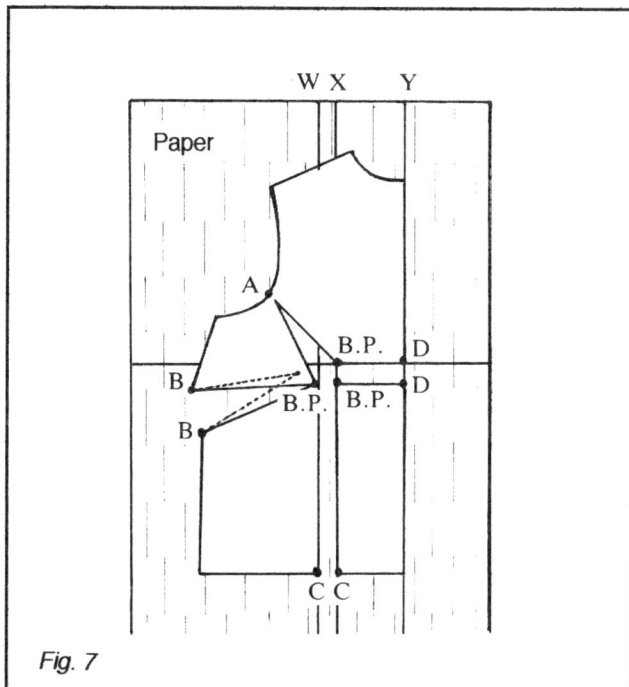

Fig. 7

the garment is constructed, but it is, at this stage, wrongly aligned.

10. Re-draw the dart, keeping the same width at the wide end but pointing it towards BP on line X and making it end 3cm(1 1/4in) short of BP.

Fold out the dart (i.e. close the dart by placing the two lines B-BP so that they are aligned together) and turn it downwards towards the waistline: then cut the paper straight down the side cutting-line. This gives the correct shape at the wide end of the dart.

The waistline is now automatically bigger. If it is too big, adjust at the fitting stage.

Adjusting Paper Patterns for Rounded Backs

Dowager's Humps appear, unfortunately, with advancing age when the top of the spine often starts to curl over to some degree. Sufferers begin to notice that their garments hems are rising at the back and that the back area of the armholes does not fit well. Extra width and extra length need to be added to the Back section of the paper pattern and this is usually achieved by making darts from either the neck seamline or the shoulder seamline.

Again, this appears complicated but is simple if you follow the instructions one step at a time. The rewards in better-fitting clothes are well worth the effort!

First, look carefully at the back of the figure for which the garment is being made. This is difficult if you are making for yourself; use a hand-mirror to see your back view reflected in a full-length mirror.

If the roundness is mainly down the centre of the back, you need darts from the neck seamline.

If the roundness is away from the centre, over the shoulder-blades, make darts from the shoulder seamlines.

In severe cases, darts from both the shoulder and the neckline may be indicated. In closely woven fabrics this doesn't look too good, but with knitted fabrics you can probably get away with it.

1. Fig. 8. Rule and then cut *two lines* on the Back pattern piece, as shown.

The first (W-X), from a point almost halfway down the armhole seamline, straight across to meet the Centre Back line at right angles.

The second (Y-Z), from EITHER
a. a point halfway along the shoulder line
                OR
b. a point on the neck seamline, roughly halfway between the Centre Back and the neck end of the shoulder-line.

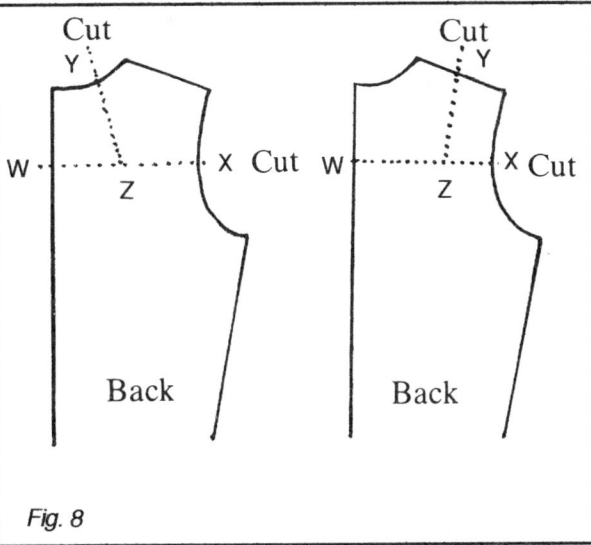

Fig. 8

Which option you choose may depend on the presence of a dart already in one of these positions, which can then be enlarged.

Note: you cannot make a shoulder dart in a design where the shoulder seamline has been dropped towards the garment Front.

2. Fig. 9. Take a sheet of plain paper and spread the cut pieces as shown to form a dart space, either from the neck (Fig.9a) or the shoulder (Fig.9b), and to give extra length down the Centre Back.

Notes

a. The Centre Back cutting line must be kept absolutely straight in line.

b.. The distance between the upper and lower sections at point W depends upon the degree of roundness; 1.25cm(1/2in) may be sufficient for mild roundness; more severely rounded backs may need 5cm(2in) or even more.

c. A small pleat will form in the seam allowance at point X.

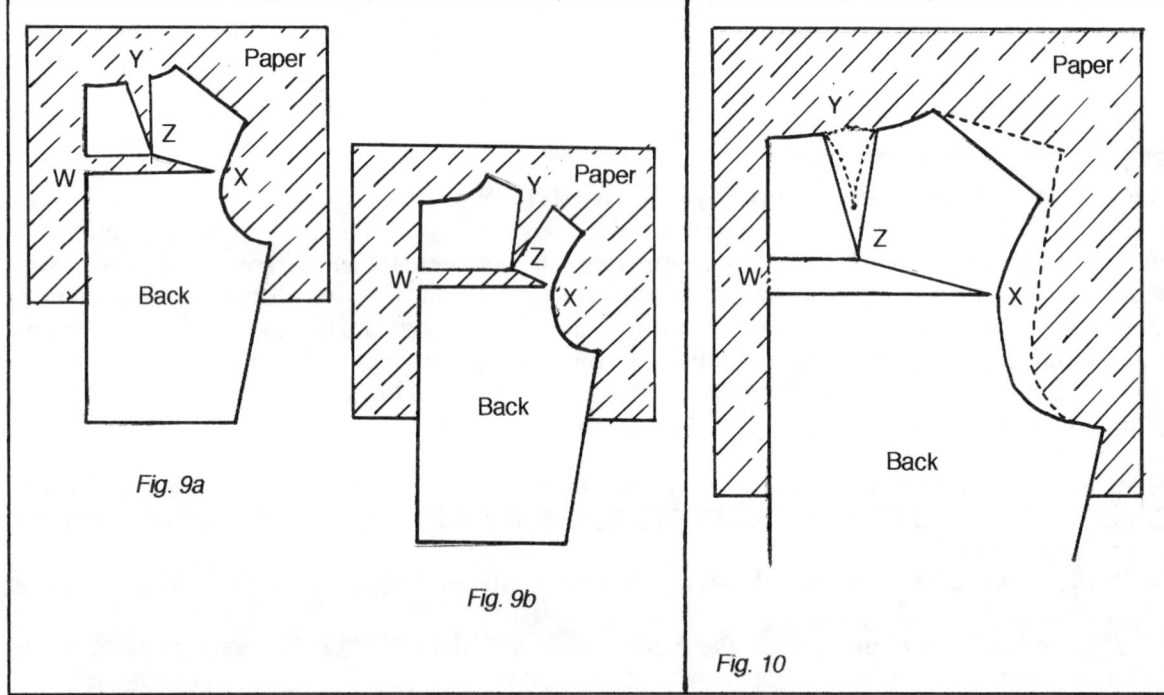

Fig. 9a

Fig. 9b

Fig. 10

3. Fig.10. Draw in the dart, as shown, making it shorter and more curved in shape than the cut made in the pattern paper.

The shoulderline now slopes down too much. Adjust it by raising the outer end until the angle is the same as it was originally. Also re-draw the armhole line, as shown, to allow more width across the shoulder blades.

4. Fig.11. If the back is very rounded below the base of the neck, it is advisable to extend the neck end of the shoulderline inwards, and the height at Centre Back upwards to raise the neckline by 1-2cm(3/8-3/4in) all round. Remember to adjust the Front shoulderline, as shown, to match.

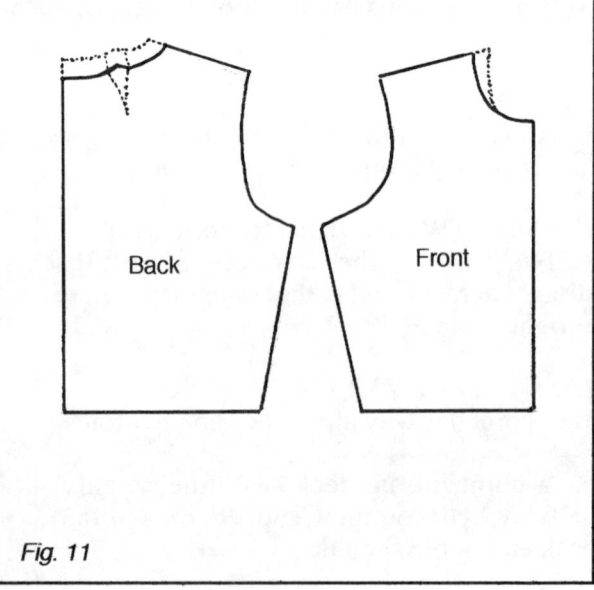

Fig. 11

CHAPTER 3

DARTS

I am devoting a short chapter entirely to the subject of darts because experience has shown me that they can so often go wrong. For cut-and-sew work, it is often possible to eliminate darts by simply easing in the fullness which the dart aims to remove. Try easing first, to see if you like the effect, and then return to the dart if you don't.

A "poke" at the end of a dart is a very common complaint in general dressmaking and, when using knitted fabrics, it is especially important that this does not happen. Fortunately it is an error which is easily overcome with a bit of forethought.

You must understand that a dart is there to shape the fabric over a curved area of the body which is **either** a *convex* shape (Eg. over hip or shoulder - as shown in **Fig.12a.b.c.**)

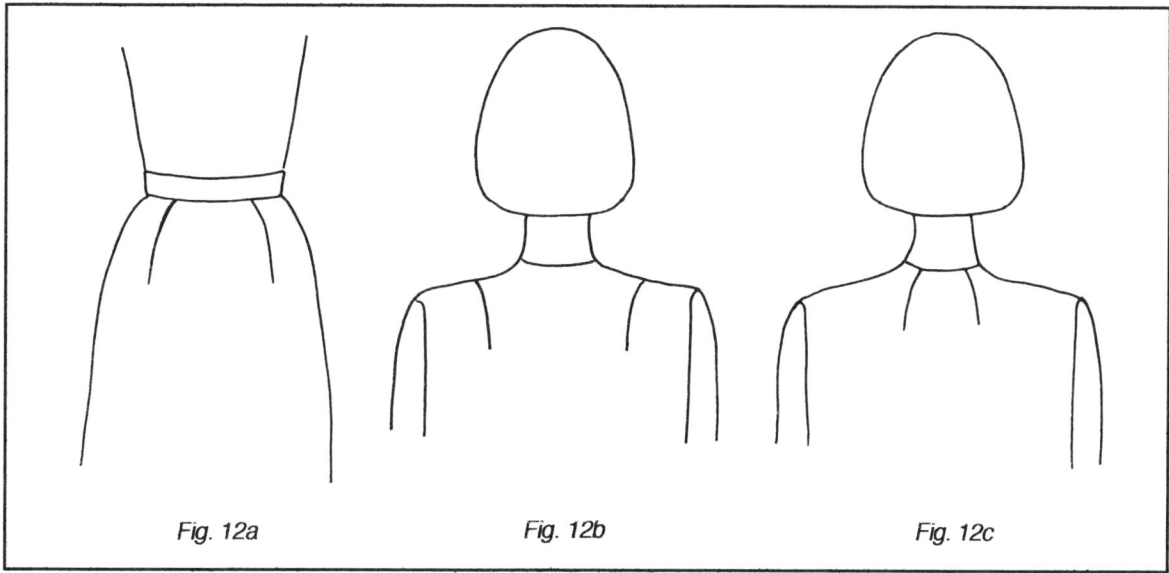

Fig. 12a   *Fig. 12b*   *Fig. 12c*

or a *concave* shape. Eg. from waist or hip level, up to and under the bust; or from the shoulder, rising up the curve of the neck - as shown in **Fig.13a.b**.

Therefore - the sewing-line of the dart is not straight, but curved.

Part of the trouble arises because, on most paper patterns, darts over the hip and stomach are frequently printed as straight lines and beginners naturally assume that they should follow the stitching lines exactly. Occasionally, even darts for concave shapes are shown as straight lines, although this is much less common.

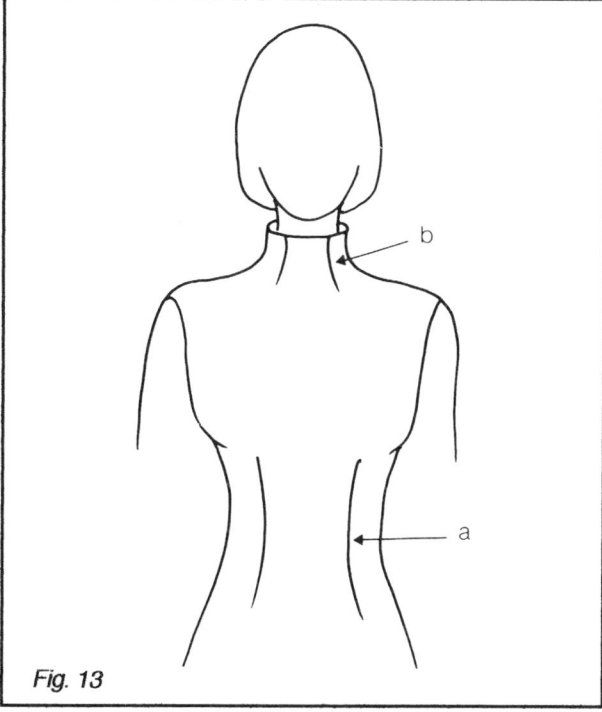

Fig. 13

To sew a dart for a convex shape

(Fig.14) Transfer all pattern lines, or the relevant dots, for the dart to the fabric, using a well-sharpened, coloured cloth-marking pencil. Fold the fabric, matching the marks at the top of the dart, and pin as shown.

Stitch from the wide end to the point, moving out towards the fold rather earlier than is indicated by the pattern lines, and then taper off very gradually so that the stitching merges into the fold without any kind of "peak". The last few stitches should be barely on the edge of the fold.

There is no need to reverse the stitching at the ends of darts: simply reduce the stitch length so that there is no danger of the stitching coming apart. and then cut off the thread ends.

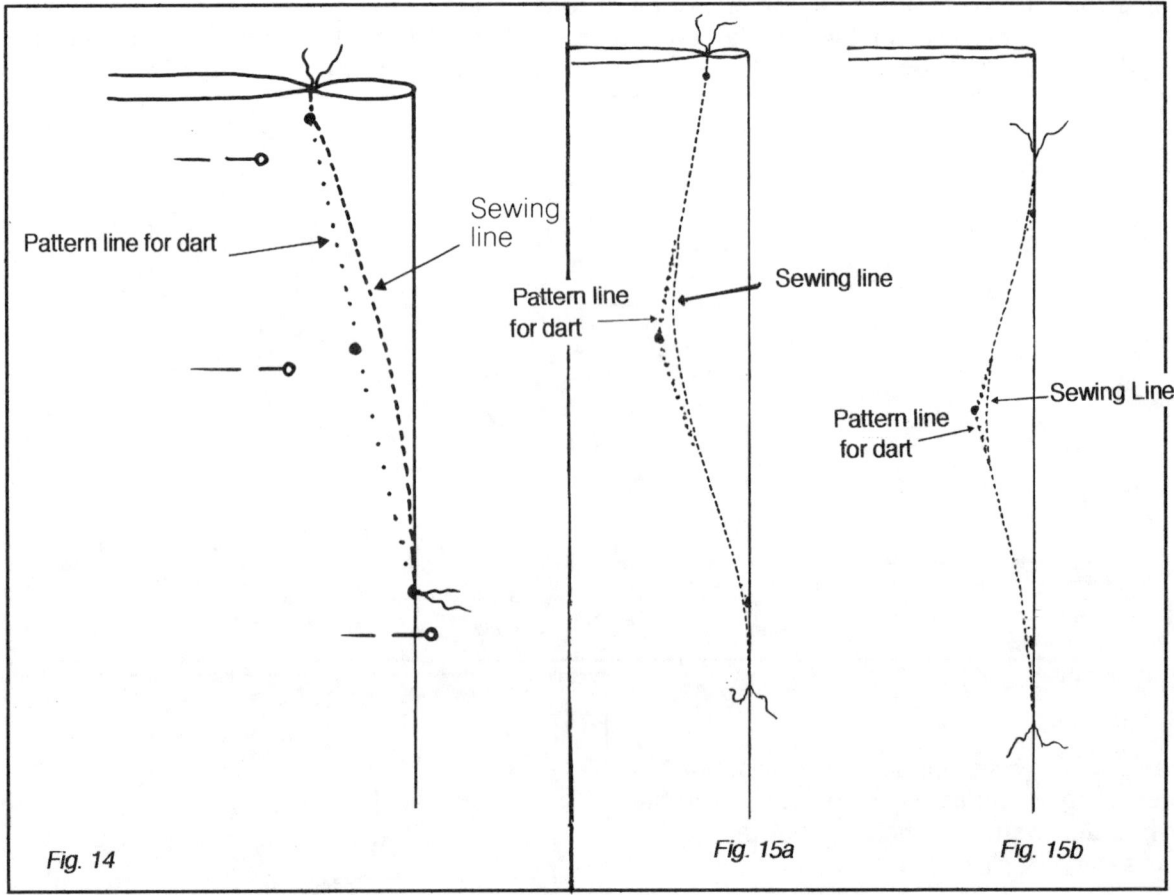

Fig. 14   Fig. 15a   Fig. 15b

To sew a dart for a concave shape

(Figs.15a and b) Transfer pattern marks and pin as shown in Fig.14.
Stitch, following the pattern lines but make sure the widest part of the dart is smoothly curved and that the end (or ends) are tapered off *very* gradually.

The length of the dart depends very much on your own individual contours, but generally waist darts over the stomach are shorter than waist darts at the back.

When trying out a new pattern, always machine-tack the darts before trying on for fitting (use a loose needle-tension so that the stitching can be pulled out easily); then be prepared to shorten or lengthen the darts as necessary.

Bust Darts break the rule!

Any dart which runs towards the bust from the upper side seam, the armhole, the shoulder, the neck, the centre-front seam, (**Fig.16a**), or from a vertical bodice seam (**Fig.16b**) *should actually be sewn as a straight line.*
     The reason for this is simply that a more pointed shape is actually needed there, to cope with the outward thrust of the bust.

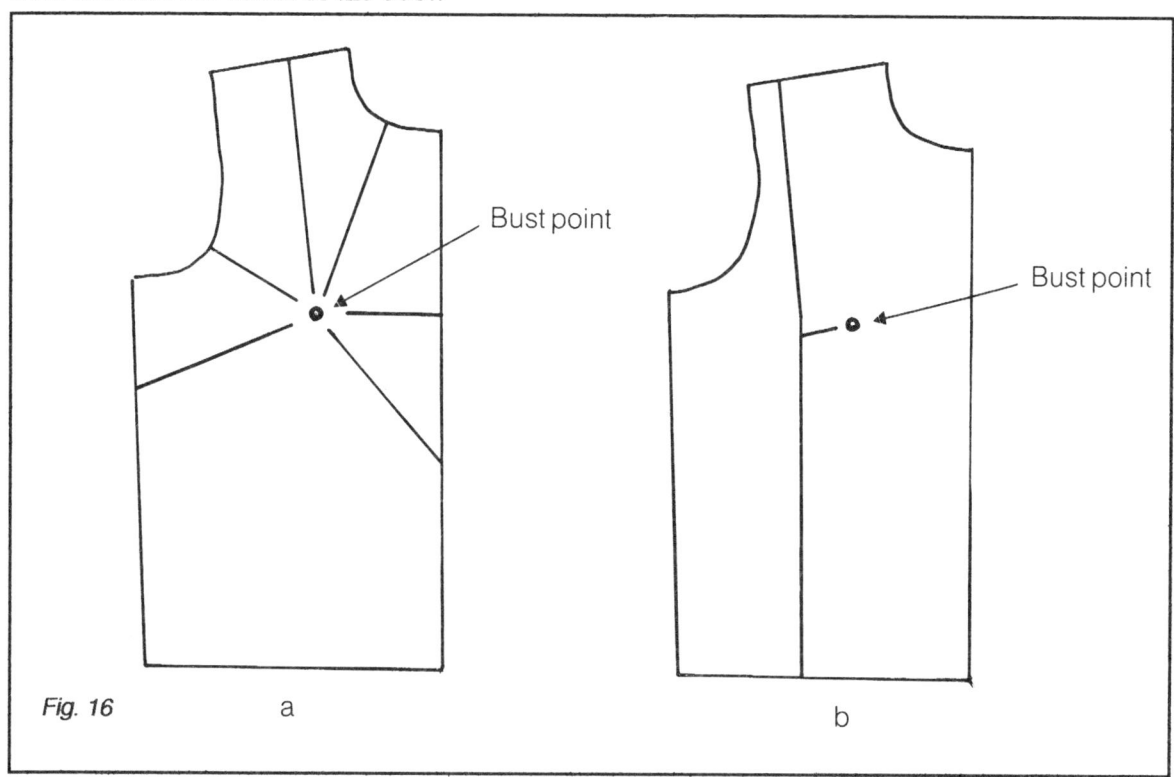

Fig. 16   a   b

Pressing darts

Remember that sewing a dart gives the fabric a three-dimensional shape; therefore the garment piece in which you have made a dart should never again be pressed out flat on a table or ironing-board. This is where the Tailor's Ham, recommended in Book 1 (p.9) comes into its own; its curved surface is ideal for the task. See p.5 and p.110 of this book for details of a kit, available on mail order, for making a Tailor's Ham
     Press on the wrong side of the fabric. *Horizontal darts should generally be pressed downwards* and *vertical darts should generally be pressed towards the centre of the body.* When lining a garment however, press the darts on the lining the opposite way to those on the garment in order to avoid unnecessary bulk. If you are using a rather bulky knitted fabric, it will probably be advisable to cut the dart down its fold and to press it open flat. Cut as near to the point as you dare without endangering the stability of the fabric.
     Note: Do check that any darts in the paper pattern are actually in the right position to fit your particular figure.
     Bust darts sometimes need to be raised for a very young physique, or lowered for the elderly.
     Back shoulder darts sometimes need to be transferred to the back neck if the shoulders are very rounded.
     Skirt darts are usually designed to fit a young figure with a sharply defined waistline, flat stomach and rounded hips; older women, whose waists and tummies have expanded but whose posteriors have gone a bit flat (I know this problem well!) need far less fabric taken out in darts.

CHAPTER 4

PIPING

I mentioned piping in Book 1 as both a decorative method of trimming and an excellent way of stabilising some of the seams and edges of cut-and-sew clothes. I did not, however, because of lack of space, enlarge on the subject; but as a number of readers have asked for more detail I am including it in this book.

Piping can draw attention to seams where you want to display their line. For example, the seamline of a yoke, or where a raglan sleeve joins the body. These can often get lost in the texture of the knit, especially when it is patterned; but when piping is inserted, the shapes immediately becomes obvious.

Piping also stabilises those seams in which it is inserted, simply because the piping cord cannot stretch; a good reason for adding it not only to yokes and raglan armholes, but also to pocket tops, neck edges (where there is no collar) and the front opening edges of coats and jackets. Having thus stabilised the edges, facings can be cut from the same knit as the rest of the garment.

Suitable fabrics for piping

Piping can be purchased ready-made but I find that I can ill afford the time involved in searching for just the right shade and thickness. It is usually much easier (and often cheaper) to find a suitable woven fabric which can be bias-cut into strips which are then used to cover plain cotton piping cord: a length of 20 to 40 cms (1/4 to 1/2yd.) by whatever the width between selvedges happens to be, will be sufficient for most purposes; the smaller the piece, the more joins you will have to make. With practice and experience you will find that you can obtain an amazingly long strip from quite small odd pieces. If you have already combined a woven fabric with the knit elsewhere on the garment, use the leftover pieces of that - providing the texture is suitable.

Avoid thick, bulky or loosely-woven fabrics for covering piping cord; in fact, avoid anything which will not stand up to a fair amount of friction. Velvet is not generally suitable unless the pile is very short and dense. Suede-cloth, on the other hand, works beautifully. So does poly/cotton poplin or gingham, fine linen-type mixtures of natural and synthetic fibres, polyester linings or polyester satin. Small candy-stripes can make very effective piping on plain knits as the stripes appear diagonally when cut on the bias grain.

I have used fine (purchased) jersey fabrics successfully for covering piping-cord. In this case it is not essential to cut bias strips; lengths cut straight across the width (from selvedge to selvedge) will have the necessary degree of stretch. I have not so far used knitted fabrics made on a domestic knitting-machine for this purpose; I think it might work but the texture and tension would need to be very fine.

The Piping cord

Fig.17. Tootal make excellent piping cord in seven different thicknesses. Choose the right thickness to compliment the garment; usually Size 1 or 2, or Size 3 for a bulky knit.

This cord is made from pure cotton, so buy more than you actually need, to allow for shrinkage. Boil in water, drain and allow to dry before using. Polyester piping cord can be obtained, and this does not require pre-shrinking, but I find that cotton cord is softer in effect.

Fig. 17 (Tootal)

To cover piping cord

If you have never done this before, do have a trial run before actually trying to do it on a garment; your results will improve enormously after a modicum of practice!

1. Cut and join bias strips, following the directions for binding strips on pp.86-87, but the width of the strips has to be calculated according to the thickness of the piping cord to be used: i.e. the width of the bias-cut fabric strip should be equal to the *circumference* of the cord plus twice the width of the seam allowances. For a size 1 cord (and allowing for 1.5cm(5/8in) seam allowances), strips 3.8cm(1 1/2in) wide are about right; thicker cord will require wider strips.

2. Fit a presser foot which will accommodate the piping cord, to your sewing-machine, instead of the normal presser foot. At present, comparatively few manufacturers (known exceptions are Bernina and Husqvarna) produce a specially designed foot for this purpose, and even these are optional extra purchases (See Book 1, p.14). In the case of the majority of sewing-machines, the zipper foot has to be used; adjust this, if possible, so that the needle can penetrate the fabric as close as possible to the cord without actually catching it in.

3. Fig. 18a. Fold the bias strip in half lengthwise, right side out, fitting the cord closely into the fold and lining up the raw edges together. Pin in position if necessary, and then machine-stitch as close as possible to the cord, using a short stitch-length (about 1 1/2).

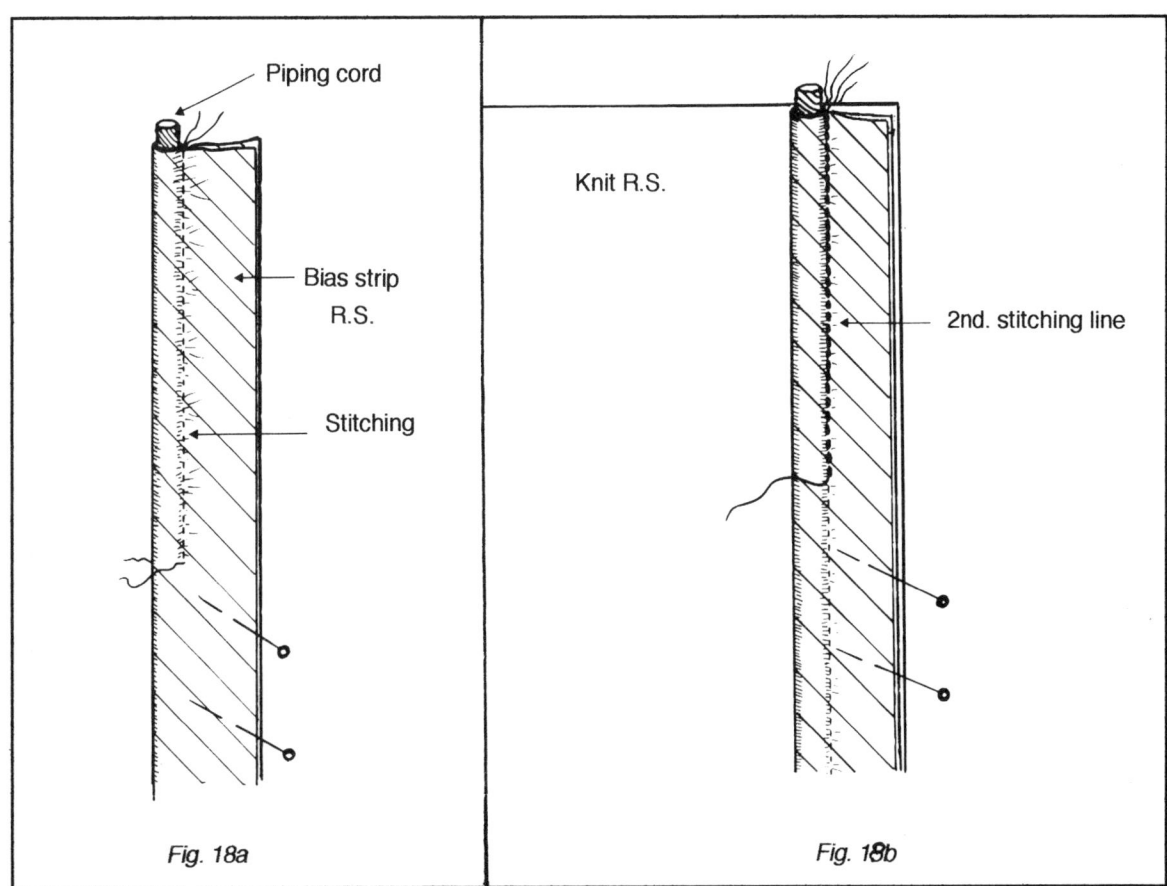

Fig. 18a   Fig. 18b

To apply the piping

Note : always stitch the piping first to whichever of the two garment pieces appears to be the more stable. Eg. on a neckline, where the facing has been interfaced with Vilene, stitch the piping first to the facing rather than to the garment which is more likely to stretch during the process.

1. Fig. 18b. Place the prepared piping on the right side of the garment piece as shown, so that the stitching line on the piping lies exactly on the seamline of the garment; if you judged the width of the strips correctly, it means that all three raw edges will lie exactly together. Pin in position taking great care to see that neither the knitted fabric nor the piping are unduly stretched out. Do this flat on a table, not in your lap!

Machine-stitch again precisely on the previous line of stitching, still using the zipper or piping foot.

2. Fig. 19a. To carry the piping round a corner, snip into the seam allowances of the covered piping at a point exactly where you will pivot to turn the corner; snip almost right up to the stitching line. The corner will be slightly rounded rather than a sharp right angle.

3. Fig. 19b. To cope with more gentle curves, make more snips in the seam allowances.

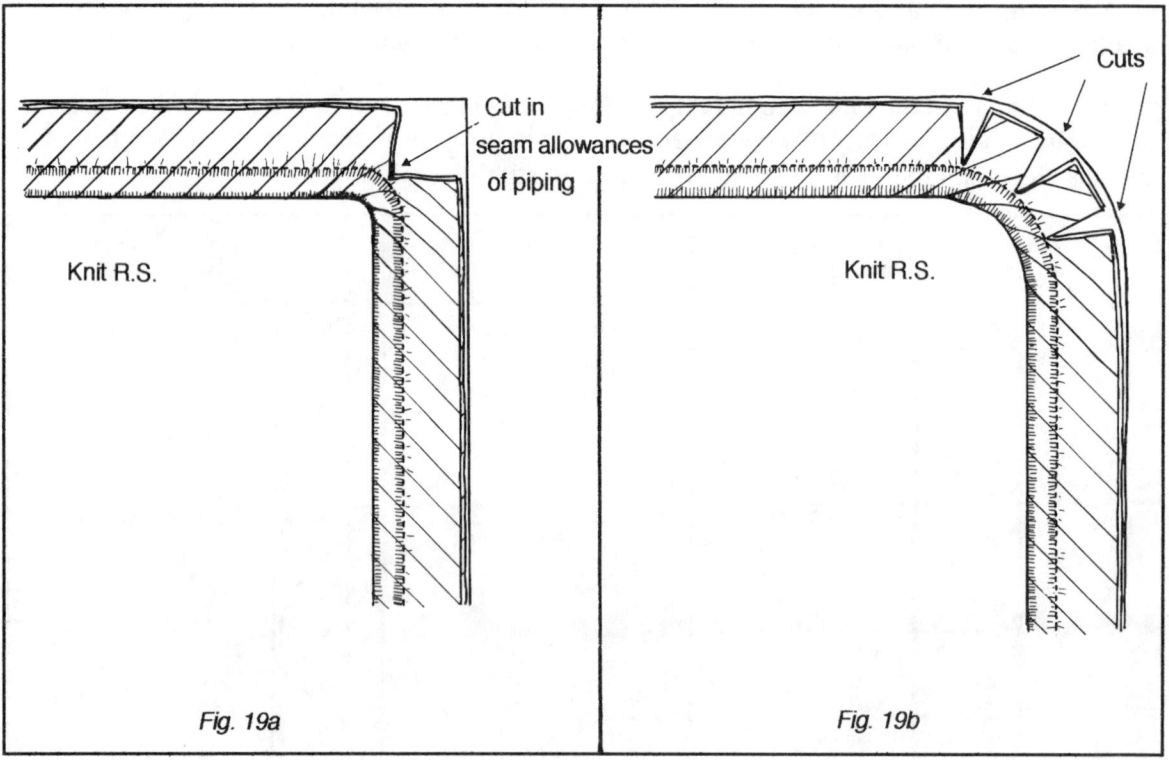

Fig. 19a   Fig. 19b

2. Take the piece of fabric to which the piping is now attached and turn it over so that the wrong side is uppermost. Place it on the appropriate garment piece, right sides together, so that the raw edges are lined up. Machine-stitch again, still using the zipper or piping foot, exactly along the line of stitching already there.

3. Trim back the seam allowances by about half and snip them wherever you have concave curves. Turn through to the right side.

4. If required, secure the seam allowances in place by understitching (see Book 1, pp63-64) or by top-stitching through all seam allowances on one side of the seamline.

Note: To avoid bulk where the ends of the piping are to be enclosed in future seams, pull out and cut off sufficient cord to leave the casing empty where it will lie within such a seam. Removing about 2mm(3/4in) is usually sufficient.

Page 19

Piping a continuous edge

To pipe a continuous edge, such as an unbroken neckline or a sleeve end, where there is no opening, start at a point where the join will be least obvious - perhaps the centre back. Remove the cord from the first 2cm(5/8in) of piping and fold the empty casing towards the raw edges, as shown in **Fig.20a.***

Start the machine-stitching just before the folded edge of the casing. When you have completed the circle, stop the stitching exactly where you started and stitch in reverse for 1.2cm(1/2in). Cut off the remaining piping strip 2.5cm(1in) from the end of the stitching and remove the cord from this loose end. Turn it towards the raw edges as shown in **Fig.20b.** Stitch in position.

If you have done this correctly, the covered ends of the piping cord meet without overlapping, so that no excess bulk occurs. You can slip-stitch the ends together invisibly with needle and thread.

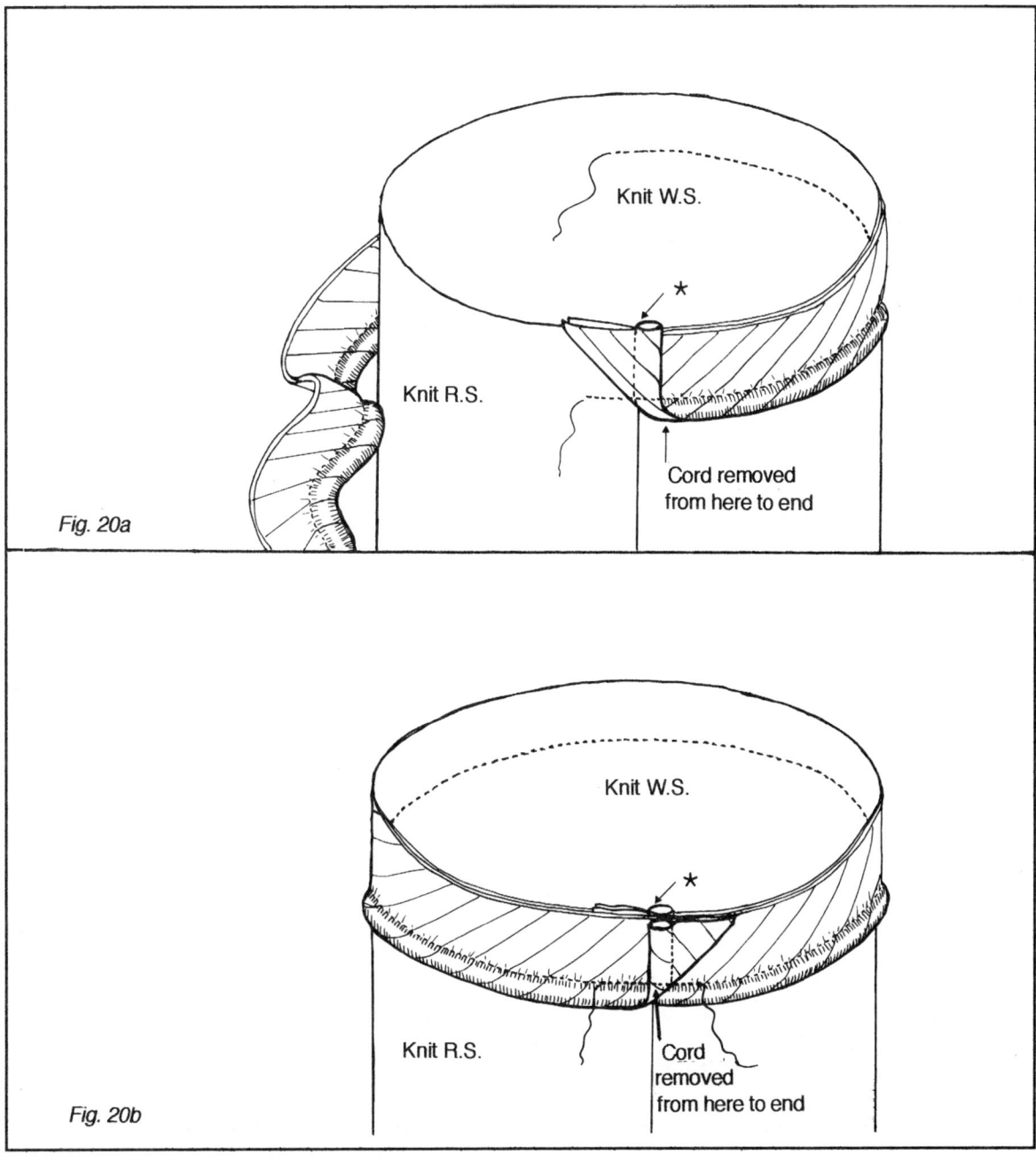

Fig. 20a

Fig. 20b

CHAPTER 5

COLLARS AND NECKLINES

Collars can vary so widely that a whole book could be devoted to this one subject. Anyone who wants to pursue the study of collar shapes and the principles of collar fitting should read the relevant chapters in Natalie Bray's Dress Pattern Designing (Crosby Lockwood Staples, London). For the purposes of this book, in which I am concentrating mainly on the use of commercial paper patterns, it might be sufficient to say that you should choose the design you want, purchase the pattern in the correct size for your figure (see Book 1, pp.19-21) and then simply follow the pattern instructions sheets.

However, the application of a collar to a garment can cause more headaches than almost any other process in its completion. You can get away with errors in other parts but a badly fitting collar simply looks like home-dressmaking at its worst! In cut-and-sew work, the added hazard of using a stretchy fabric increases the chances of getting it wrong; so, start by anticipating the possible problems and taking positive steps to avoid them.

Planning the collar

Check the fitting of the collar if you are in any doubt about that; some people know in advance that the collar is going to be their particular fitting problem!. It might be worth cutting the collar in a piece of old sheeting and simply trying it on to see how it fits and whether or not you actually like its shape.

Fitting problems in collars usually occur only when the pattern has been purchased in the wrong size. However, if you happen to have a neck which is larger or smaller than average for your size and also want a buttoned-up collar to fit perfectly, it is worth checking the actual length of the neck seamline between the centre front marks on the collar and then comparing it with your own measurement. Take care to see that you measure your neck exactly where the neck seamline will come - not higher or lower. Then make the collar longer or shorter accordingly, by adding to, or subtracting from, the paper pattern. Divide your alterations so that you make small differences to front, back and each side of the collar, rather than just adding or removing a large chunk at centre back which will make the collar unbalanced.

If an adjustment has been made to the collar, the garment neckline must be altered to fit it. Lowering it slightly will enable it to accommodate a longer collar; raising it slightly will enable it to accommodate a shorter collar. Check the lengths of the two neck seamlines, between the centre front. marks, to make sure that they are identical.

Likewise, if the garment has been altered at the neckline, the collar will need to be adjusted to fit accordingly.

Stabilising the collar

The collar should be stabilised so that neither it nor the neckline of the garment can possibly stretch. This can be done in one of several ways:

1. When both layers of the collar are cut from knitted fabric, one of them can be interfaced with a non-stretch, woven interfacing such as fusible cotton muslin, or sewn-in lawn or organza. Remember that a non-woven interfacing, such as fusible knitted nylon, or any of the Vilenes, can still stretch a little.

2. The upper layer of the collar can be cut from knitted fabric and the under layer (the collar facing) can be cut from a woven fabric chosen to match, tone or contrast with the knitted fabric. A fusible or sew-in interfacing can be used as well if necessary.

3. Both layers of the collar can be cut from a carefully chosen woven fabric. This is a technique I have used a lot simply because the contrast in texture between knitted and woven fabrics is so effective and pleasing. Co-ordinate by using the woven fabric again elsewhere in the garment, perhaps to cover buttons, make a belt, or for buttoning bands.

4. A collar can be made from a single layer of knitted fabric, perhaps having the edges bound with bias-cut woven fabric, or with real or fake suede. To stabilise the neckline in this case, the neck facing, if there is one, should be cut from woven lining fabric and interfaced with Vilene Ultrasoft lightweight to make it a little firmer, without adding bulk. If there is no neck facing, the neck seamline should be covered with an applied strip of woven braid or ribbon, cut to the correct length.

Cutting and making up the collar

There are several aspects of making collars which are worth studying briefly; some understanding of these will not only provide a foundation of extra background knowledge which is not generally provided in pattern instruction sheets, but will also help you to solve problems when they inevitably occur.

For instance, you can, with safety, always alter the shape of the outer edge of a collar if you wish. **(see Fig.21 below.)** As long as you have not altered its neck edge, the collar will still fit the neck of the garment. Old patterns with out-of-date collars can often be re-used in this way. With experience you can readily change one type of collar for another but always remember that the collar must be designed or adapted to fit the neckline upon which it is to be placed. This generally means that the seamline on the neck edge of the collar must be adjusted so that it becomes precisely the same length as the neck seamline on the garment, between the points where the ends of the collar should be placed.

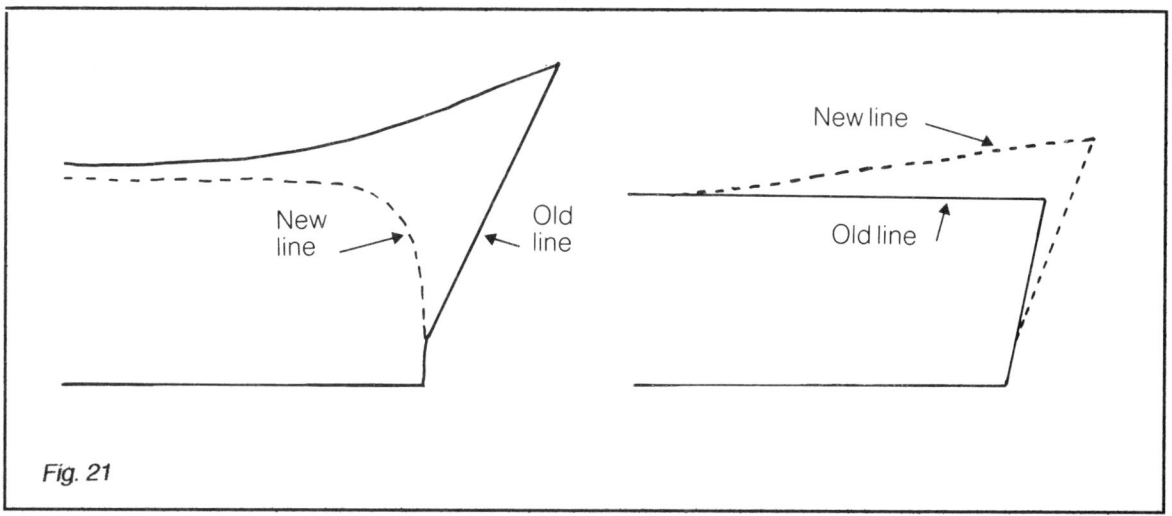

Fig. 21

Sewing the two layers of a collar together

Note: get the terminology right!
   "collar" refers to the top layer, the one which will be on view when the garment is complete;
      "collar facing" refers to the under part of the collar which is usually hidden when the garment
         is complete.
   "interfacing" refers to the stiffening and/or stabilising fabric which lies between the
         collar and the collar facing.

A problem occurs when making shirts and dresses because the collar and the collar facing, which are sewn together before being applied to the garment, are usually both cut from the same pattern piece. This leads to some difficulty in getting the finished collar to roll properly, with the seamline on its outer edge rolled neatly just underneath, rather than showing on the edge - or, even worse, actually rolling up and over on to the upper side of the collar. In fact, to achieve a neatly rolled effect, *the collar facing needs to be slightly smaller than the collar.*

Page 22

The following process solves the problem - but it must be emphasised that these instructions are for *dressmaking*. In *tailoring* the collar construction is quite different: see p.23.

1. If interfacing is required, add it to the collar. It should be cut on the same pattern piece so that the edges match exactly - not, as some pattern instructions suggest, with the seam allowances removed; it needs to be included in the seam when this is machined.

2. Fig.22. Draw the pattern markings (notches, dots, centre back line, centre front marks, etc.) on to the interfacing, using a sharp soft lead pencil or a cloth-marking pen. Mark, also, the points at the outer corners of the collar, where you will actually be turning the corners when sewing. A clearly marked dot here, on which to pivot around the needle, will help tremendously when the work is under the machine presser foot.

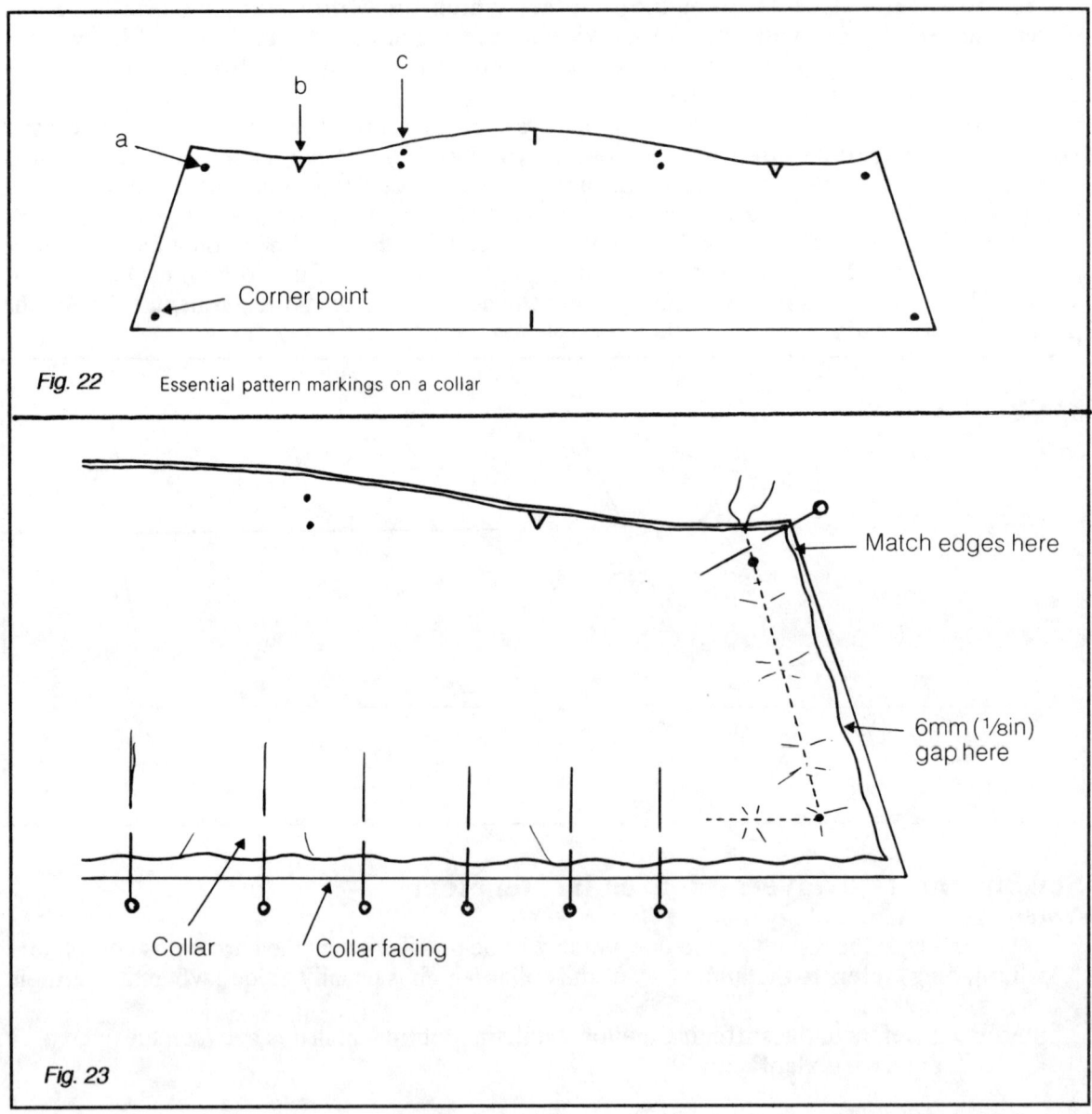

Fig. 22   Essential pattern markings on a collar

Fig. 23

3. Place the collar on top of the collar facing, right sides together, carefully matching the ends of the collar pieces at the neck edge. Pin these points exactly together - see **Fig.23.**

4. Fig.23. Pin the remaining outer edges of the collar to the corresponding edges of the collar facing, as shown, with the collar pushed slightly inwards, making it pucker a little and creating a gap of approximately 3mm(1/8in) between the outer edges of the two pieces. Do this all around the outer edges of the collar, easing it slightly (and stretching the collar facing a little) to make it fit.

Note: if the fabrics are very thick and bulky, you may need to push the collar edges inwards by 6mm(1/4in).

Use plenty of pins to hold the two layers together securely; one every half inch is not excessive. Leave the neck edge alone.

5. Machine along the collar seamlines as shown. Sew with the collar on top and the collar facing underneath. (Having the interfaced piece immediately under the presser-foot helps to reduce stretching problems.) Use a small stitch-length because you will have to reduce the seam allowances to a minimum before turning the collar; large stitches would allow the knit to fray.

Check, after stitching, that there are no faults in the seam. It is all too easy to make little tucks accidentally; if this has happened, simply unpick about 2.5cm(1in) either side of the fault, re-arrange the fabrics, and re-stitch.

6. Trim the seam allowances and turn the collar to the right side.

7. Push the seamline out from the inside with a large knitting needle, taking care not to pierce through. Press the collar carefully and thoroughly, rolling the seam on the outer edge so that it is just hidden on the under side of the collar.

Constructing Tailored Collars

When making coats and jackets you will probably have a "collar facing" pattern which is already slightly smaller than the "collar" pattern. The "collar facing" may be cut on the straight grain but could equally (and more correctly) be cut on the bias grain. The construction method is also different: a "soft tailoring" method is used whereby the collar facing is attached to the coat, the collar attached to the facings, and only then are the two outer edges of the collar sewn together. At this stage, it is certainly advisable to use the same technique of pushing the collar further in than the collar facing, even if your collar facing pattern *is* cut smaller - simply because of the thickness of the knit. (See p.27-28 for further information on Tailored Collars)

Attaching collars.

In general, follow your pattern instructions for attaching collars but I do want to emphasise three simple rules for ensuring success, whatever the style. Follow these and your collars will always look professional.

Rule 1. *Look for, and transfer to the fabrics, all the pattern marks on the neck edge of the garment and on the neck edge of the collar; i.e. all dots, circles and notches. Also mark the centre back line on both collar and garment.*

These marks are vitally important and cannot be safely ignored! They have been carefully placed in position by the pattern-maker precisely to within a millimetre of where they should be, so you must be equally precise about transferring them to the fabrics.

Look again at **Fig.22** where these marks are illustrated;

a. The mark on the front neck edge of the garment where the finished ends of the collar are to be placed.

b. The notches on the neck edge of the garment and the corresponding notches on the neck edge of the collar.

c. The dots, on the neck edge of the collar, roughly halfway between centre back and the collar ends, which indicate the shoulder-line. These have to be positioned exactly on the shoulder-line of the garment when the collar is attached. (Note: your garment could possibly have a "dropped" shoulder seam, in which case there will be a mark on the garment neck edge indicating where the true shoulder-line lies.

Rule 2. *See Fig.24a and b*
Before attempting to attach the collar, stay-stitch the neck seamline on the garment and then snip the neck seam allowance all round, cutting almost to the stay-stitching.

"Stay-stitching" means straight machine-stitching on a very short [1-1 1/2] stitch length; it is usually mentioned in the pattern instructions but that paragraph is all too frequently either ignored or misinterpreted! The reason for stay-stitching is simple - it stops the knit from fraying when the snipping is done. "What snipping?" I hear you ask in horror! The reason for the snipping may not be quite so obvious, but you have probably already discovered that when the neck of the garment is a definite concave curve and the neck edge of the collar is either straight or even a convex curve, *the neck edge of the collar often appears to be too long to fit the neck edge of the garment* . Making cuts in the seam allowance, from the outer edge, in towards (and almost up to) the stay-stitching, all around the neck edge of the garment, enables you to stretch it out into a straight line - and so the collar fits quite easily!

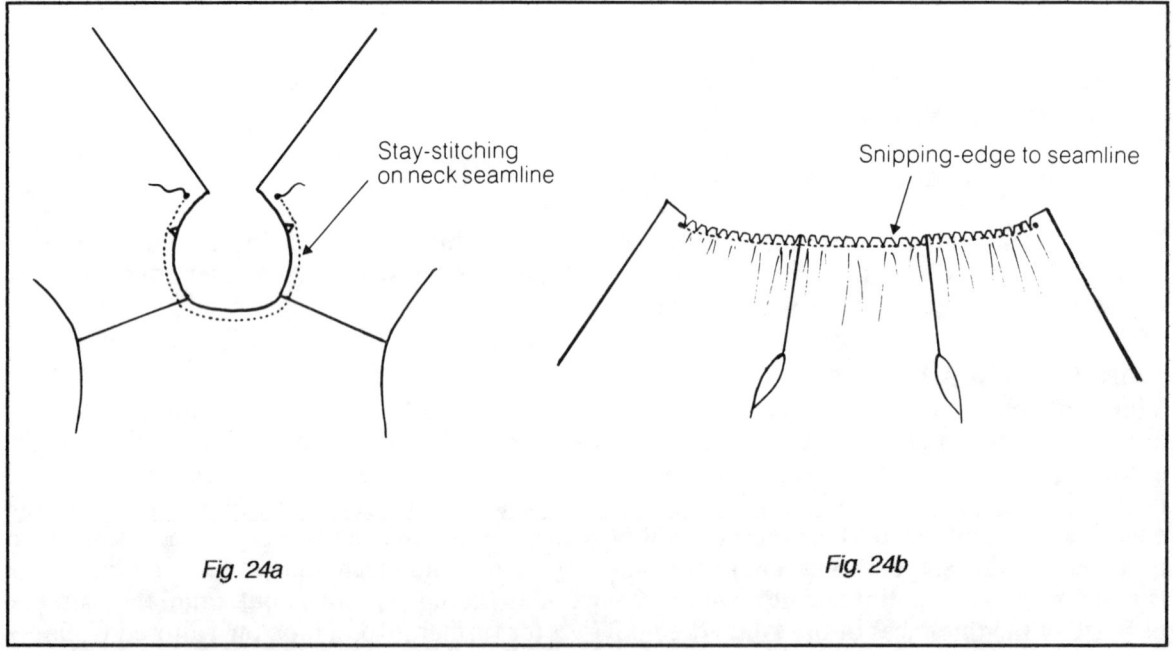

Fig. 24a   Fig. 24b

Rule 3. *Match all the dots, notches and centre back lines **precisely** when pinning the collar to the neck edge of the garment.*
"Near enough" is simply not good enough - try to acquire the attitude of a precision engineer! Also make sure that the edges of the seam allowances lie exactly together; it is all too easy to let one of them slip down.

FUNNEL COLLARS.

This is a type of collar which can very easily be added to any circular neckline, and it works particularly well with knitted fabrics. You can even rejuvenate old sweaters by removing the old collar and adding a new funnel collar, in the original yarn if you still have some, or in a contrasting shade or texture. Collars like this are, in fact, often to be found in expensive boutiques as separate items which can be worn over any sweater, dress, coat, etc., without being sewn on at all. The same idea, but cut deeper, becomes a "wimple" which can be pulled up right over the head.

No interfacing is used. Do some experimenting before committing yourself because a lot can depend on the thickness and texture of the knit; you also need to try out the effect to see if it actually suits you.

Page 25

To make a funnel collar

1. Fig.25a. Draw out a pattern in the shape of a rectangle.
A-B equals the measurement of the neck seamline on the garment.
B-C can be whatever depth of collar you want: it could be quite shallow, or it could rise up the neck and then turn over and down, once or even twice, depending on the thickness of the knit.

2. Fig.25b. Add seam allowances to all four sides of the rectangle. Mark the straight grain line as shown. This collar could, alternatively, be cut on the bias grain.

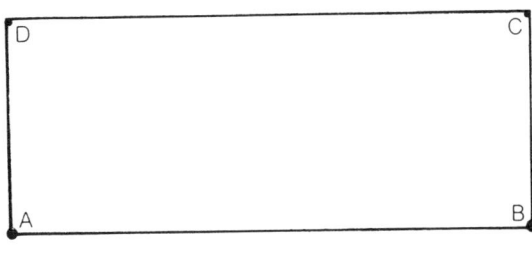

Fig. 25a

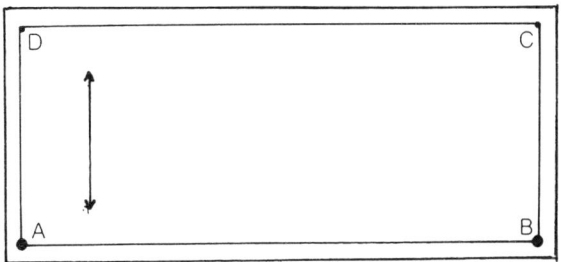

Fig. 25b

3. Cut the collar from the knitted fabric using the paper pattern you have just made.

4. Fig.26.
Sew up the vertical seam, A-D to B-C, right sides together. This seam would need to be neatly finished as it may be partly visible.

5. Turn in and hem the top edge of the collar, or neaten it with the help of an overlocking machine. Take care not to stretch it out too much but also aim at a finish which will allow it to stretch out a little if necessary.

6. Holding both the garment and the collar wrong side out, place the collar inside the neck of the garment, so that the seam in the collar is placed at centre back of the neck and the raw edges of the neck seam allowances lie exactly together.

Note: *the wrong side of the collar must face the right side of the garment.*

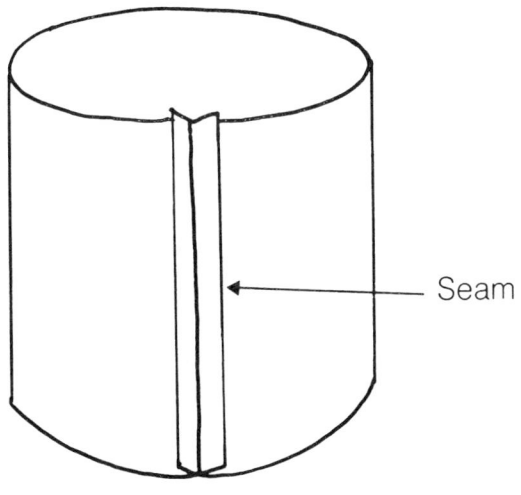

Fig. 26

7. Fig. 27. Pin as shown and stitch the collar to the garment. Neaten the seam allowance with over-edge stitching, or overlocking, but take care not to stretch out the neck seam any more than you can help. If it does stretch badly, thread a double length of fine shirring elastic through the neatened seam allowances.

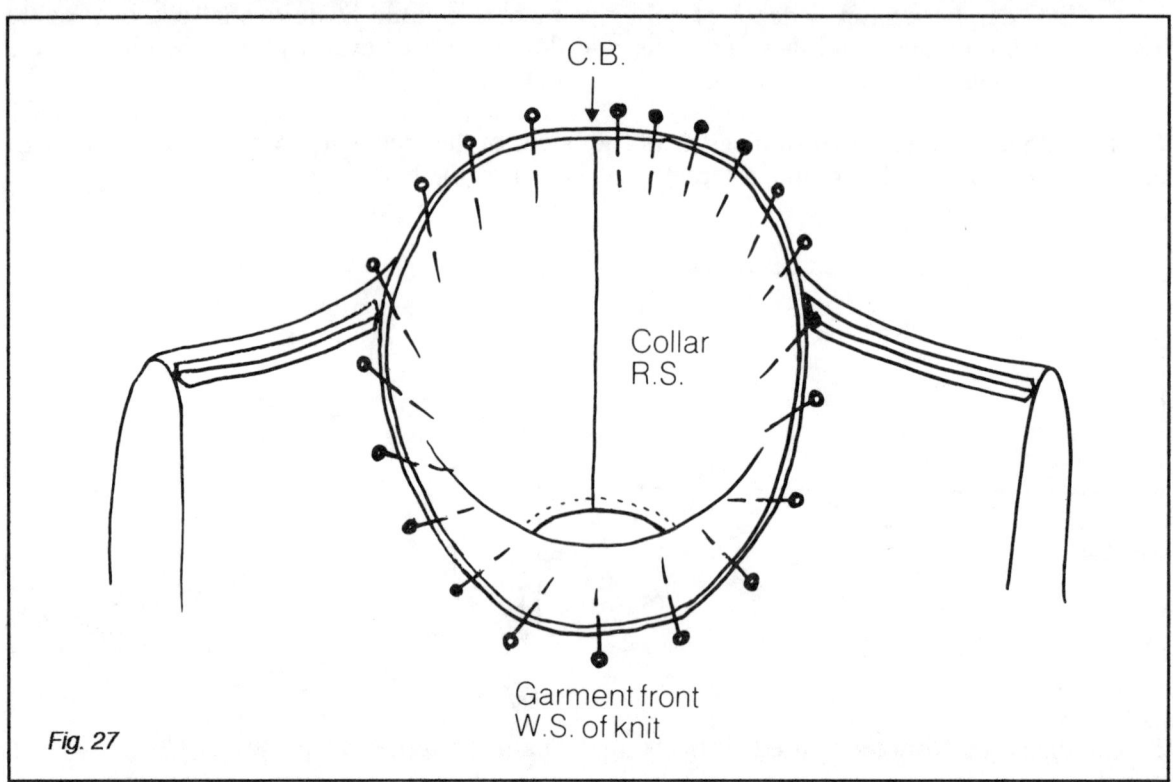

Fig. 27

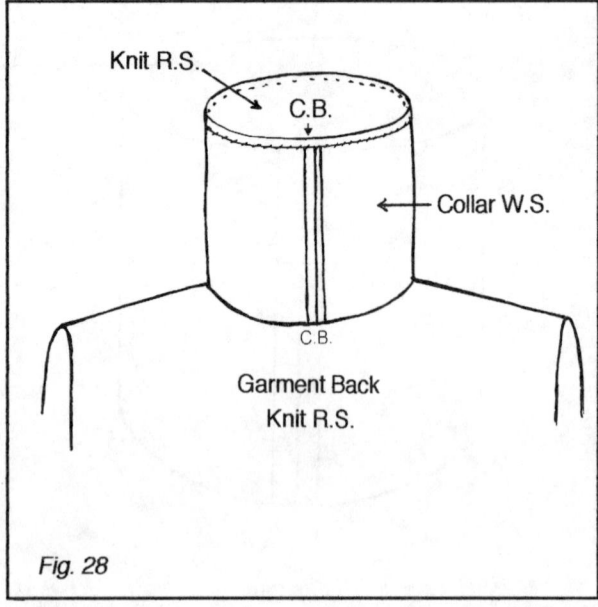

Fig. 28

8. Fig. 28. Turn the collar upwards from the neck and then roll the top edge down over the seamline.

Here are several variations on this idea. You can probably invent more.

a. The neck edge of the collar can be placed on the right side of the garment, right sides together and stitched; the top edge of the collar is then turned over to the wrong side. of the garment and hemmed in place over the seam allowances. This collar is now of double thickness and can either rise straight up the neck, or, if cut deeper, can rise up, turn over and fall down to the right side like a polo-neck.

b. The collar, cut as a much more shallow rectangle and made up as in "a" above, could take the form of quite a narrow band, and this could be stiffened if required, by the addition of interfacing. The effect of this is a stand-up "ring" collar.

c. The collar can be cut in two sections shaped as in **Fig.29a.**; line A-B is exactly half the measurement of the neck seamline. The two seams are sewn up and the collar is attached to the garment as shown in **Fig.29b**, with one seam lined up with each side of the neck. This produces a softer collar which falls lower on the garment.

d. Making the neck edge of the collar slightly larger than the neck edge of the garment, and then easing it on to the seamline, also makes for a softer, more draped collar.

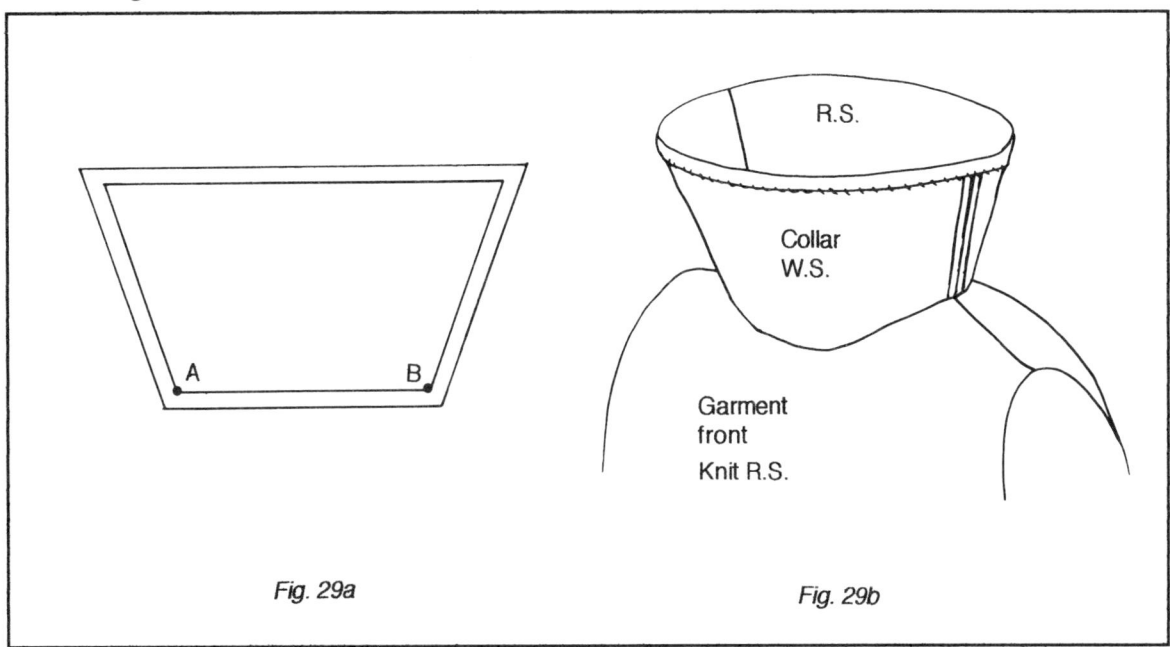

Fig. 29a   Fig. 29b

INTERFACING AND SHAPING TAILORED COLLARS

Collars on tailored coats and jackets are constructed by special tailoring methods; a good dressmaking pattern should give sufficient detail to enable you to get them right but if you are left in doubt, consult the chapter on tailoring in the Readers Digest Book of Sewing, or the Vogue Sewing Book. (See Appendix 1 for other recommended books) In these cases, the collar facing should be interfaced, rather than the collar itself. A non-stretch, iron-on interfacing such as fusible cotton muslin may be sufficient, but you may have to search for some of the fusible tailoring canvases, which are manufactured in a variety of weights and textures, to give more stability and firmness to heavier knits. Take care to avoid over-stiffening the fabric and making it too heavy.

To ensure that the finished collar is going to be neatly rolled and well-shaped, the collar facing and the interfacing should be pad-stitched together along the lines shown in **Fig.30.**

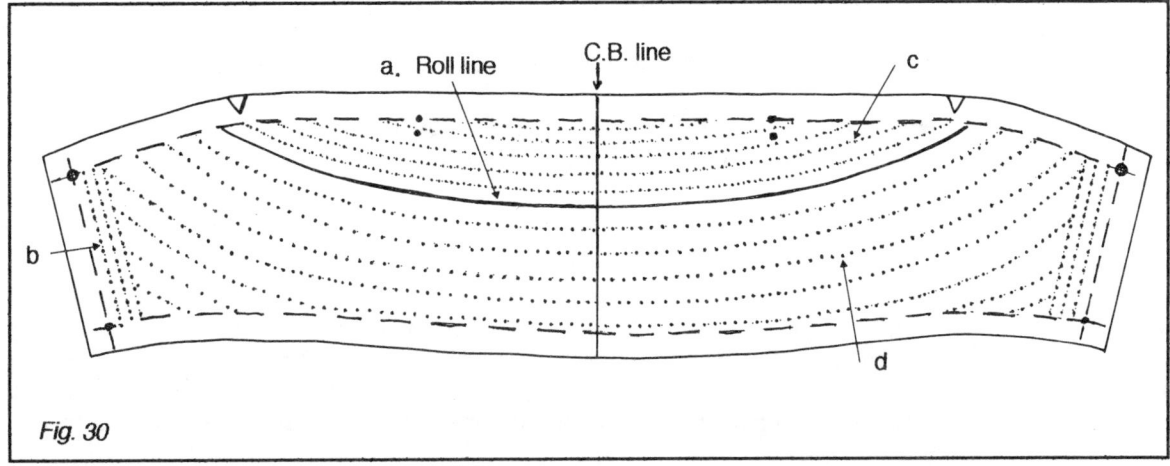

Fig. 30

TO PAD-STITCH

1. You should find that the roll line of the collar is marked on the paper pattern for the collar facing, as shown in **Fig.30a**. Transfer this line from the pattern to the interfaced collar facing, using a cloth-marking pen or a soft lead pencil.

2. Fig.31. Pad-stitch along the marked roll-line first, to establish it. To do this, hold the collar, interfacing on top, curving it over the fingers, and take small stitches which cross the line at right angles. Use a thread which matches the collar facing fabric exactly. These stitches should sew into but not right through the collar facing fabric.

Note: For *small pad-stitching*, the needle should pick up about 3mm(1/8in) of fabric and stitches should be 6mm(1/4in) apart.

For *larger pad-stitching*, the needle should still pick up only 3mm(1/8in) but the gaps between stitches can be 1.2cm(1/2in) or more.

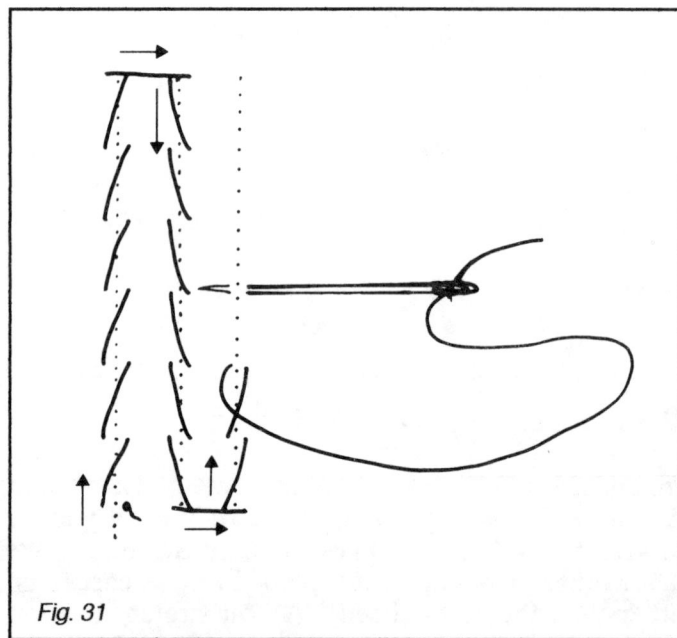

Fig. 31

Sew firmly but not too tightly; you should aim at a curved shape; try to avoid letting it become crinkled or tucked. Stitch down one line, then take a stitch sideways and continue stitching up the next line, and so on. Do not take the pad-stitching over into the seam allowances.

3. Make three lines of small pad-stitching parallel with the collar ends. (point b. in **Fig.30**)

4. Fill in the area between the roll-line and the neck edge (point c. in **Fig.30**) with small pad-stitching, and the area between the roll-line and the outer edge of the collar (point d. in **Fig.30**) with larger pad-stitching, following more lines drawn on the interfacing as shown.

T-SHIRT NECKLINE

The T-shirt neckline is made by cutting a straight strip of the knit *parallel with the rows* and even in width: the ends are sewn together to form a circle which is then folded in half lengthwise and sewn to the already cut out neckline. This is fully described and illustrated in Book 1, pp 70-71.

The knit for this band should obviously have a reasonably stretchy texture; therefore I would not advise attempting this with knit-woven or Fairisle fabrics. Ideally, use plain stocking-stitch, specially knitted ribbing, or even (if you can find the right shade!) the purchased manufactured ribbing which is sometimes on sale in haberdashery stores.

FACED NECKLINES FOR KNITWEAR

Finishing a neckline with a facing is a very common dressmaking technique which is also a useful Cut and Sew method; in Book 1 (p 63-64), instructions were given for applying facings cut from purchased woven fabrics to necklines of garments *cut* from knits. Several of my students have asked how they can use this neckline on garments which they have knitted from a knitting pattern and where, of course, they have no dressmaking paper-pattern pieces. So here goes!

Assuming that the knitted pieces are not yet sewn together, you can use them just like a paper pattern. The following instructions and diagrams refer to a V-neck with no front or back openings, but they can easily be adapted to any other shape.

1. Start with the Front (if the garment is already assembled then you will have to do some careful folding and pinning to isolate the Front, as far as possible, from all the rest.) The piece must lie absolutely flat and straight; *check carefully that the rows are at right-angles to the stitches all over the neck and shoulder area.* Make sure that the neck is not stretched out more than it should be. If you have problems getting the piece into shape, steam and press it lightly.

2. Lay the Front on the paper, as shown in **Fig.32a.**; the centre front of the knit should lie parallel with the vertical edge of the paper, and the rows should be parallel with the horizontal edge. Hold in place with pins or weights.

3. Trace the shoulder, neck and front edges on the paper, as shown, as a line A-B-C-D
   A-B and C-D should both measure 7.5cm(3in).

4. Repeat this procedure with the garment Back, as shown in **Fig.32b.** tracing the line W-X-Y-Z. W-X and Y-Z should both measure 7.5cm(3in).

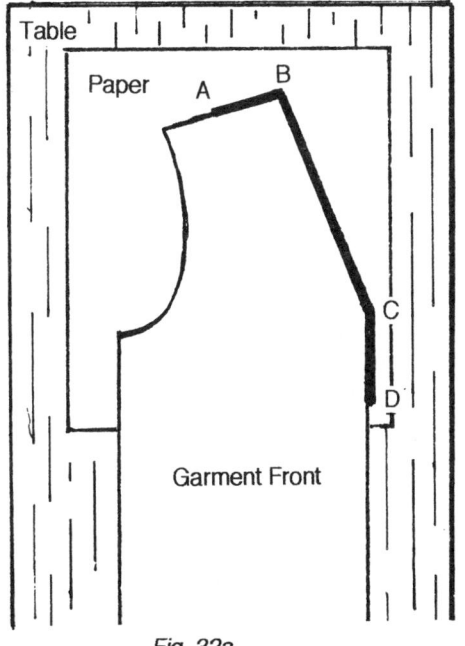

Fig. 32a

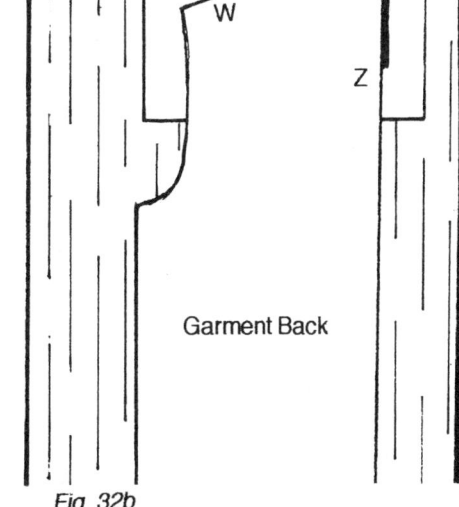

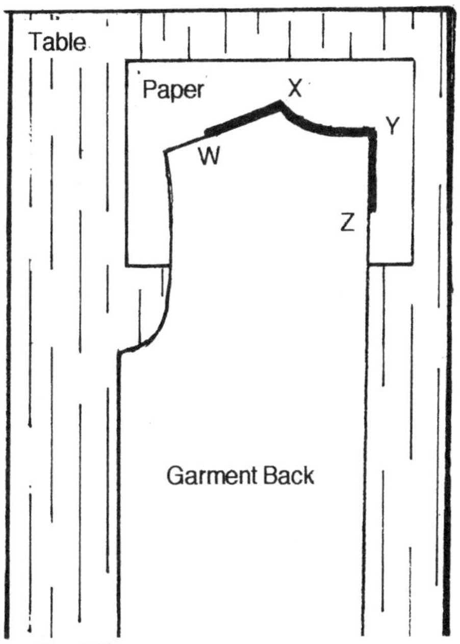

Fig. 32b

5. Remove the knitted pieces and "tidy up" the drawn lines; use a ruler for the ones which should be straight.

6. Fig.33a and b. Add 1.5cm(5/8in) seam allowances to the shoulders (at A-B and W-X) and draw in the remaining dotted lines as shown.

The straight line A-E should be parallel with and 7.5cm(3in) from line B-C.

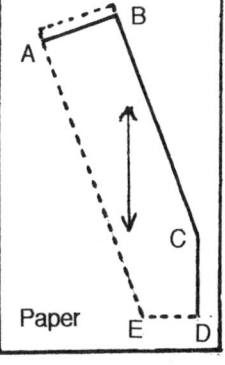

Fig. 33a

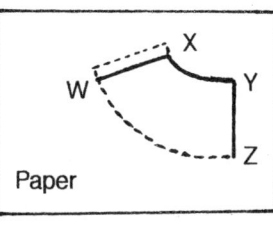

Fig. 33 b

> The curved line W-Z should likewise run 7.5cm(3in) from line X-Y.
> The line E-D should meet the line D-C at right angles.
> Draw in a "straight grain" line parallel with line C-D.

You now have paper patterns for cutting facings for this neckline. Cut them from lining fabric in a colour to match the knit, or use any other woven fabric such as poly/cotton, lightweight linen, etc. that you might be using as some other part of the outfit.

Note: Full instructions for interfacing and applying such facings are given in Book 1, p.63-64

Variations.
a. If the garment opens down the front, remember to add seam allowances to the centre front line - similarly add to the centre back line if the opening is at the back.
b. The facing can be continued down the entire length of open-front edges and can even continue all around the hem if required, with seams at the sides joining the front facings to the back facing.
c. A collar can be sewn to the neck seamline before the facing is attached.
d. Piping, lace, or a frill can be sewn to the neck seamline before the facing is attached.

"<u>REAL</u> CUT AND SEW NECKLINES" FOR KNITWEAR

I spend a very large portion of my life teaching and talking to machine-knitters at clubs and classes and invariably someone will ask me "Can you help me with cut-and-sew necklines?" Of course, they are referring to a *knitwear* process whereas my particular field is *dressmaking;* Fortunately, there are a number of highly qualified machine-knitting tutors who write on the subject of cut-and-sew necklines for knitwear, so there is no need for me to try to tell you about a process of which I know very little indeed!

However, I am aware that, for most knitters, the problem invariably seems to be the sheer terror of having to cut into their knitting with a pair of scissors. When I do *dressmaking*, all the knitted fabric has been thoroughly steam-pressed, so the fibres are well bonded together and therefore less likely to fray - so I have no fear of cutting. When you make *knitwear*, the pieces are unlikely to have been pressed (particularly if the yarn is acrylic) so the chances of the knit fraying are obviously higher - hence the panic.

Here are a few suggestions which may prove helpful.
1. If you are afraid the knitting is going to fray, then *steam* the area you are going to cut before start to cut. Use a really powerful steam-iron and "hover" it *just above* the knit, blowing hot steam into it and pressing the area gently with your fingers. Or use Kamalini Trentham"s Steamer to do the same job. This technique fluffs up the fibres and makes them cling together more closely so that fraying is unlikely to happen.

2. The smooth yarns are, of course, more likely to fray than the hairy ones. In this case I suggest you tack a piece of Vilene Stitch'n'Tear to the wrong side of the neck area. This will give it a firm, non-stretch base so that you can now make a line of zigzag machine-stitching around the proposed neckline. Stitch only one line, using a medium stitch width and a medium stitch-length. Then cut out the neckline and gently tear away the Stitch'n'Tear.

3. If you have an overlocker the job is simplicity itself. Tighten up the differential feed to avoid undue stretching of the fabric; ideally, first check the stitch length and differential by machining on your original tension swatch. Mark the proposed cutting line for the neck, then feed it it into the overlocker, guiding the marked line into the knife. This is fully described and illustrated in Book 1 on p67-69.

CHAPTER 6

<u>**SLEEVES**</u>

Sleeves which are cut as part of the body of the garment, such as raglan or dolman sleeves, necessarily have to be there when you do your first fitting, and are then fairly easily adjusted - providing your pattern was the right size in the first place. The troubles which usually beset home dressmakers arise when sleeves are cut separately and then set in on an armhole seamline; mistakes in this area can, so easily, label the finished article as "home-made".

Checking the armhole seamline *First, some warning notes!*
1. *Always try the garment on -**after** the bodice has been completed, including the neckline*. The reason for this is that sewing on the collar and/or neck facing immediately stabilises the neckline, so that it will not stretch out of shape when you try the garment on.

2. Do not, at this stage, make any attempt to set in the sleeves. Tacking the sleeves in before this fitting is generally a complete waste of time because you simply do not know where the upper end of the armhole seamline should actually be. My own experience of fitting clients and students has shown me that most women need to have the top of the armhole seamline moved in a little towards the neck.

3. Shoulder seams should always be taped when sleeves are to be set in. Failure to do this will result in the shoulder seam being stretched down by the weight of the sleeve, and consequent dropping of the sleeve-head down over the arm.

4. The style of the garment has to be taken into account before you decide on the best position for the top of the armhole seamline. If in doubt, read the designer's description which should be included with other details on the back of the pattern envelope, and/or study the illustrations on the front and in the instruction sheets. Here are some general guidelines to go with the diagrams on the next page.

   Fig.34a. Wearing the garment, tuck a thin book under the armpit and hold it in place there while you look in a mirror. An imaginary line continuing straight up from the book is where the armhole seamline should normally be.

   Fig.34b. *Plain set-in sleeve*. Mark the imaginary line with a line of pins, graduating from where the seamline already lies at the underarm curve, to the shoulder line. Continue the pin-line over the back shoulder, merging back into the original seamline where necessary; take care not to make the back too narrow.

   Fig.34c. *Puffed sleeve*.. The line should come a little further in towards the neck, so that the top of the arm will help to support the gathered top of the sleeve.

   Fig.34d. *Exaggeratedly square shoulders*. The shoulder seam will be rather longer than usual, extending outwards to meet the sleeve-head, beyond the normal set-in sleeve line. The shoulder seam may also be higher than usual at the outer end in order to accommodate the necessary shoulder-pad. If you really feel that this kind of shoulder shape does not suit you, you will probably need to lower the outer end of the shoulder seam slightly and also bring the top of the armhole seamline inward.

   Fig.34e. *Dropped shoulders*. Here the armhole seamline is deliberately allowed to fall over the end of the shoulder, down the arm.

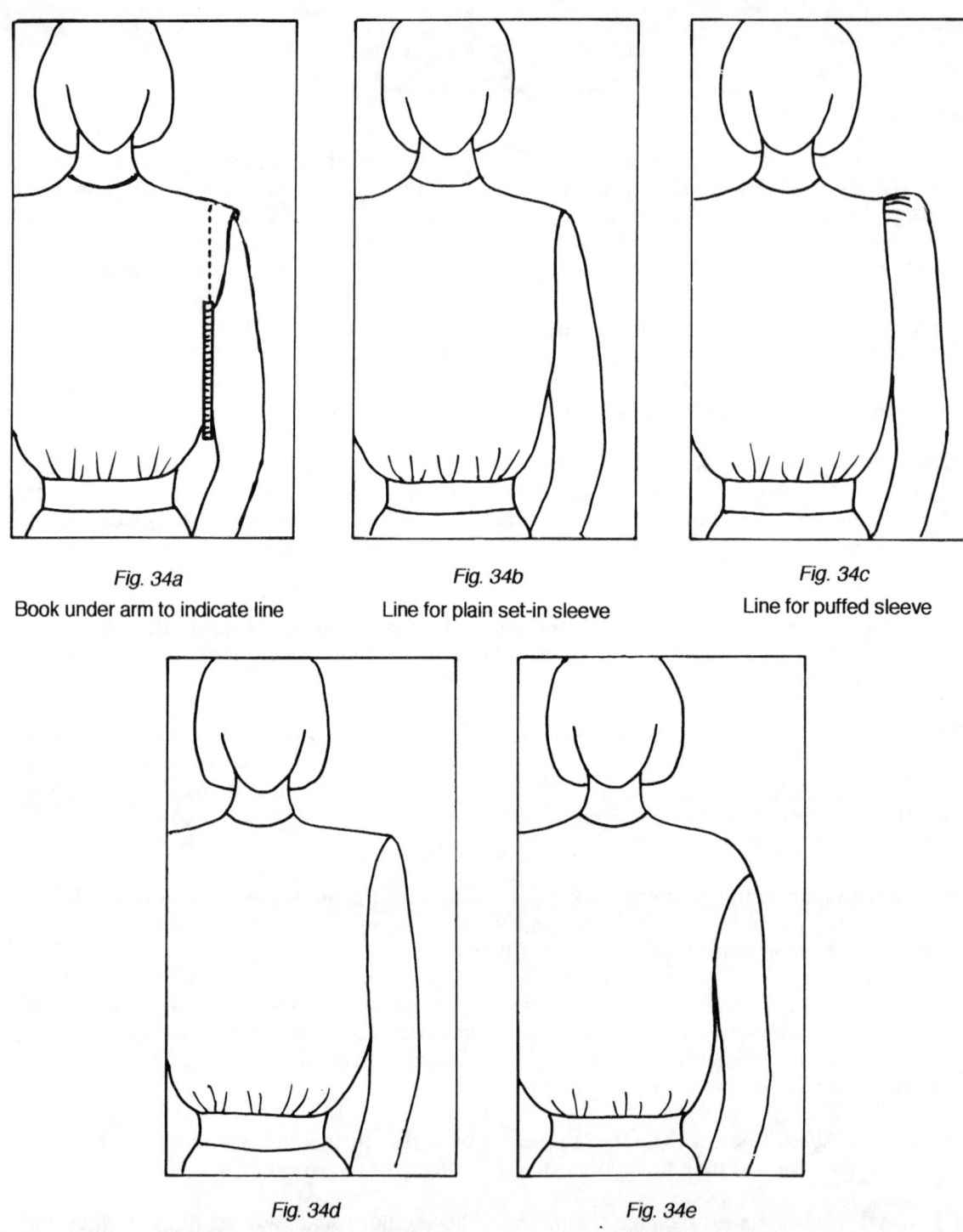

Fig. 34a
Book under arm to indicate line

Fig. 34b
Line for plain set-in sleeve

Fig. 34c
Line for puffed sleeve

Fig. 34d
Line for extended square shoulder

Fig. 34e
Line for dropped shoulder

Whichever of these variations applies to your particular pattern, some adjustment may be needed in order to obtain a perfect fit for your particular figure.

Remember *that adjustments to the armhole seamline should only be made on the armhole (on the body of the garment) and never to the top of the sleeve.*

5. Mark the adjusted armhole seamline with a tacking thread and then trim off any excess seam allowance, leaving an exact 1.5cm(5/8in) all round.

***Note*:** it is a good idea to keep these trimmings; pin them to a piece of paper and label them carefully - "Left shoulder Front", "Left shoulder Back', "Right shoulder Front" and "Right shoulder Back". Then you will be able to see exactly how much to remove from the shoulder when you construct the lining, or a repeat version of this garment.

6. The armhole should be stabilised by stitching narrow tape or ribbon to the seamline on the wrong side. Full instructions for doing this are given in Book 1, p40-41.

PREPARING THE SLEEVE-HEAD
Here is a foolproof method to help less experienced dressmakers to overcome that old problem of trying to fit what appears to be too much sleeve into too little armhole! By the way, don't let anyone tell you that "with knitted fabrics it is easy to put a sleeve in because you can simply stretch the armhole to fit it"! If you do that you will have a very ill-fitting armhole - and, in any case, you should have already stabilised the armhole with tape so that it *can't* stretch.
Note: do not sew up the sleeve seam yet - you need to keep it flat as in **Fig.35** below.

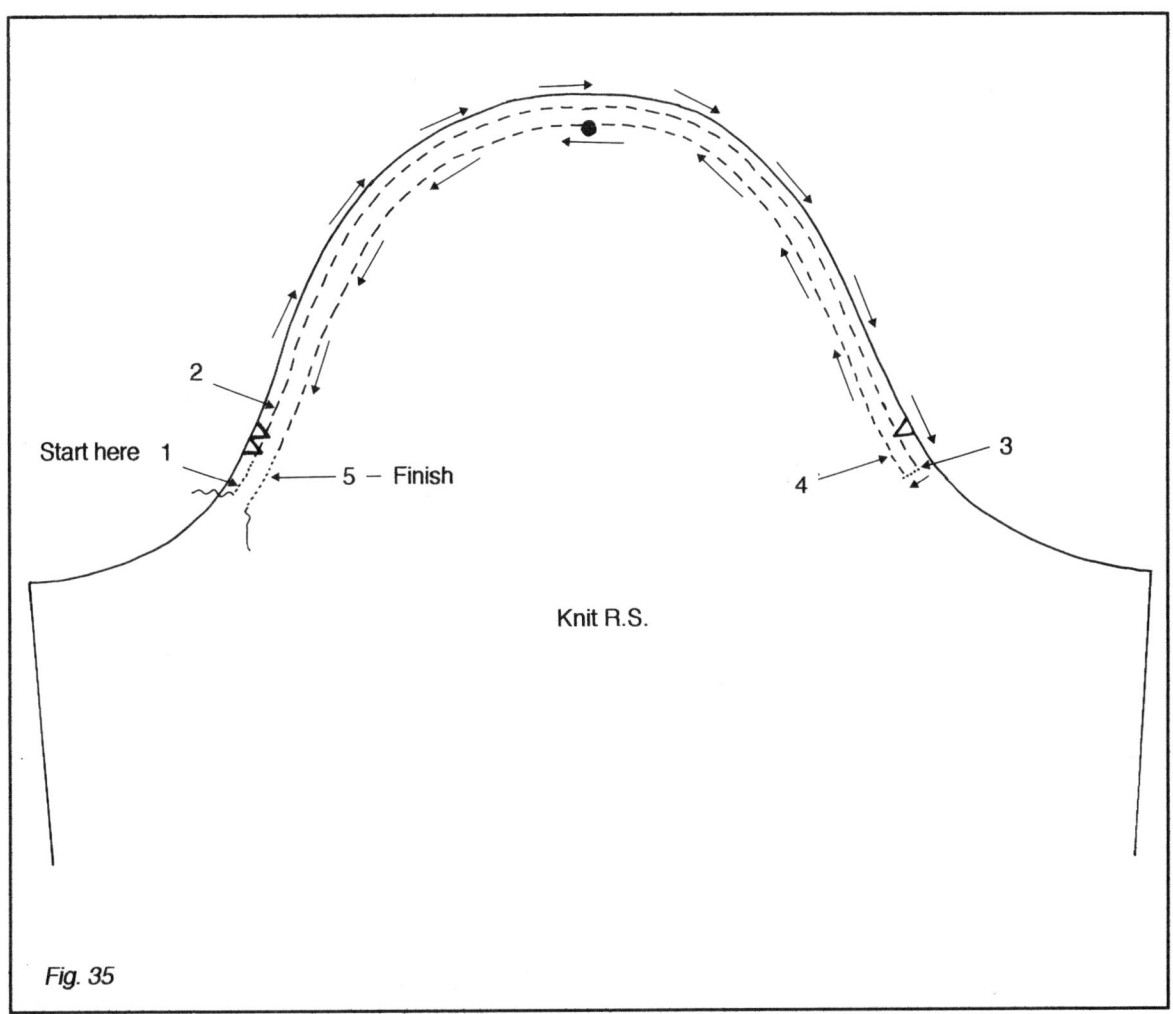

Fig. 35

First test out your sewing-machine stitch tension.

   1. Take a small, spare piece of your knitted fabric (single layer) and, with the stitch-length set at its *longest*, stitch straight for about 15cm(6in). Do not secure the thread ends.
   2. Now pick up the thread which came from the bobbin, on the underside of the fabric, at one end of the line of stitching, and try to pull it up. The fabric should gather up quite easily. If it does not, loosen the tension a little on the needle thread and repeat the test until it does pull up easily.
   Note: I have come across a few students with temperamental sewing-machines who find they can do the pulling-up more successfully on the needle thread - so be warned!

Now follow Fig.35 carefully: each step is numbered on the diagram on p.33.
1. Place the sleeve right side up; starting at the inner curve on one side of the sleeve-head, 6mm(1/4in) in from the edge and parallel with it, make a few very small machine stitches (for about 1cm(3/8in)) to make the ends secure.

2. Change to the longest straight-stitch your machine can do and stitch around the sleeve-head, keeping 6mm(1/4in) from the edge, until you reach the inner curve on the other side.

3. Change back to a very small stitch-length, turn and stitch inwards until the seamline is reached - i.e. 1.5cm(5/8in) from the edge.

4. Change to the longest straight-stitch, turn and stitch along the seamline until you reach a point opposite your original starting-point.

5. Finish off with a few very small stitches.

6. Fig.36. Hook up one stitch on each of the two lines of the bobbin threads (on the wrong side of the sleeve) at the top point of the sleeve, using a pin; ease them gently out into two loops. The outer line of stitching will need to be pulled up rather more than the inner line. Keep pulling and easing until you have a nicely shaped top to your sleeve without producing pleats or gathers. Do not tie the loops because you may need to adjust the easing later.

   If the sleeve is actually intended to be gathered into the armhole, of course the loops will have to be pulled up much further and gathering will then occur.

7. Now stitch the sleeve seam for several inches below the underarm point. On a long sleeve it is advisable not to sew the seam right to the lower end if you are going to have to make a sleeve opening. You can always complete the seam once the opening is finished.

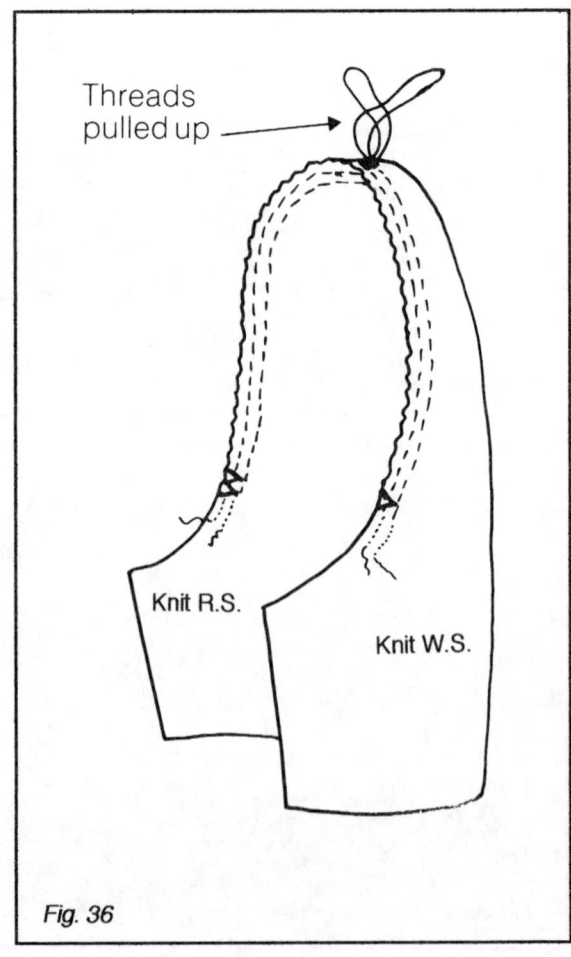

Fig. 36

INSERTING THE SLEEVE INTO THE ARMHOLE.

Fig.37. Helpful hints:
a. Work on the sleeve side, not the body side.
b. Place all the pins *across* the seamline, not parallel with it. Take care to keep the edges of the two seam allowances exactly together.
c. It may be necessary to either loosen or tighten the ease-stitching on the sleeve head to make it fit the armhole but remember that a plain set-in sleeve should have no visible gathering or pleating.
d. In the case of a puffed sleeve, aim to keep most of the gathering within about 7.5cm(3in) either side of the shoulder line.

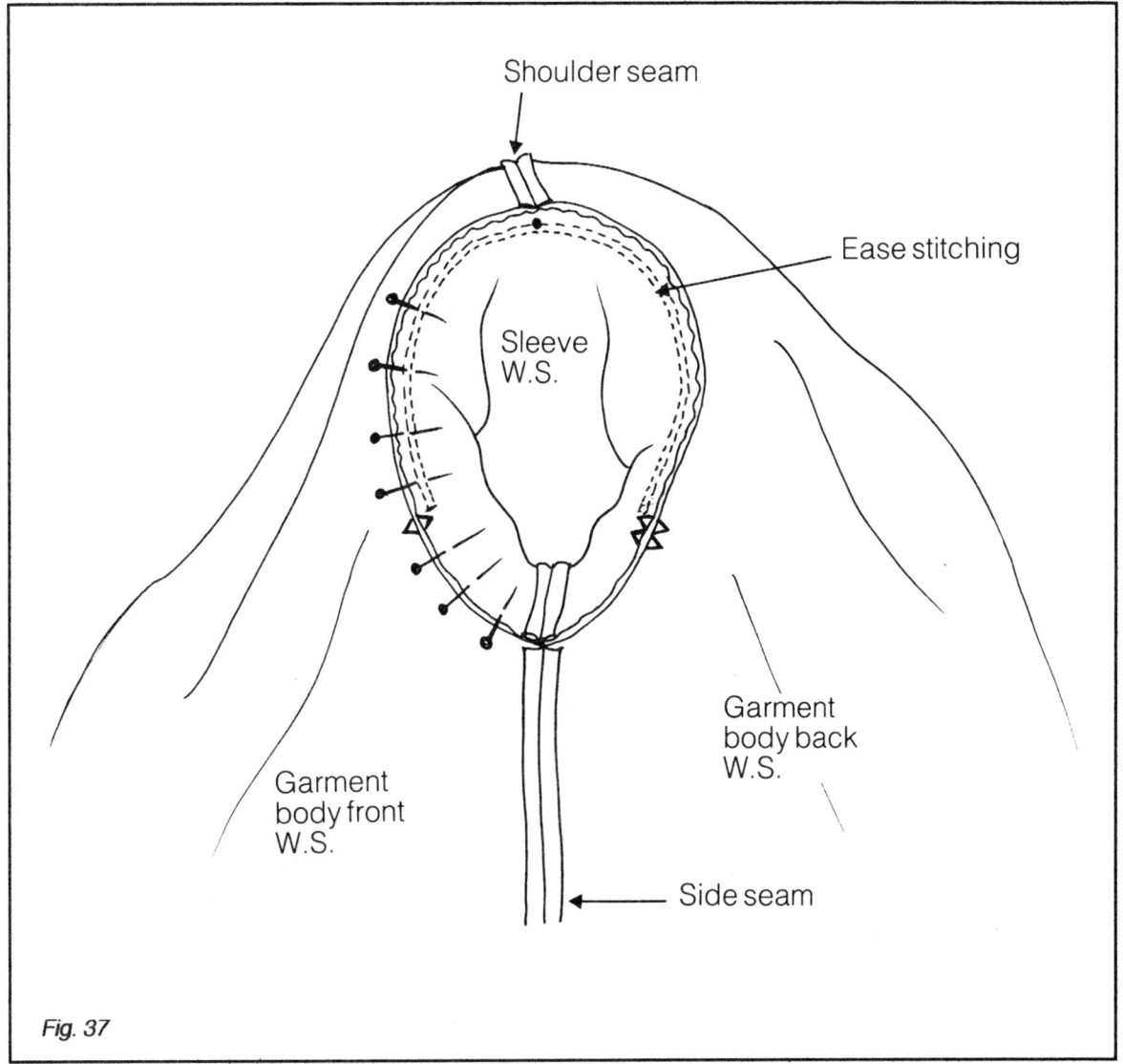

Fig. 37

Work in the following order:
1. Turn the garment wrong side out and the sleeve right side out.
2. Pass the sleeve through the armhole until the top edge of the sleeve meets the armhole edge of the garment.
3. Match and pin the underarm points.
4. Match and pin the dot at the centre top of the sleeve to the shoulder seam (or shoulder line) of the garment.

5. Match and pin the one notch at the front of the sleeve to the one notch at the front armhole, and the two notches at the back of the sleeve to the two notches at the back armhole.
6. Continue pinning until the sleeve is held in place all round the armhole.
7. *Either* - machine-stitch the seam, removing the pins just as they approach the presser foot,
   or - tack by hand, using fairly small stitches so that the fabrics will not slip, and follow this with machine-stitching. Start and finish at the underarm seamlines.
Now for the acid test - assuming that your stabilising armhole tape was positioned correctly, you should now find that the armhole seamline runs exactly along the centre of the tape! Don't panic if it doesn't - just re-position the tape where you have missed it.)

Suggestions for Neatening the Armhole Seamline

In the case of a dress or shirt, simply oversewing or overlocking the armhole seam allowances will probably be sufficient; in the case of a well fitting garment, reduce the seam allowance by half its depth around the under arm curve, but still leave the full seam allowance around the top of the armhole as this helps to support the top of the sleeve.

If you are making a coat or jacket, where the inside could be on display, you will probably want to make a neater job of it. Consider binding the trimmed seam allowances with a bias-cut strip of matching lining fabric, or perhaps silk or poly/cotton. See Chapter 12 of this book for instructions on binding. Consider, perhaps, knitting a matching narrow strip for binding.

The armholes can be sewn with lapped seams which are finally top-stitched on the right side. See Book 1, for details on p51, and illustration on p50.

The armhole seamline can be made on the right side of the garment, the seam allowances pressed open flat and then trimmed back to 6mm(1/4in): flat braid is then applied to cover the seamline and seam allowances, carefully eased to fit around the curves. See Book 1, p46.
Note: usually, the armhole seam allowances are turned out towards the sleeve, but you should check this with your pattern instructions sheets in case there are any design variations.

CHECKING THE LENGTH OF THE SLEEVE

Try on the garment. If you are going to use shoulder pads, slip them in position now as these will alter the length of the sleeve. Shorten, by cutting off from the lower end, if necessary, but check that you can bend your elbow easily. If, despite careful planning, you find that it is going to be too short, you can then plan a cuff, or lengthen any cuff which has already been planned.

MAKING A SLEEVE OPENING

A sleeve which is to have a buttoned cuff, or which fits snugly at the wrist, will need an opening at the lower end. Do this, preferably, before the sleeve seam is completed because it is so much easier to do it on flat fabric.
If, you design your own garment, remember that the opening should usually be on the back quarter of the sleeve; see **Fig.38**.

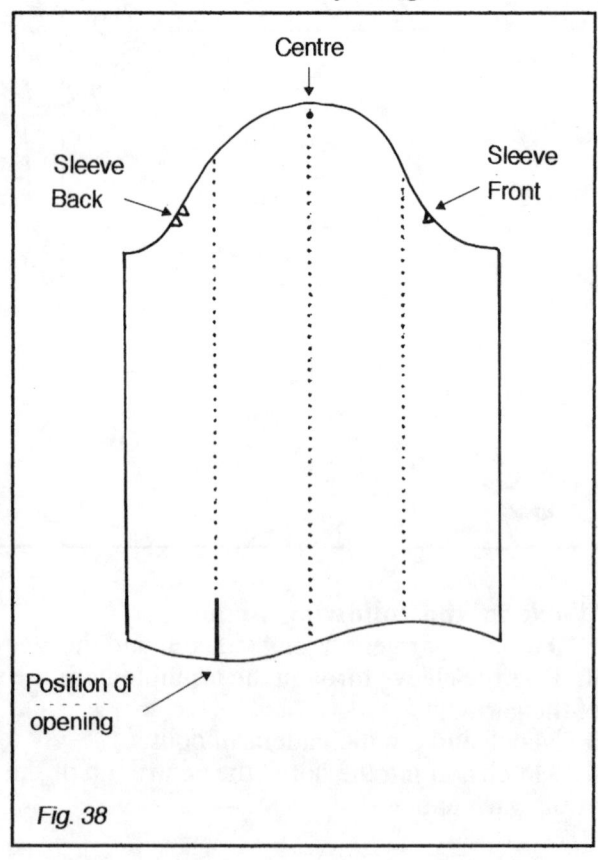

Fig. 38

Here are two methods of finishing these openings which work well on knitted fabrics.

The first is very simple and the second slightly more complicated, but both require careful and accurate machine-stitching ... and that comes with practice!

In both cases, a finely woven fabric (Eg. cotton gingham, linen, poly/cotton poplin, polyester lining, etc.), should be used to give a firm and secure finish to the knit without adding too much bulk.

Method A.

1. **Fig.39a.** Mark the position of the opening on the right side of the sleeve.

2. **Fig.39b.** Cut a rectangle of woven fabric approximately 7cm(2³/4in) wide, by 4cm(1¹/2in) longer than the required length of the opening. Oversew, or overlock, the raw edges on three sides as shown.

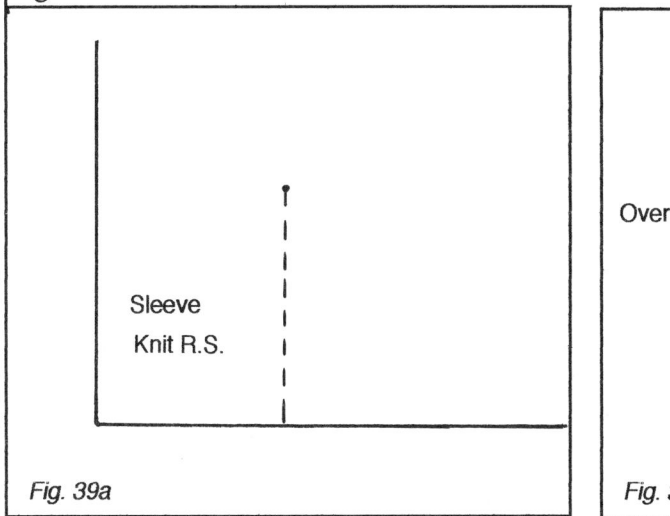

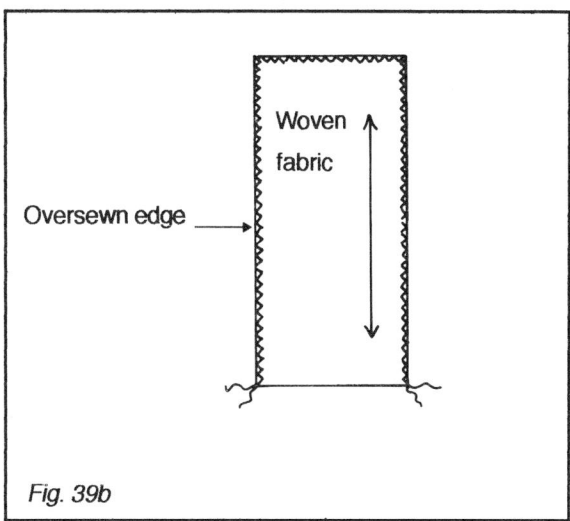

Fig. 39a

Fig. 39b

3. **Fig.39c.** Centre the woven fabric piece over the marked position on the knitted sleeve, right sides together, and pin in place. Draw the line of the opening on the wrong side of the fabric piece, using a cloth-marking pen or pencil.

4. **Fig.39d.** With the stitch-length set at very small (about 1 to 1¹/2) stay-stitch around the pencilled line, keeping about 9mm(³/8in) away from it at the lower end and making a narrow U-shaped bend (not a sharp point) at the top.

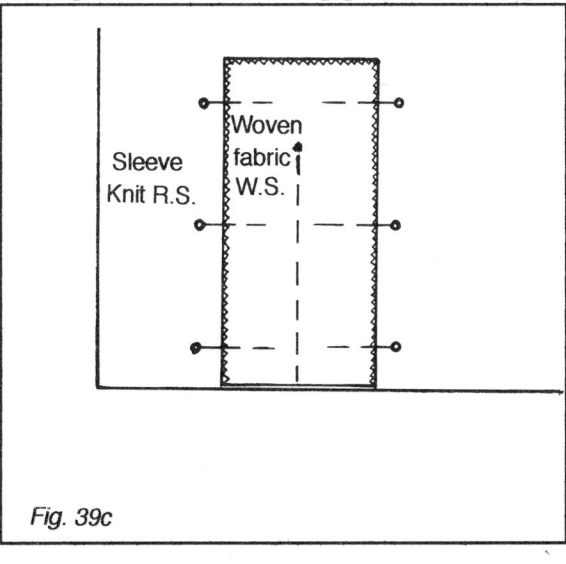

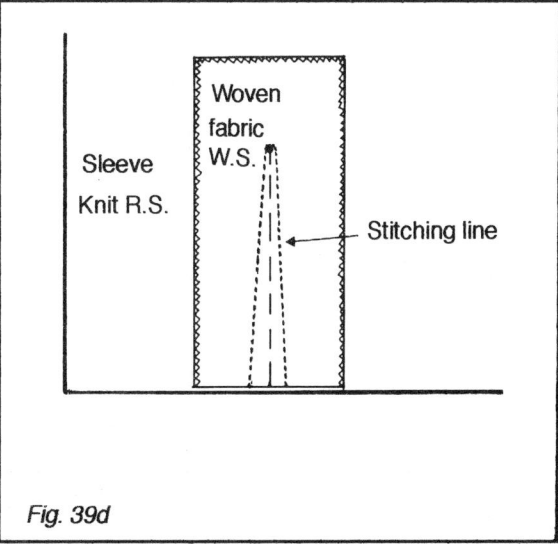

Fig. 39c

Fig. 39d

5. Fig.39e. Cut carefully between the lines of stitching, right up to the stitching at the top, stopping only just short of it.

6. Fig.39f. Turn the woven fabric piece through to the wrong side of the sleeve, rolling the seamline slightly to the wrong side so that it is invisible from the right side. Press well. Tack the lower edges of the woven fabric piece to the lower edges of the knitted sleeve on both sides of the opening. Blind-hem the top of the woven fabric piece to the knit to hold it in place.

Note: when the cuff is attached, the two edges of this type of sleeve opening should meet but should not overlap.

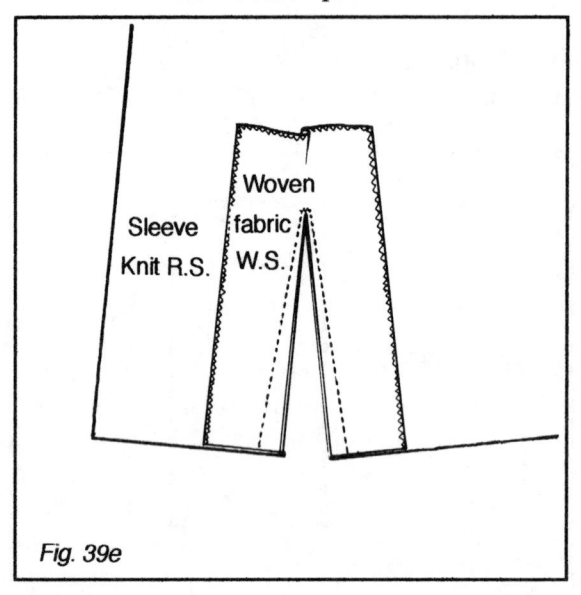

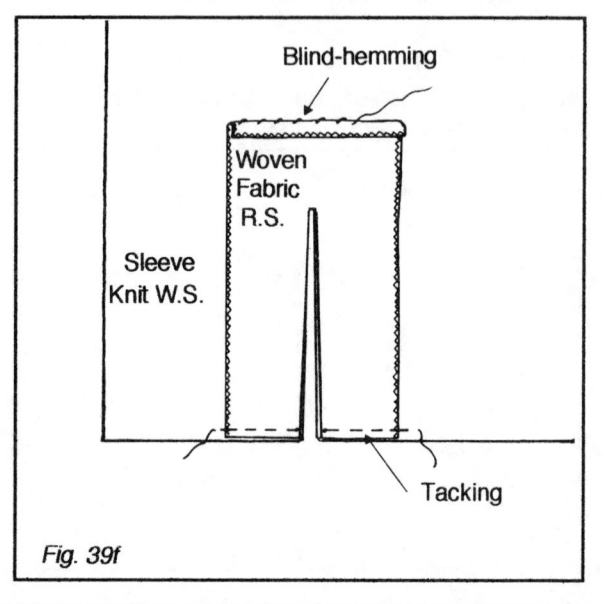

Fig. 39e

Fig. 39f

Method B

1. Fig.40a. Mark the position and length of the opening on the wrong side of the sleeve.

2. Fig.40b. With the stitch length set at very small (about 1 to 1 1/2) stay-stitch around the marked line, as in Method A-4.

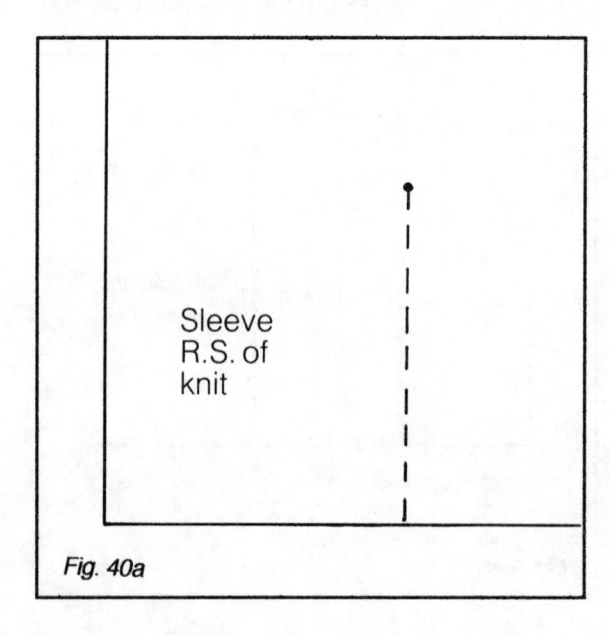

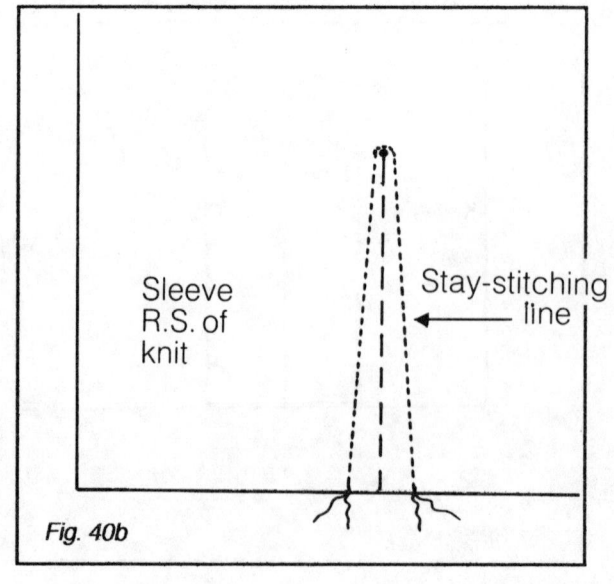

Fig. 40a

Fig. 40b

3. Fig.40c.
Cut as in Fig.39e.

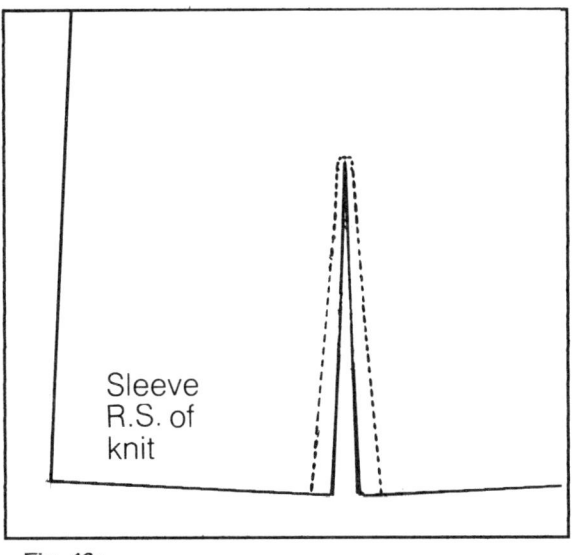

Fig. 40c

Fig. 40d

Woven fabric binding strip

4. Fig.40d.
Cut a straight-grain strip of woven fabric, 4.5cm(1¾in) wide, by twice as long as the proposed opening. This is your binding strip.

5. Fig.40e.
Open the cut slit out into a straight line and lay it, wrong side down, on to the right side of the binding strip.

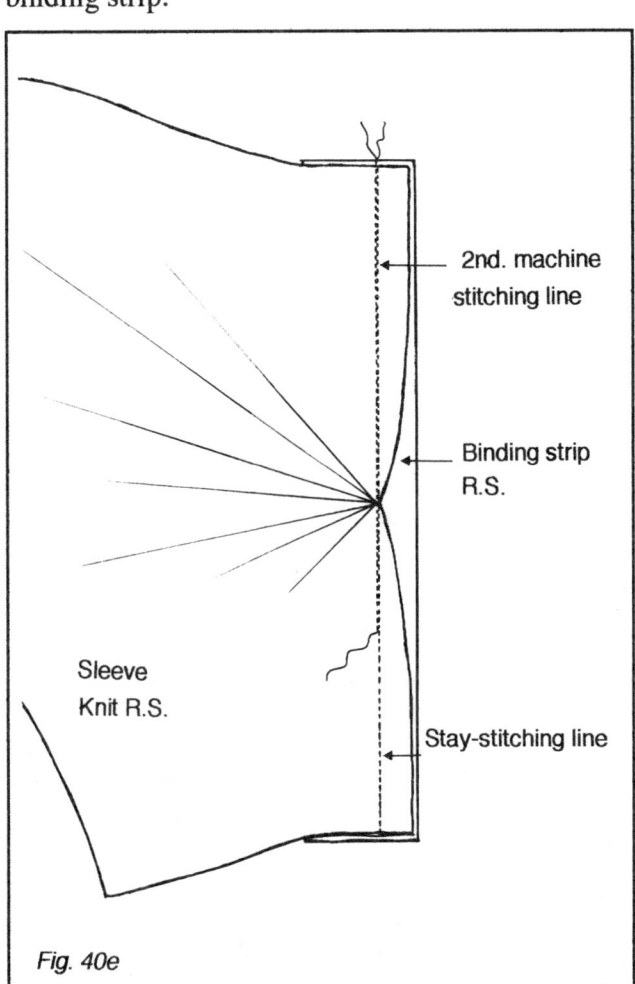

2nd. machine stitching line

Binding strip R.S.

Sleeve Knit R.S.

Stay-stitching line

Fig. 40e

Position it -
so that the line of stay-stitching lies exactly parallel with the edge of the binding strip.

Pin in position.
Then machine again -
exactly along the stay-stitching line.

Take care to avoid catching in the folds of the knitted sleeve when you reach the middle of the line.

6. Fig.40f.
Fold and press the free edge of the binding strip 9mm(3/8in) to the wrong side.
Roll this folded edge towards the right side of the sleeve until it just barely covers the stitching line. Pin and top-stitch in place.

7. Fig.40g.
To finish, turn one side of the bound opening to the inside of the sleeve; which side depends upon which sleeve you are working on.
Remember that the front of the sleeve should overlap the back.

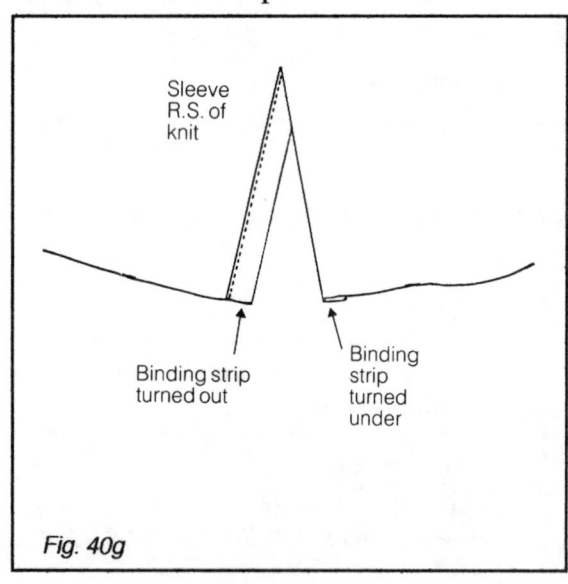

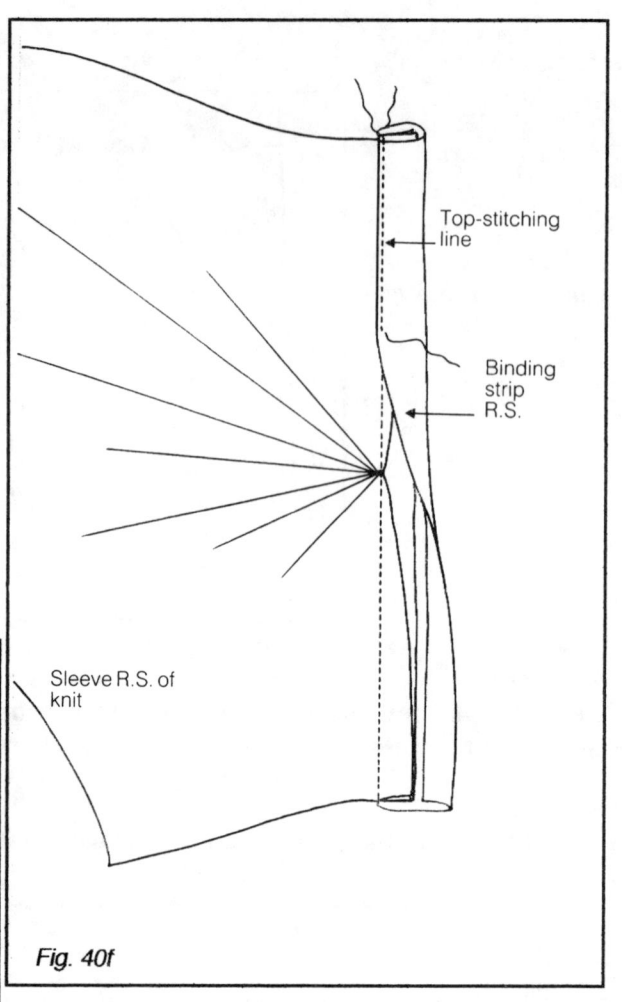

Fig. 40g

Fig. 40f

Completing the sleeve seam
When the opening is completed, the sleeve seam can be sewn up and pressed. The cuff should then be attached.

CUFFS

Cuffs come in many forms and you probably have adequate instructions for making them in the instruction sheets given with the pattern you are using, but, in case you are designing your own garment, here are some simple guidelines.

Making a buttoned cuff
A shirt-type cuff can be made of knitted fabric which has been interfaced to make it stable and reasonably firm - but do beware of ending up with something which is far too bulky! A possible solution to this problem is to make a cuff in two parts - the outside layer of the knit and the inside (the cuff facing) of lining fabric or some other thin woven cloth. Alternatively, consider making the cuff entirely of woven fabric, perhaps matching the collar, the front buttoning band and the binding used for the sleeve opening.
Combining woven fabrics with knits in this way is both practical and attractive; a variety of effects can be achieved by mixing the textures and the colours - rough with smooth, plain with pattern, matt with shine, etc.

Here is a simple one-piece cuff which could be cut in woven fabric, or even a fine, interfaced knit:

1. Cut two identical rectangles.
    Length = measurement of wrist, plus a total of 8cm(3 1/4ins) for ease, overlap and seam allowances.
    Depth = twice the desired depth of the finished cuff, plus 3cm(1 1/4in) for seam allowances.

2. Mark a foldline along the centre of the cuff lengthwise.

3 **Fig.41a.** Cut and apply interfacing to fit just over half the cuff, so that it extends approximately 1.2cm(1/2in) over the marked foldline. *Note* that the half which is completely interfaced is termed *the cuff* and the other half is termed *the cuff facing*.

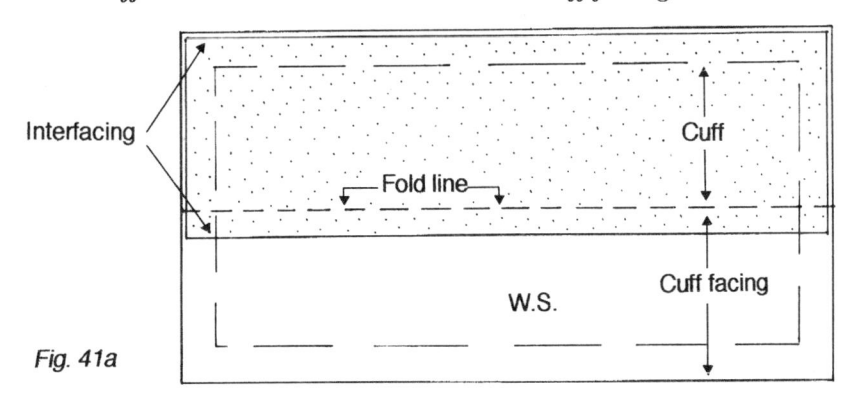

Fig. 41a

4. **Fig.41b.** Press the interfaced seam allowance of the cuff to the wrong side. Tack if necessary and then trim to 6mm(1/4in).

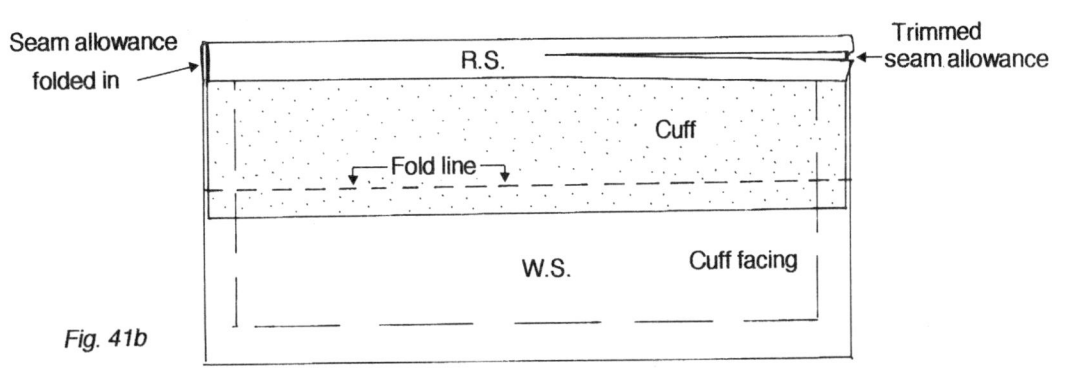

Fig. 41b

5.   **Fig.41c.** Fold the cuff, right sides together, along the foldline. Stitch the end seams, using a fairly short stitch-length, and trim the seam allowances to 6mm(1/4in).

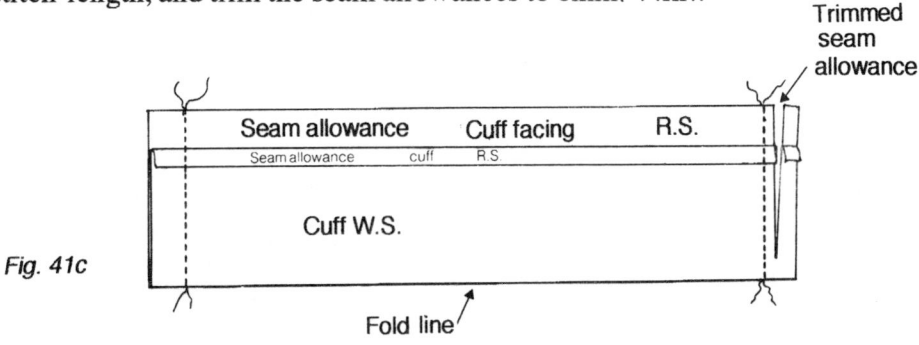

Fig. 41c

6. **Fig.41d.** Turn the cuff to the right side, pushing out the corners gently. Press.

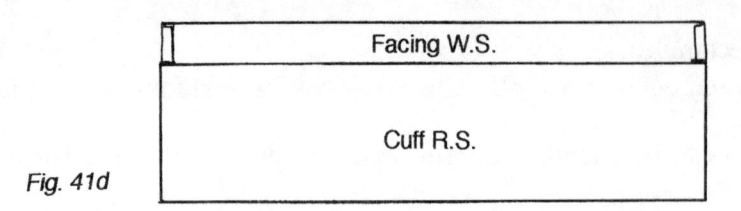

Fig. 41d

Facing W.S.
Cuff R.S.

Note: A cuff made in two fabrics (knitted and woven) would, of course have to be cut in two halves with a seamline between cuff and cuff facing, where I have illustrated a foldline

Attaching a cuff to a shirt-type sleeve

1. Turn the sleeve inside out.

2. **Fig.42a.** apply the right side of the seam allowance on the cuff facing to the wrong side of the seam allowance on the sleeve end, matching the edges of the seam allowances. Line up the cuff ends with the edges of the sleeve opening. Pin carefully, as shown, adjusting the gathering (or pleating) on the sleeve to fit the cuff. Tack if necessary. Machine stitch (small stitch-length) and trim the seam allowances to 6mm(1/4in).

3. **Fig.42b.** Turn sleeve and cuff to the right side and pin the turned-in seam allowance of the cuff to the sleeve, so that it just covers the previous seamline. Top-stitch in place, carrying the stitching right round the entire cuff edge if desired.

Note: if a plain finish, with no visible stitching on the right side, is required, attach the cuff to the right side of the sleeve first and then hem the facing to the wrong side by hand.

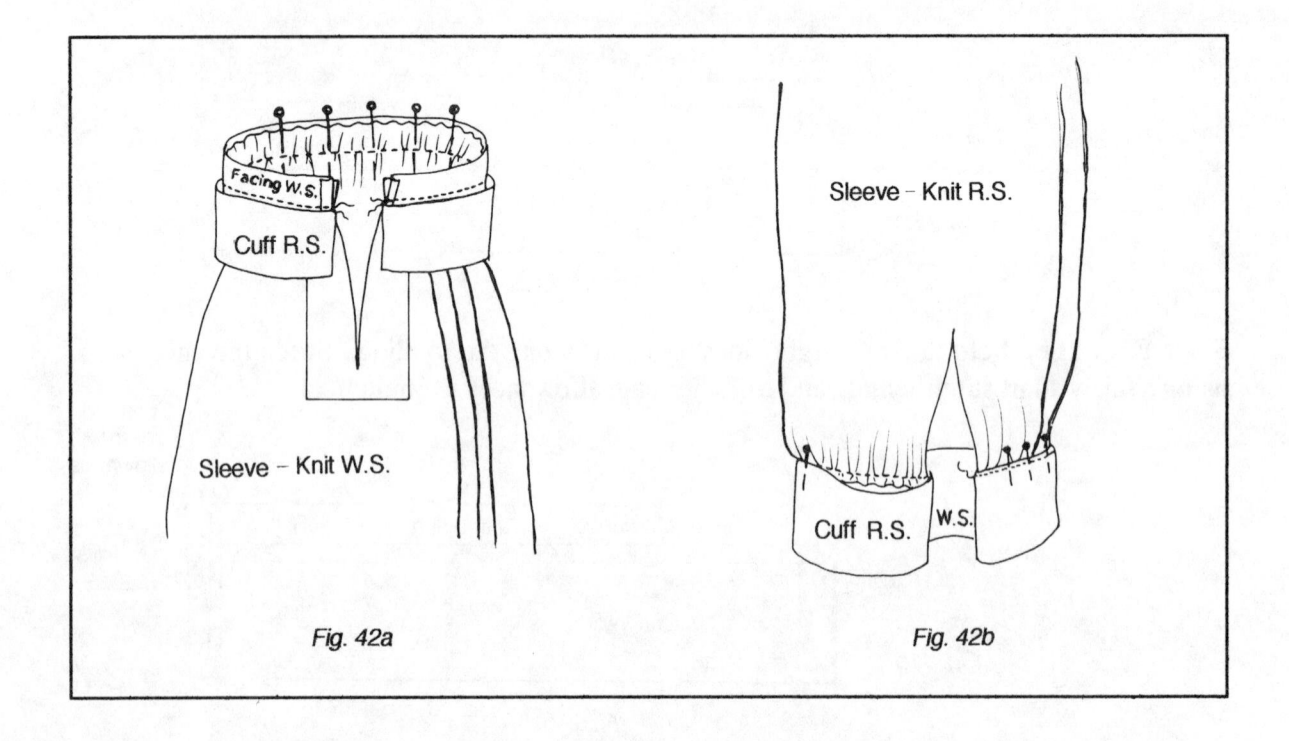

Fig. 42a

Fig. 42b

Other types of cuff

Cuffs which will stretch and therefore do not need an opening in the sleeve above them, can be cut from purchased ribbing available from some haberdashers. This should be cut to the correct length to fit comfortably around the wrist, sewn into a circle, stretched out to fit the lower end of the sleeve and sewn with zigzag stitching and overlocking. Similar cuffs can be made from your own knitted fabric providing it still has a fair degree of stretch quality after pressing, and it is not too bulky. (This method, detailed below, is fully illustrated in Book 1, p70 - the technique is just the same as that used for T-shirt necklines)

1. Cut a strip across the knitted fabric, keeping straight along one row.
    Length = long enough to fit comfortably around the wrist (or wherever the sleeve should finish) and for the hand to pass through, plus two seam allowances.
    Depth = twice as deep as the desired depth of the finished cuff plus two seam allowances.
    Note: do not use interfacing here because you need to retain the stretch quality of the fabric.

2. Stitch the ends of the strip, right sides together, to form a circle.

3. Fold the circle in half lengthwise and stitch the raw edges together with a zigzag stitch, keeping 6mm(1/4in) from the raw edges.

4. Pin the raw edges of the cuff to the right side of the sleeve end, stretching out the sleeve to fit. (If the sleeve is very full it may need to be gathered first.) Sew with zigzag stitching (medium length and width), trim the seam allowances and oversew, or overlock and trim together. Turn the cuff downwards.

An elasticated cuff
Fig.43
This is useful for bomber-type jackets and can be made by turning up a hem allowance at the bottom of the sleeve, approximately 5cm(2in) to 7.5cm(3in) deep, and dividing this hem into several channels by making lines of straight machine-stitching parallel with the lower edge; a length of fairly narrow elastic, to fit the wrist, is then inserted into each channel.

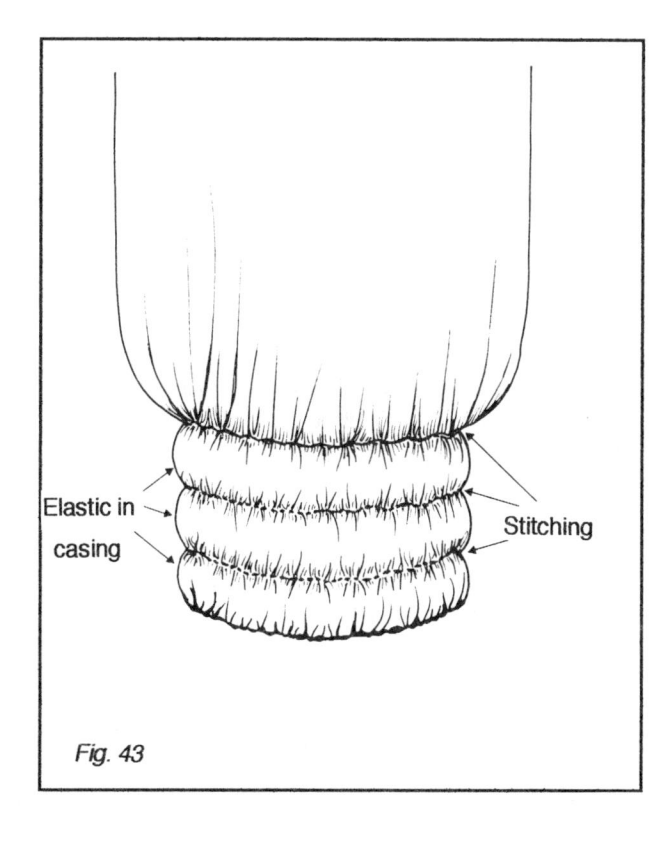

Fig. 43

CHAPTER 7

SHOULDER PADS

Shoulder pads are an essential part of the current fashion scene but are far removed from the cumbersome affairs made of horsehair which gave us the military look (or in some cases, the "spiv" look!) during World War Two. Many women, however, are now reluctant to use shoulder pads, fearing that they may look like an escapee from an American soap opera; this is a pity because the average British rather pear-shaped figure is generally enormously improved by making the shoulders appear wider and straighter.

I suggest therefore that whenever you make a garment you simply try out the effect of padding out the shoulders with anything handy - spare fabric, tissues, a skein of wool - and then look at the result in a good mirror. If your dressmaking pattern was designed for shoulder pads (check on this in the instruction sheets) then you actually have a gap there which should either be filled with a pad, or removed by taking in the outer end of the shoulder seam and moving the armhole seamline inwards towards the neck. Even if no shoulder pad is suggested in the instructions, a small one usually improves the line tremendously. Just try it.

BUYING SHOULDER PADS

Be careful to select the correct shape and size for the garment you are sewing. For example, a pad designed for a set-in sleeve simply will not fit properly in a raglan sleeve, and there is a slightly different shape designed for drop-shoulder seams. Remember too that a coat will generally need a much larger and thicker pad than a dress.

Home dressmakers often have difficulty in finding shoulder pads in the variety of shapes and sizes demanded by the pattern designers.

Vilene have completely re-designed their range, as follows:
1. 'Luxury Soft' pads (these are more suitable for knitwear than dressmaking)
2. 'Covered Contour Moulded' pads:
   Note: both the above types are available in raglan and set-in shapes and are composed of foam, covered with knitted nylon, but both are limited to only one size.
3. 'Traditionally Structured' pads are designed for lined garment where they will be hidden between the outer layer and the lining. These also come in both raglan and set-in types, are beautifully shaped and are available in both small and medium sizes.

Other manufacturers' shoulder pads are to be found so you should check on what is available in your local haberdashery store. *always bearing in mind the particular shoulder shape of the garment you are making and the size it requires.*

Here are some guidelines:

1. *For set-in sleeves*, remember that, to fit the garment properly, the pad should not be merely a semi-circle as in **Fig.44a.**

The outer edge (A-B) should be curved to fit the armhole of the garment, as shown in **Fig.44b.**

The shoulder line should be clearly indicated by a mark or notch, and the Back portion should be longer than the Front portion.

So, when you buy a pair of shoulder pads for set-in sleeves, they should be different - one for the Left Shoulder and one for the Right Shoulder!

Fig. 44a

Fig. 44b — shoulder line, Back, Front

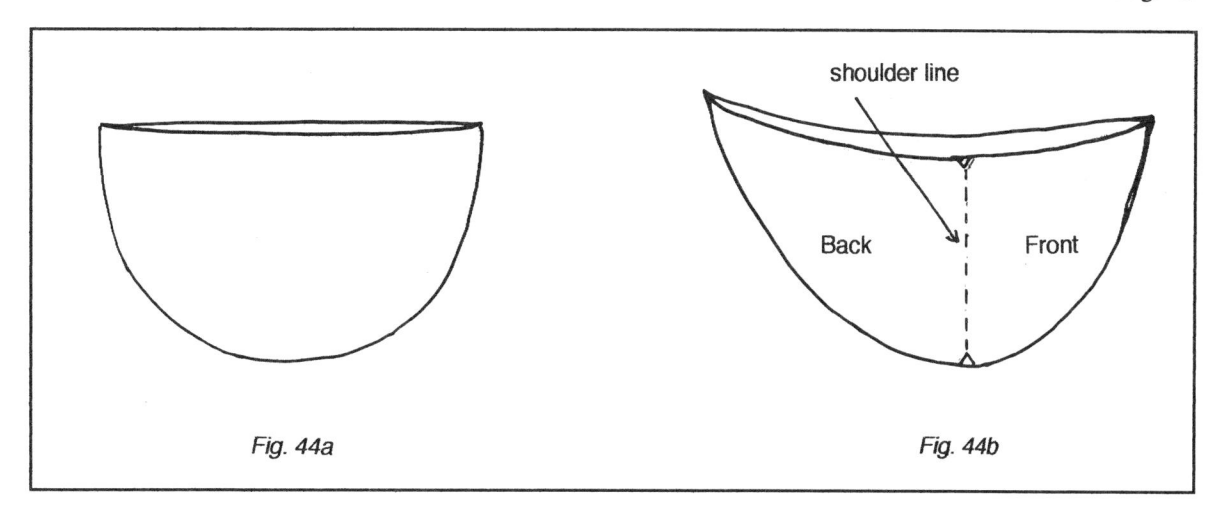

2. If the shoulders are to be very much raised, you may find it advisable to add a small pad to the underside of a larger one; use fabric glue, or slipstitch with a needle and thread, to keep them together. This is often an excellent idea if you happen to have one shoulder much higher than the other!

3. The rounded edges of the pads should be gently tapered off so that they do not show as visible lines on the outside of the garment. Avoid any pads which have thick, lumpy edges.

4. Remember that shoulder pads which are to be sewn into a garment which is going to be dry cleaned should be suitable for dry-cleaning; likewise, if the garment is to be washed, the pads must also be washable.

Alternatively try making your own; Vogue and Butterick sell excellent paper patterns for shoulder pads in a wide range of styles.

COVERING SHOULDER PADS

Purchased pads made of polyester foam with no outer covering, need to be covered with some kind of fabric before sewing into a garment, otherwise they simply get torn by the needle and thread. If they are going to lie between the main fabric of the garment and a lining, they can be covered with virtually anything which is soft, flexible and thin; butter muslin, nylon tricot or even fabric cut from the wide end of an old pair of nylon tights.

Purchased pads which already have a fabric covering, or which are constructed of some material into which you can sew, will need no further covering if they are going to be hidden by the garment lining.

If the garment is to be unlined then the pads should be covered with the same knitted fabric as that from which the garment is cut.

For a set-in sleeve

1. Fig.45a. Take a sufficiently large square of fabric (cut straight with the grain) and mark a line between diagonally opposite corners, on the wrong side of the knit.

2. Place the thicker edge of the pad along the marked diagonal line.

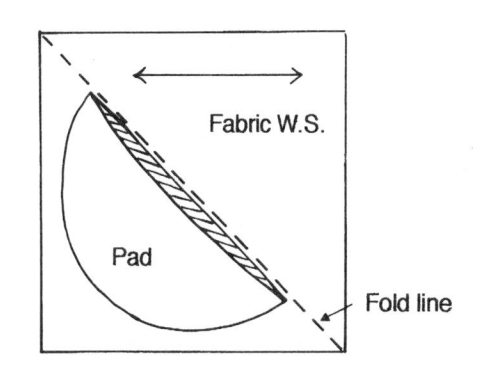

Fig. 45a — Fabric W.S., Pad, Fold line

3.   Fig.45b. Fold the fabric over and pin the two layers together all around the rounded edge of the pad as shown. Because the covering fabric is now on the bias grain you can mould it to fit the pad closely. Take care to retain the curved shape of the pad - don't flatten it! It is wise to pin just fractionally inside the edge of the pad so that the stitching which follows will catch in the pad so that it will not eventually be left floating around loose inside the cover.
    Machine-stitch where the pins lie, removing each pin as you get to it.

5.   Fig.45c. Trim off the surplus fabric leaving a small seam allowance. Oversew or overlock the raw edges together and mark the centre line

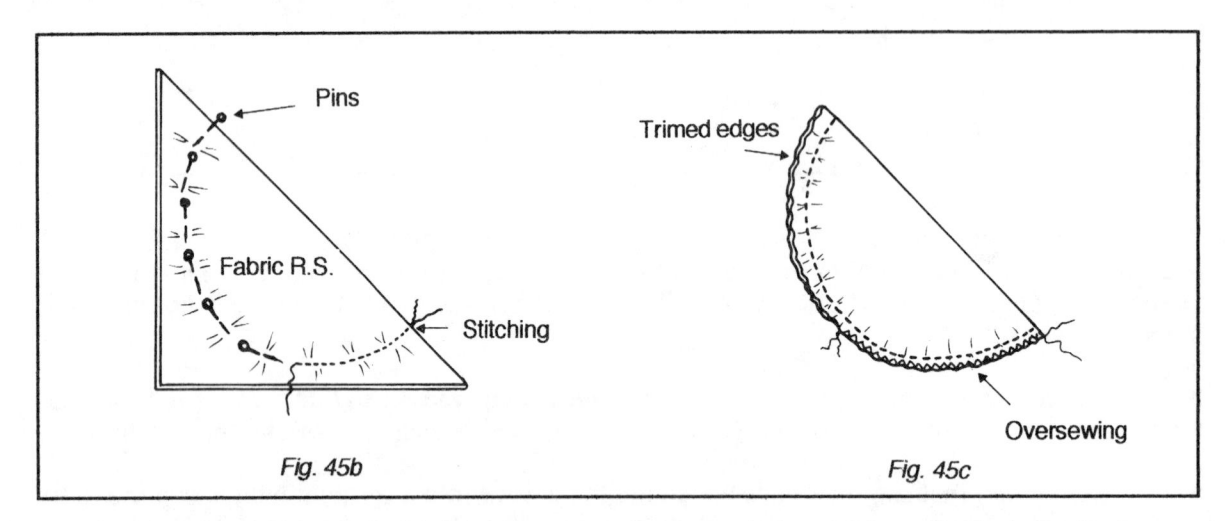

Fig. 45b   *Fig. 45c*

For a raglan or dolman shaped sleeve

1.   Cut two or three separate pieces of knitted fabric for each pad - one (or possibly two seamed together) for the top and one for the under surface. These knit pieces should still be cut on the bias grain
2.   Mould the knit pieces carefully, both under and over the pad, in order to keep the shaping correct. Slip-stitch to hold the knit into the hollow under the pad, if necessary.
3.   Oversewing should be carried all around the pad in this case.

SEWING IN SHOULDER PADS

Note: always sew in (or, at least, pin in) your shoulder pads *before* making a final decision on the sleeve length, because the pads will lift the sleeves a little.

For a set-in sleeve

1.   Mark a line on the upper side of the pad, exactly along the 'shoulder-line' (this could be indicated by a cut notch in a manufactured pad, and might, or might not, be in the centre), from the outer (thick) end to the inner (thin) end. Use pencil, pins or thread to do this marking.

2.   On the inside of the garment, place this marked line exactly along the shoulder seam* (see note below), *with the thick end of the pad extending 1.5cm(5/8in) out into the sleeve head.* If you have left the full 1.5cm(5/8in) armhole seam allowance, you will find that the thick end of the pad lines up neatly with the edges of the seam allowances. Pin the pad in position from the right side of the garment, placing the pins at right angles to the seamline and just catching the shoulder seamline to the marked line on the cover of the pad.
**Note: if you have no shoulder seam, or you have a 'dropped' shoulder seam, the shoulder-
        line of the pad must be aligned with the shoulder-line on the garment body .*

You will find that this is marked on your paper pattern). You then have to catch the pad to the garment wherever you can do so invisibly.

3.   Try the garment on to check that the padding looks right. Adjust if necessary.

4.   From the right side of the garment, hand stitch, using small back-stitches 1.25cm(1/2in) apart, exactly along and into the shoulder seamline, catching the seamline to the cover of the pad. Take care to catch in only the cover of the pad - do not take the needle into the pad itself or you may distort its shape. Providing you use a carefully matched thread this stitching should be totally invisible.

5.   Repeat this invisible stitching around the armhole seamline, from one end of the pad to the other.
Note: If the thick end of the pad is not sufficiently curved to fit the armhole seamline, it may be wiser to secure the pad only along the shoulder seamline, leaving the ends of the pad to 'float' independently.

For a raglan or dolman sleeve.
As there is no conventional armhole line you will need to try on the garment in front of a mirror in order to find the point where the outer end of the pad should go. It should fit comfortably over the end of your shoulder, making a smoothly rounded shape and supporting the sleeve. The shoulder line of the pad should be attached to the shoulder seam with invisible stitching while the remainder of the pad is left to 'float'.

SHOULDER PADS - NOT SEWN IN - AND INTERCHANGEABLE!
Shoulder pads are becoming expensive so this idea could save you money. It also solves the problem that looms when you want to wear a shoulder-padded top under a shoulder-padded jacket under a shoulder-padded coat; you can end up looking like the Incredible Hulk!
So, if you habitually wear one basic colour (eg. beige or navy-blue), try covering your shoulder pads with a knit in that colour and then simply stitch a strip of Velcro (the hook side) to the top of the pad, along the shoulder line. This will then cling sufficiently well to almost any garment made from knitted fabric. Of course, it doesn't work if the garment is lined!

ANOTHER USEFUL SHOULDER PAD HINT
If your garment is made from any kind of 'see-through' fabric, (eg. knitted lace) then your shoulder pads should be covered with a fabric which matches, as closely as possible, the colour of your own skin. Black shoulder pads showing through black lace, over pale skin, look really awful!

SIMPLE HOME-MADE SHOULDER PAD

Note: this method should be used only for small pads (for dresses, tops, etc.) because the thick edge of the pad cannot be curved to fit the armhole well.

1.   **Fig.46a.** Cut a square of knitted fabric (or lining fabric) and three squares of polyester wadding or Vilene non-fusible Fleece (see p6), graded in size as shown. The layers should be loosely tacked (or fused with fabric glue) to each other and to the fabric square, to keep them in place.

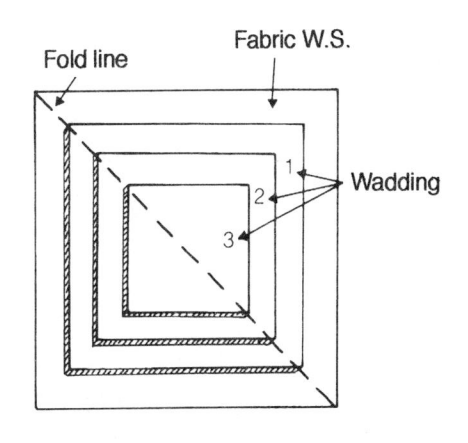

Fig. 46a

2.　Fig.46b.
Fold diagonally and stitch along the two straight sides as shown.

The same kind of pad can be made by cutting oval or circular shapes instead of squares.

Remember that pads filled with polyester wadding must never get involved with heat pressing, because that flattens the wadding irretrievably.

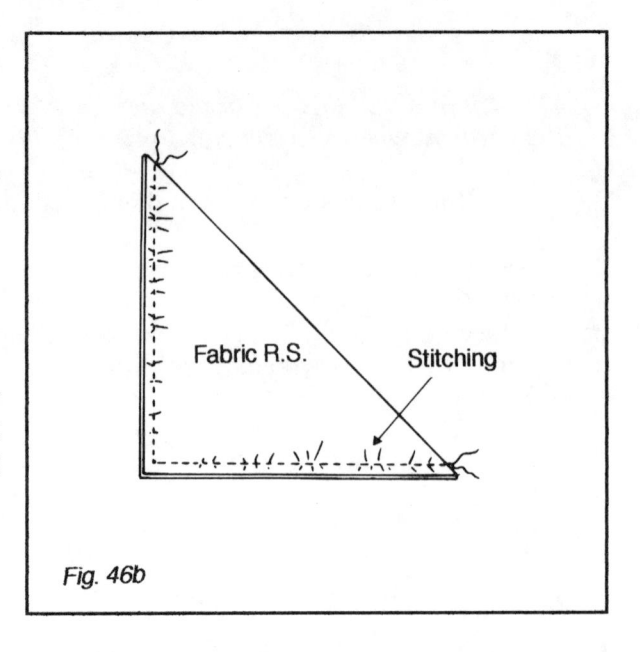

Fabric R.S.　　Stitching

Fig. 46b

SUPPORTING THE SLEEVE TOP WITHOUT PADDING UP THE SHOULDER

If you already have rather square shoulders you may want to avoid adding conventional shoulder pads and yet the sleeve head may need a little support. Also, if the top of the sleeve is actually gathered or pleated, some form of support to hold up that gathering is vital.

Suggested methods

a. Make little sausage-shaped bags, stuffed with wadding, yarn or small bits of knitting.

b. Sew in a folded strip of stiff, sew-in Vilene.

c. Fig.47. Take some fairly stiff petersham ribbon (about 2.5cm(1in) wide) and pleat it into a slightly curved, fan shape, about 10cm(4in) long.
　Machine-stitch along the shorter edge, and then sew this to the top of the armhole seamline, with the fanned-out pleats extending out into the top of the sleeve.
　This can also be made from firm, sew-in Vilene interfacing, stiff tulle or organza.

Sew the supporting pad, whichever method is used, just along the top of the armhole seamline, directing most of it out towards the sleeve.

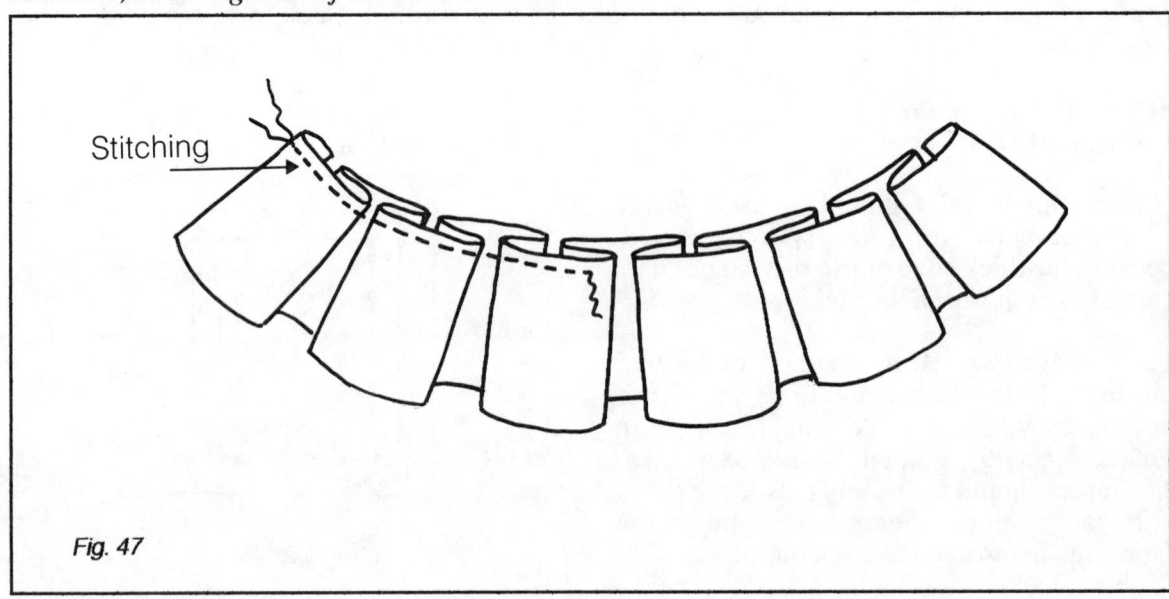

Stitching

Fig. 47

CHAPTER 8

POCKETS

Some people don't like pockets and never seem to need them. I feel positively deprived if I do not have a pocket somewhere around my person to give me instant access to my reading glasses, handkerchief, car keys, etc. However, pockets are not always utilitarian; they can be an aesthetically pleasing part of the style and shape of the garment even if they are never actually used.

It is rarely safe to assume that you can simply slap a pocket on at a late stage in the making up process; they need careful planning and, depending upon the type of pocket, some degree of expertise in their execution. The dressmaking pattern you are using will probably give you sufficient instruction in how to cut and apply the particular kind of pocket used in the design, but as you will have the additional problem of coping with knitted fabrics, these instructions may not be totally adequate.

Here are several general points which it may be helpful to consider.

1. *Check the position of the pockets* by pinning the pattern for the pocket to the pattern for the garment front: hold this up against you (positioning the shoulder and centre-front lines correctly) and have a look in a mirror. Is the pocket at the right level for you? Is it perhaps just where it will make your worst feature look even worse? Is the opening wide enough for your hand to enter comfortably? Do you like it? If there is anything you need to alter, do it now, to the paper pattern, before starting to cut the knit.

2. *Consider the weight of the pockets*. Are they likely to stretch the knit to which they are going to be sewn: this is a definite possibility, for instance, where a patch pocket is going to be lined and interlined, and therefore becomes heavier than the main fabric. In this case, the front of the garment will probably have to be interfaced to give it strength and stability, either over its whole area, or simply over the part where the pockets are to be attached. The type of interfacing used would depend upon the style of the garment and the weight of the knit. On a dress, fusible knitted nylon or fine fusible muslin would be sufficient, but in the case of a coat or jacket, fusible tailoring canvas would probably be more suitable.

3. *Avoid the 'droopy pocket' syndrome!* A patch pocket made of the knit alone, could possibly become "baggy" if it is going to be used much. Consider this and perhaps decide to line it, using purchased polyester lining fabric.

4. *Avoid stretched out top edges on your pockets.* It is perfectly permissible to construct a patch pocket from the knit alone, leaving it unlined, but care must be taken to see that the upper (opening) edge does not then stretch out of shape. The top of the pocket could be faced on the inside with purchased woven fabric, or it could be finished with an applied band of woven fabric on the outside. Where the pocket facing and the pocket are cut as one piece, the pocket facing could be interfaced with Vilene Fold-a-Band. Pockets can be bound with straight-cut binding, bias binding, braid, or with ribbon - just along the top edge, or around the entire pocket edge.

5. *Use purchased, woven, minimum-bulk fabrics where you can.* Any part of the pocket which is hidden away inside the garment (i.e. the 'bag' part of an inset pocket), should be cut from a thin but stable, woven fabric such as polyester lining, cotton poplin or strong calico; this helps to limit the bulk and makes for a harder-wearing pocket.

6. *Do you really need pockets?* If not, you could achieve the effect of pockets by simply making faced flap shapes and sewing them on. Or perhaps you would prefer pockets in the side seams rather than patch pockets. Feel free to make your own adaptations to the original design of the paper pattern - but always considering suitability and practicality.

JETTED, WELT OR INSET POCKETS - WITH OR WITHOUT FLAPS

These vary greatly in style, shape and construction technique, so you need to follow carefully the directions in your chosen paper pattern, or to consult a good dressmaking manual.

Here are some general hints to make the job easier

1. *Interface the knit firmly*, because jetted, welt or inset pockets are made rather like very large buttonholes and a firm non-stretch basis is essential. In addition to any interfacing you have already applied to the knitted Front pieces, firm, non-stretch, fusible interfacing should be applied to the wrong side, over an area extending at least 5cm(2in) all around the proposed pocket opening. This process presents three great advantages to make your life easier!
    a. The knit is now stable over the entire pocket area.
    b. All the tiny thread ends which could otherwise fray when the pocket slit is cut close to the stitching, are now firmly stuck down.
    c. The pattern lines, dots, circles, etc. which are your essential guides in constructing this kind of pocket, can now all be drawn on the interfacing with a sharp, soft pencil (or a cloth-marking pen) and a ruler.

2. Make a line of machine-stitching, very accurately, around the rectangle which marks the opening, following the lines you have ruled on the interfacing; doing this marks precisely the guidelines you need on the right side of the garment!

3. For jetted pockets, consider cutting the binding strips (the lips of the pocket) from a firm woven fabric rather than attempting to make them from knitted fabric; you may perhaps be planning to use this fabric elsewhere on the same garment, possibly to cover piping cord, make a collar and cuffs, or as a buttoning band   This makes sewing easier and reduces bulk.
    Note: a useful tip here - when folding and pressing the binding strip, in half lengthwise, stick the two layers together with Wundaweb: the strips are then much easier to handle without danger of fraying.

LINED AND INTERFACED PATCH POCKETS.

Patch pockets and bag-shaped pockets hidden behind seams are the two types you are most likely to want to add to any garment when you do not actually have a pattern to help you, so I am including detailed instructions for these. As with all cut-and-sew processes, it is wise to have a dummy run first, using odd pieces of fabric.

To make a patch pocket

1. **Fig 48a.** Draw and cut out a paper pattern for your pockets as shown. The dimensions are your own choice but should be in correct proportion to the garment to which the pockets will be applied; if in doubt, cut paper to what you think should be the size and shape of the finished pocket and pin it to the garment and check the effect.
    The pocket shown has rounded corners but of course they could be square if desired. Draw the finished shape first, add the pocket facing at the top (this is roughly a quarter of the depth of the finished pocket), and then add 1.5cm(5/8in) seam allowances all round.

Note: be very accurate - use a ruler and measure to the nearest millimetre.
    Rounded corners can be drawn around a wine glass or a saucer.

2. Fig 48b. Draw and cut out a paper pattern for the pocket lining. This is exactly the same as the pocket pattern but does not have the pocket facing area above the foldline. Do not add a seam allowance to the top edge.

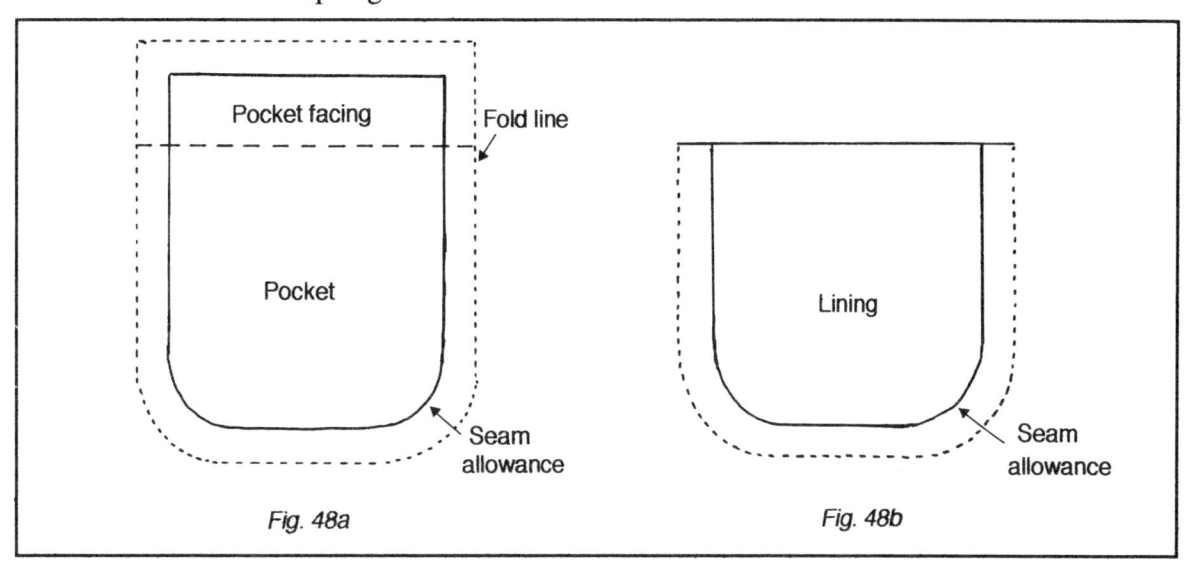

Fig. 48a

Fig. 48b

3. Cut out the pocket pattern in knitted fabric and the lining pattern in lining fabric. When doing this, take great care to keep the grainlines straight, eg. the rows of knitting parallel with the pocket top and the stitch lines parallel with the pocket sides. Any mistakes here will show up badly on the finished garment! Mark the foldline on the wrong side of the pocket fabric.

4. Fig.48c. Interface the pocket. This could mean covering the entire area of the pocket, including the facing, with a fusible interfacing such as knitted nylon, Vilene Ultrasoft in an appropriate weight, or cotton muslin. As the lining will do the job of eliminating the stretch factor, you might consider interfacing only the facing area. In most cases, lightweight Fold-a-Band placed along the foldline, as shown in this diagram, will be sufficient.

5. Fig 48d. Pin the top edges of the pocket and the lining, right sides together, and stitch on the 1.5cm(5/8in) seamline *leaving a 5-8cm(2-3in) gap in the stitching*. This is the gap through which you will turn the pocket right side out later on - so don't forget it!

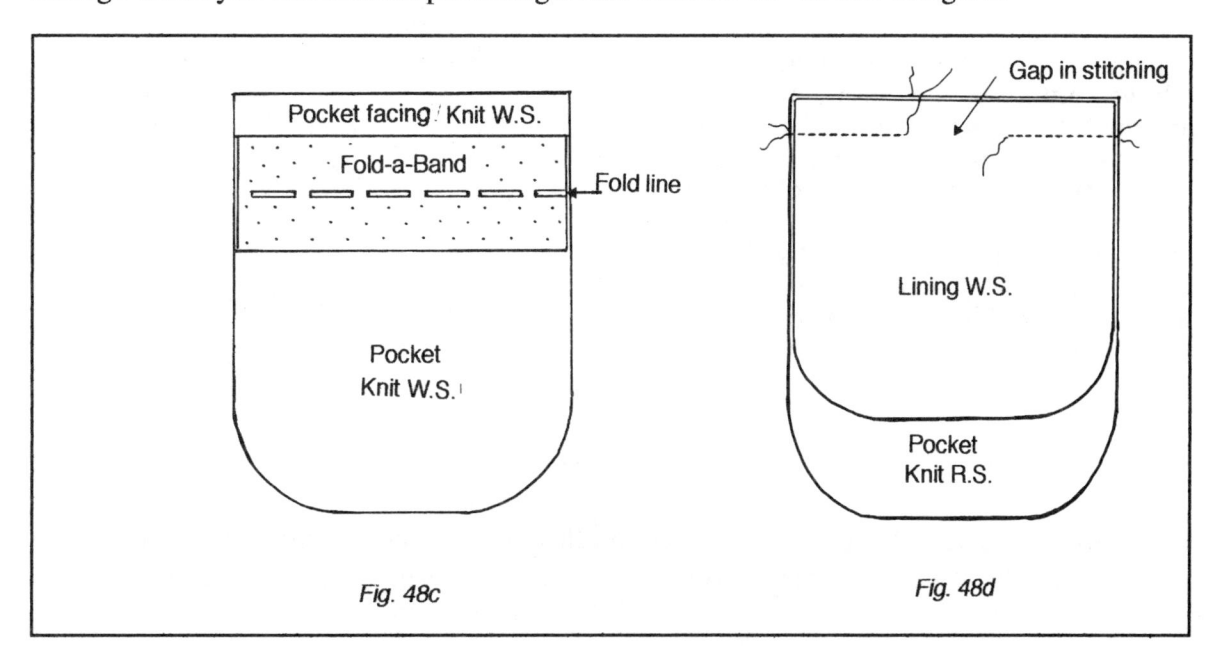

Fig. 48c

Fig. 48d

6. Fig. 48e. Pull the lining downwards until the fold at the top of the pocket is exactly on the foldline (or on the slits in the Fold-a-Band). Press the seam allowances downwards as shown. Make sure that the lining is lying straight and flat on the pocket. Trim off any excess lining fabric, so that the edges are exactly even all round.

7. Fig 48f. Turn the pocket over so that the knit side is facing you; push the knit slightly *inwards*, pinning as you go, so that the edge of the lining projects about 3mm(1/8in) beyond the edge of the knit. The effect of this is to make the pocket fabric slightly larger and looser than the lining fabric; the seamline around the pocket edge will then roll neatly to the underside when the pocket is complete.

Machine-stitch, using a short stitch-length, 1.5cm(5/8in) from the edge of the knit, around the three sides as shown. Trim the seam allowances back to 6mm(1/4in).

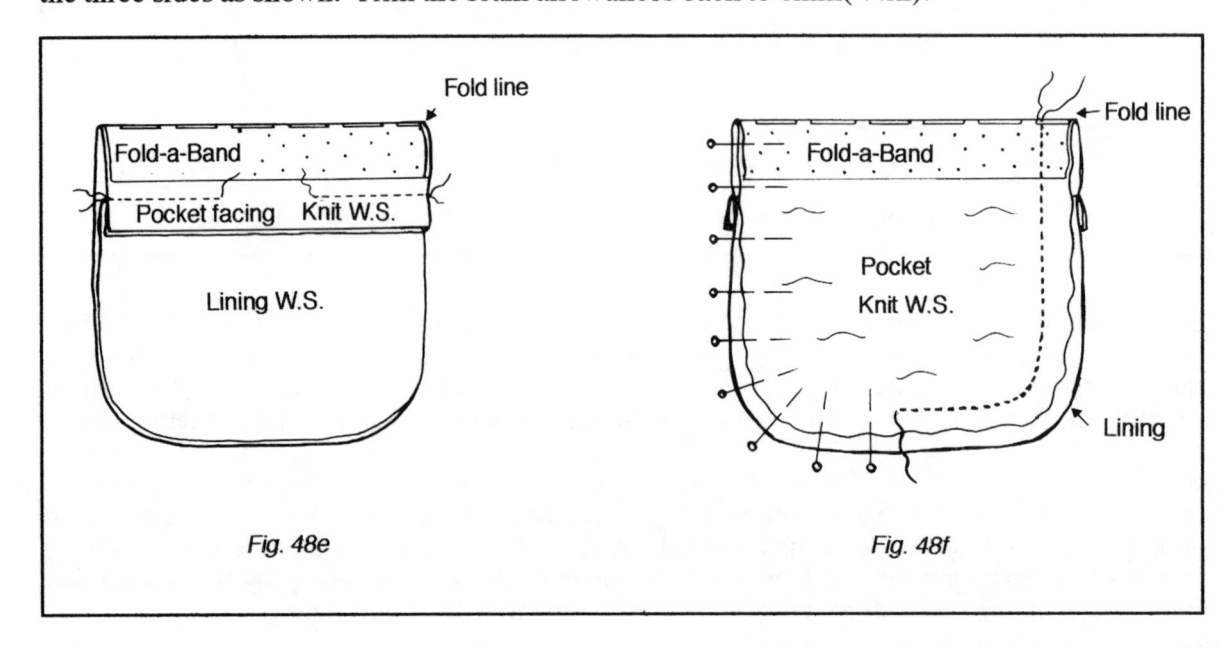

Fig. 48e

Fig. 48f

8. Fig. 48g. Turn the pocket through the gap to the right side. Using blunt scissors or a large knitting needle, push out the corners and the seam all around, from the inside. As the lining is now a little smaller than the pocket, the seam should have rolled well to the lining side of the pocket. Press well, using steam and a pounding block if necessary. With a needle and matching thread, slip-stitch the lining to the facing where the gap was left.

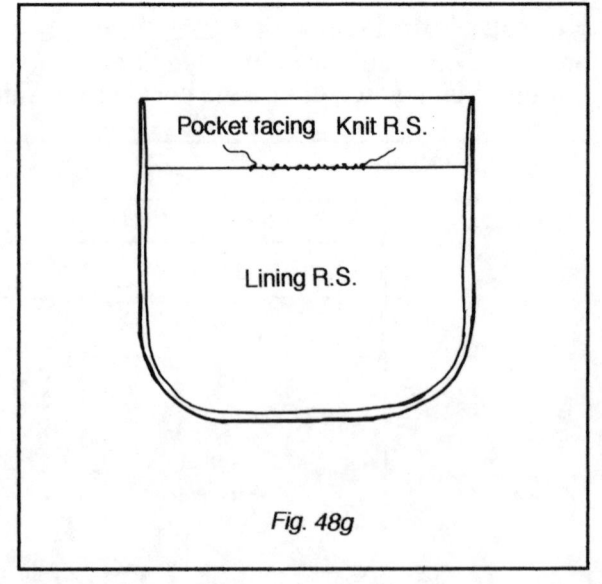

Fig. 48g

9. If an inner top-stitching line is required, do this now before attaching the pocket to the garment. Stitch about 1.25-2cm(1/2-3/4in) from the outer edge, through all thicknesses.

To apply a patch pocket

1. Fig.49a. Pin-mark a line on the garment to show where the top of the pocket should be. This line should run precisely along one row of the knitting, unless the pocket is intended to be placed at an angle. In most cases the pocket sits squarely on the garment so this marked line will also be exactly at right angles to the centre front. line.

Place the pocket with its top edge exactly on the marked line. The pocket edge nearest to the centre front line should be exactly parallel with the centre front line. The lower edge of the pocket should be exactly parallel with the hem (assuming that the hem is intended to be straight and not angled). Depending on the shape of the garment, the remaining side of the pocket might (or might not) be parallel with the side seam.

2. Fig.49b. Pin the pocket to the garment as shown, pushing the edge of the pocket inwards just a little, so that it is very slightly "cupped". It should not lie absolutely flat on the garment fabric. The reason for this is simple when you think about it: the garment is going to fit around the body - *a convex curved surface*; therefore the outer layer of fabric (the pocket) must be slightly larger than the under layer (the garment). If you sew your pocket flat on to the garment, there will be puckers in the fabric behind the pocket when you wear it.

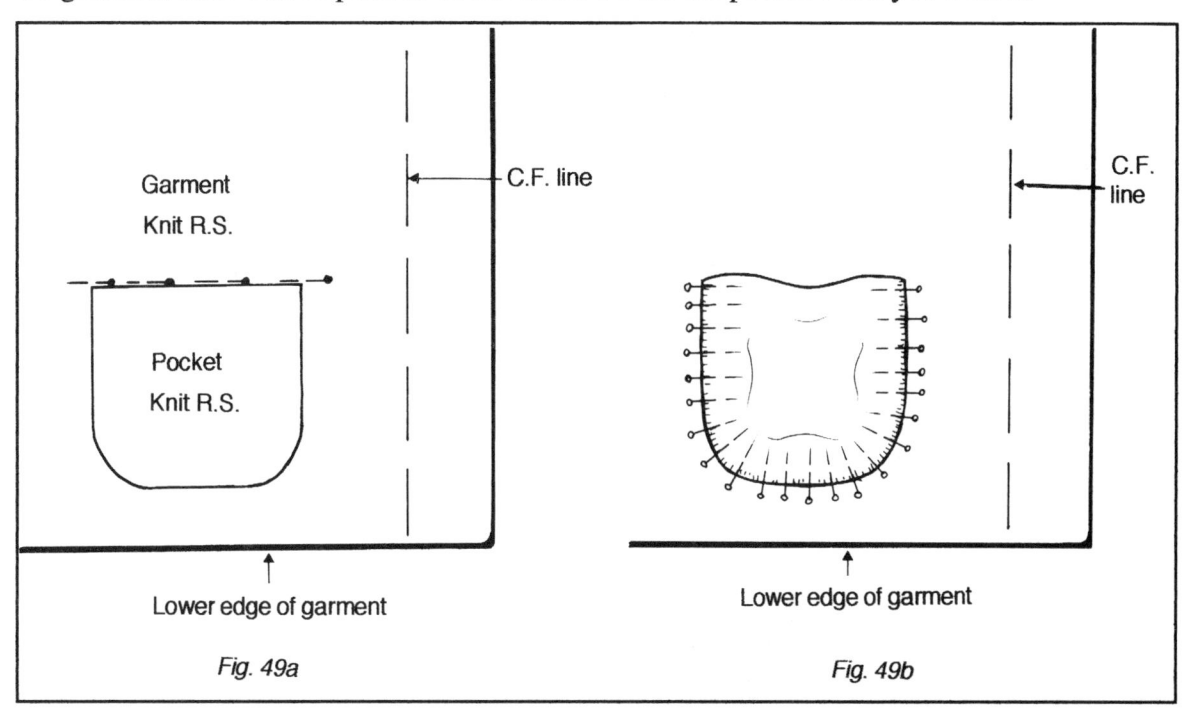

Fig. 49a *Fig. 49b*

3. Fig.50 shows several ways of top-stitching the pocket in position. Use an appropriate stitch length and remove pins as each one nears the presser foot. Also see Note on next page.

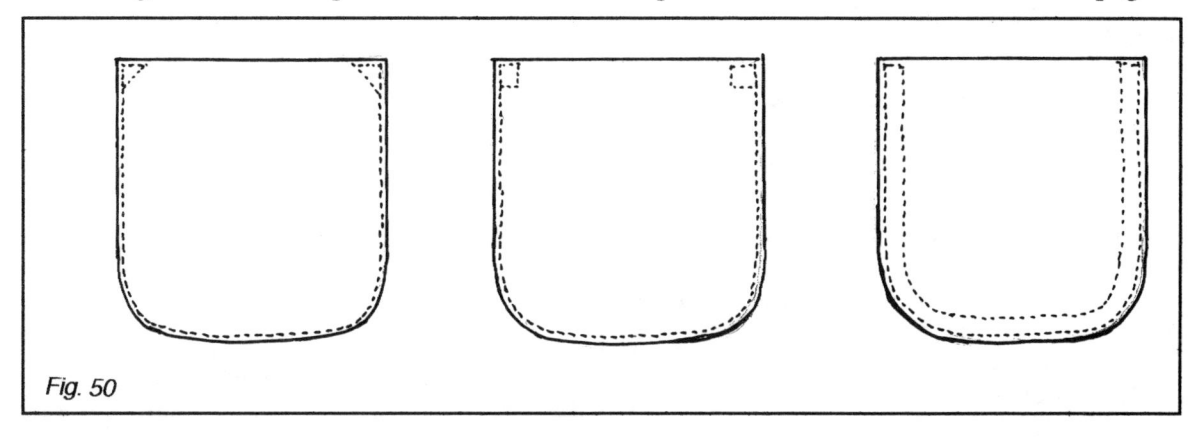

Fig. 50

Note: it may be necessary to tighten up the tension on the needle thread of your sewing-machine, when executing this top-stitching, because of the collective thickness of the several layers of fabric. If in doubt, try out the top-stitching for a short distance, remove the work from the machine and look at the underside; if there are loops there, you need to tighten the top tension.

Alternatively, the pocket can be secured by hand from the wrong side of the garment front, by back-stitching securely into the seam allowances, so that no stitching shows on the right side.

To match precisely the pocket position on the other half of the garment front place the two halves wrong sides together, matching all the edges exactly. Push pins straight through at the two top corners of the pocket and mark where these come through on the other side. Then check again by comparing measurements from the garment edges.

POCKETS IN SIDE (or side-front) SEAMS.

These are a very convenient form of pocket which can be used in any dress, skirt, coat or jacket. By unpicking the appropriate seam, you can even add them, as an afterthought, to a finished garment and this includes conventional knitwear.

General notes:
1.   Use woven fabric for the pocket pieces rather than the knit used for the rest of the garment; the woven fabric then stabilises the knitted fabric around the pocket opening so that it cannot stretch out of shape. It should match the colour of the knitted fabric as closely as possible, and should be strong without being thick or bulky. Polyester lining fabric is generally good for this purpose.

2.   *A problem can occur; the pocket fabric may show inside the opening when the garment is worn, especially if it fits fairly closely.* If you have used a woven fabric elsewhere in the outfit, for collar, cuffs, etc., you could use the same fabric for the pockets and their visibility might then be acceptable.

3.   **Fig.51a.** Otherwise, you should aim to avoid the problem by a bit of planning at the cutting-out stage; simply allow an extension to each garment piece where the pocket will be attached.

The width of the extension should be about 4.5cm(1³/4in) and the length, 11cm(4¹/4in) longer than the required opening.

This extension will need to be stabilised (by fusing a non-stretch interfacing to the wrong side) or the pocket opening will stretch out of shape.

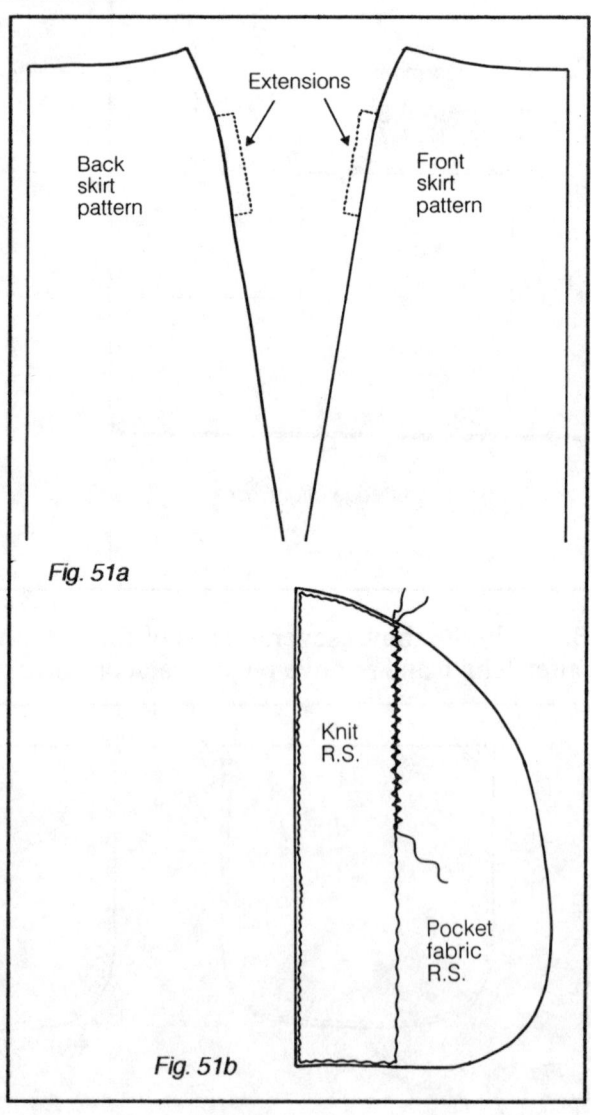

Fig. 51a

Fig. 51b

4. Fig.51b. If you have already finished cutting out and there are no extensions to the side seams (as described in para.3 on the previous page), or if you are adding pockets to a finished garment, you will probably need to cover the straight edge of each pocket section with a strip of the knit about 5cm(2in) wide; this should be stitched on flat, as shown, (not turning in the edges), using a short-length, full-width, zigzag machine stitch.

To cut a side-seam pocket

The following instructions are for pocket extensions applied to the Right Front and Right Back sections of a skirt, i.e. for one pocket in the right side seam. Adapt the instructions to make a left-hand pocket.

1. Fig.52. Draw and cut out a paper pattern for the pocket pieces as shown.

A-B is the measurement of the pocket opening and so must be long enough to allow the hand to slip through with ease.
B-C is the depth of the pocket "well"; about 7.5-10cm(3-4in) is usually sufficient.
B-D is roughly 12.5-15cm(5-6in).

Add 1.5cm(5/8in) seam allowances all round. Draw in a straight-grain line - this must be parallel with line *A-B-C*.

2. Using this paper pattern, cut out two pocket sections from the purchased woven fabric. This is just for one pocket: for two pockets you will need to cut four sections.

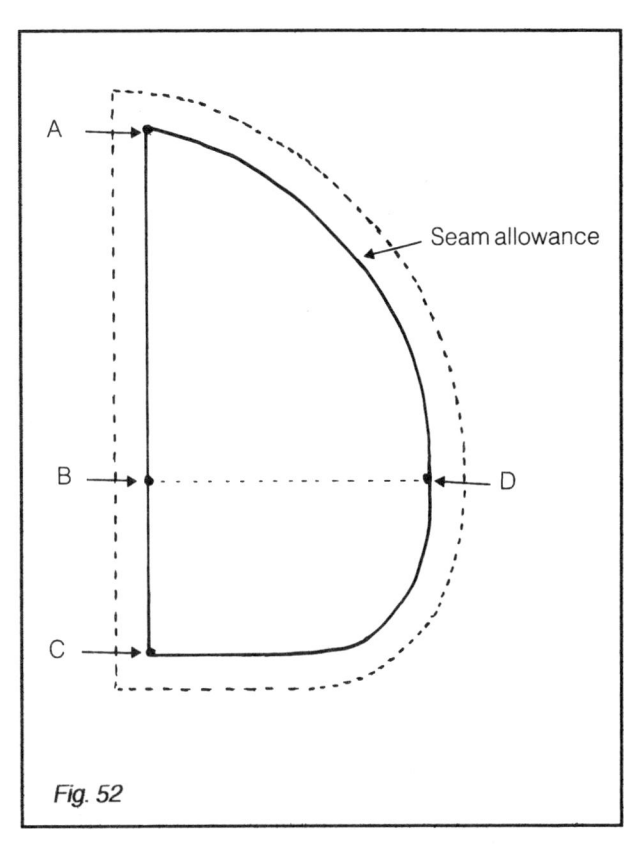

Fig. 52

To sew a side-seam pocket

1. Fig.53a. Place the pocket pieces on the skirt extensions, right sides together, matching the straight edges. Pin and then machine-stitch as shown.

Note: if there are no skirt extensions, the edge of the pocket should be aligned with the edge of the skirt and stitched in place taking only a minimal seam allowance - *not* the usual 1.5cm(5/8in).

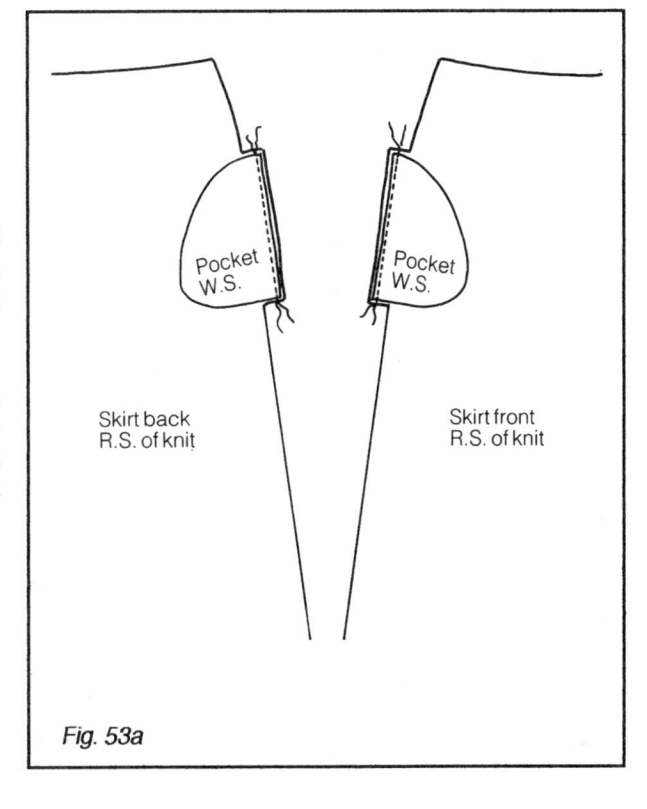

Fig. 53a

2. **Fig.53b**. Turn the pocket sections over and outwards.

Both seam allowances should be pressed towards the pocket sections.

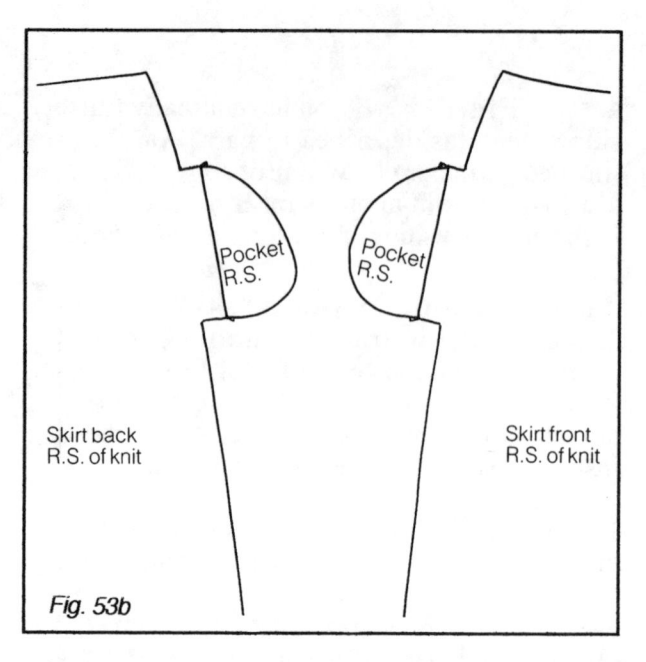

Fig. 53b

3. **Fig.53c**. Place the two skirt sections right sides together, matching the top and lower ends of the side seam, and the pocket edges. Pin firmly, and then machine-stitch as shown.

4. **Fig.53d**. Trim the seam allowances around the curved edge of the pocket and oversew or overlock them together.
Snip the *back* skirt seam allowance, as shown, at both ends of the pocket opening, so that the completed pocket can be pressed towards the garment front. The seam above and below the pocket can then be pressed open flat.

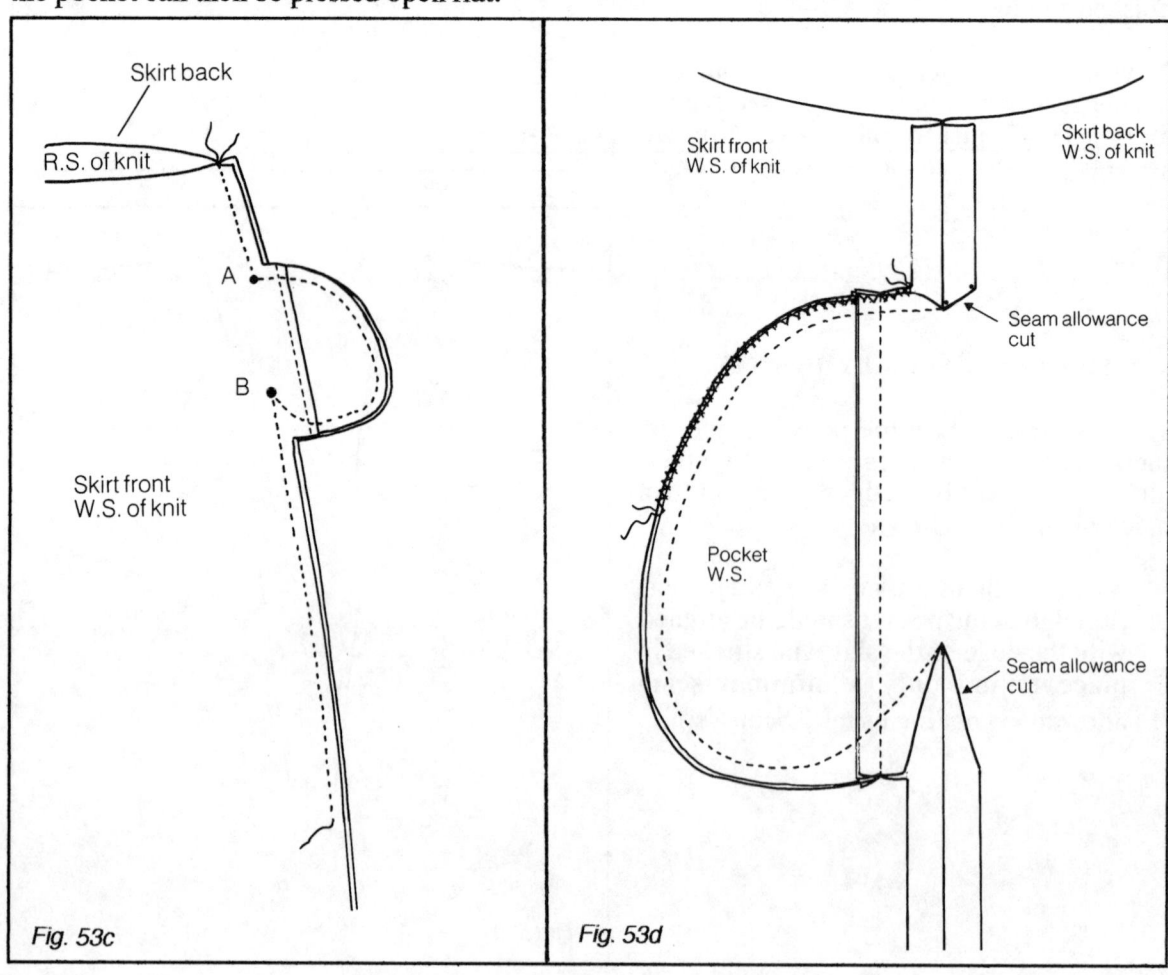

Fig. 53c

Fig. 53d

Page 57

5. Fig.53e.

On the right side, using machined *satin stitch* (stitch width at medium, and stitch-length very short), stitch from the seamline towards the skirt front, for about 1.2cm(1/2in), through all thicknesses.

This stitching not only holds the pocket in position towards the front of the skirt, but also strengthens both ends of the pocket opening.

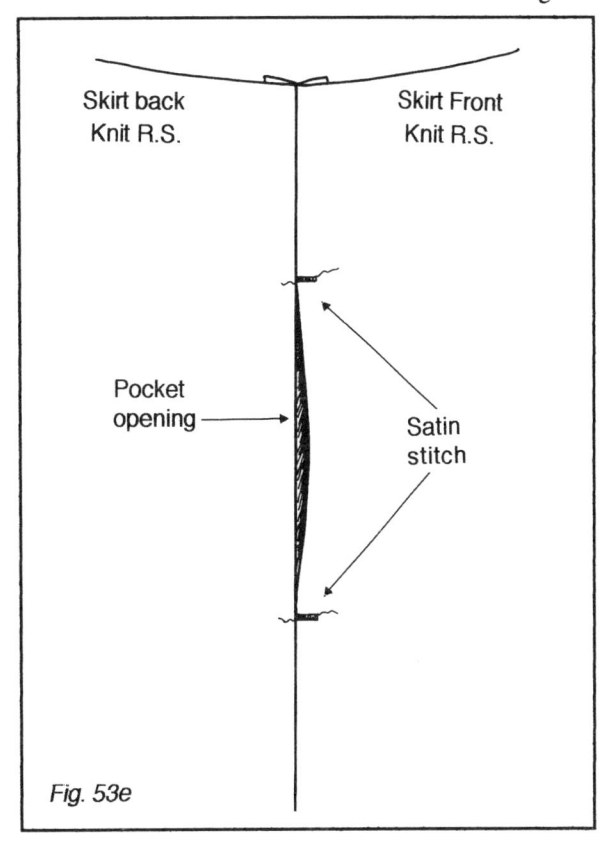

Fig. 53e

ZIPPED POCKET IN KNIT WHERE NO SEAM EXISTS

Here is another kind of pocket, one which I have found useful in cut-and-sew projects such as anoraks, or in fact in any casual clothes where a zipped-up pocket is an asset. Its great advantage is that you can put it anywhere on the knit, regardless of where the seams are. It can be added to an already made child's pullover as a safe place to keep lunch money or a bus ticket. You will need a 10-15cm(4-6in) zip, and a small piece of fairly thin but strong woven fabric for the pocket bag (eg. calico, cotton poplin, polyester lining).

    Advisory note: please do a practice one, using an old tension square, before trying it on a precious garment!

1. Mark the proposed position of the pocket opening on the garment. The length of the opening will be exactly the length of the zip you will be using to close it (not including the zip tape extensions) The line can be straight with the grain of the knitted fabric or at any other angle you choose. See examples in **Fig.54a,b and c.** If you decide to make it parallel with either the rows or the stitch lines, be accurate - it could look dreadful if even slightly crooked!

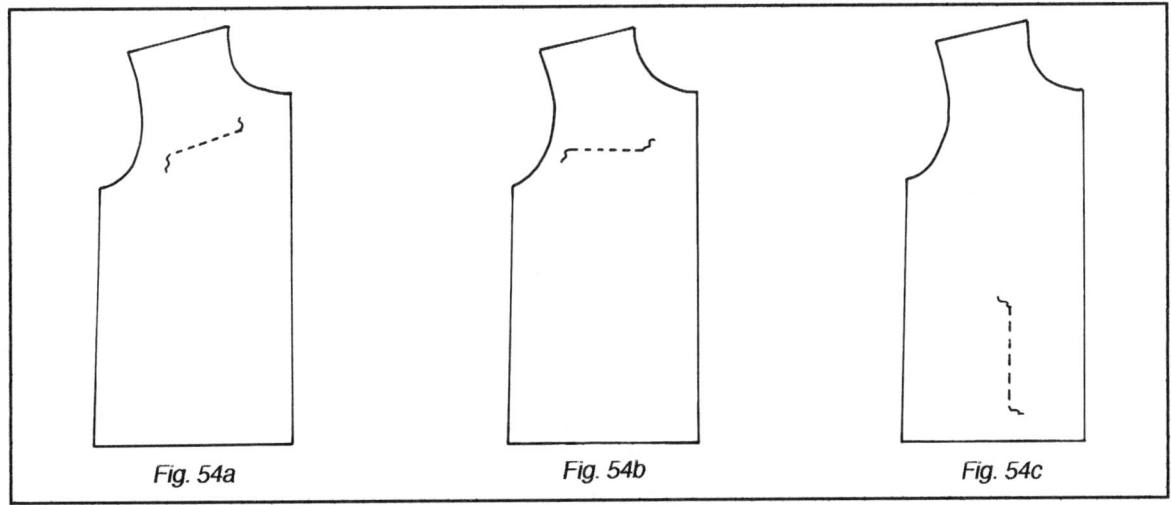

Fig. 54a *Fig. 54b* *Fig. 54c*

Page 58

2. Cut two identical pieces of the woven fabric for the pocket bag. The shape is indicated in the examples shown in **Fig.55a,b and c,** which relate to the various pocket positions shown in **Fig.54.** There should be about 4cm(1½in) of fabric surrounding the marked line on the opening end of the pocket; the depth of the pocket is your own decision.

Mark the line of the pocket opening with a pencil and a ruler, on the wrong side of one of the pocket pieces, making it the same length as the marked line on the garment.

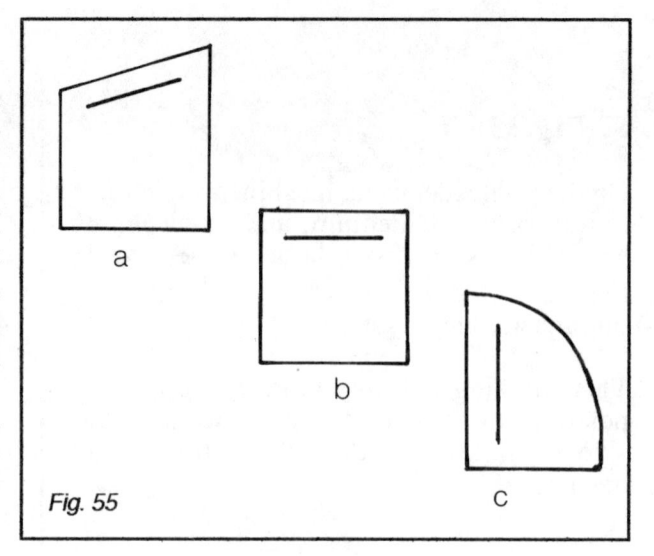

Fig. 55

3. Fig.56a. Place the pocket piece which has the opening line marked on it, on the garment, right sides together, so that the marked lines lie exactly together. Pin in position.

4. Fig.56b. Machine-stitch, using a very short stitch-length all around the marked line (the very short stitch-length is essential to sew all the fibres down firmly so that fraying will not occur when the slit is cut). You will be sewing a rectangular shape, the short sides of which will touch the ends of the line; the long sides should be parallel with the line and a fraction more than half the width of the zip teeth away from it. Start the stitching at some point on one of the long sides, and overlap this when you have completed the circuit.

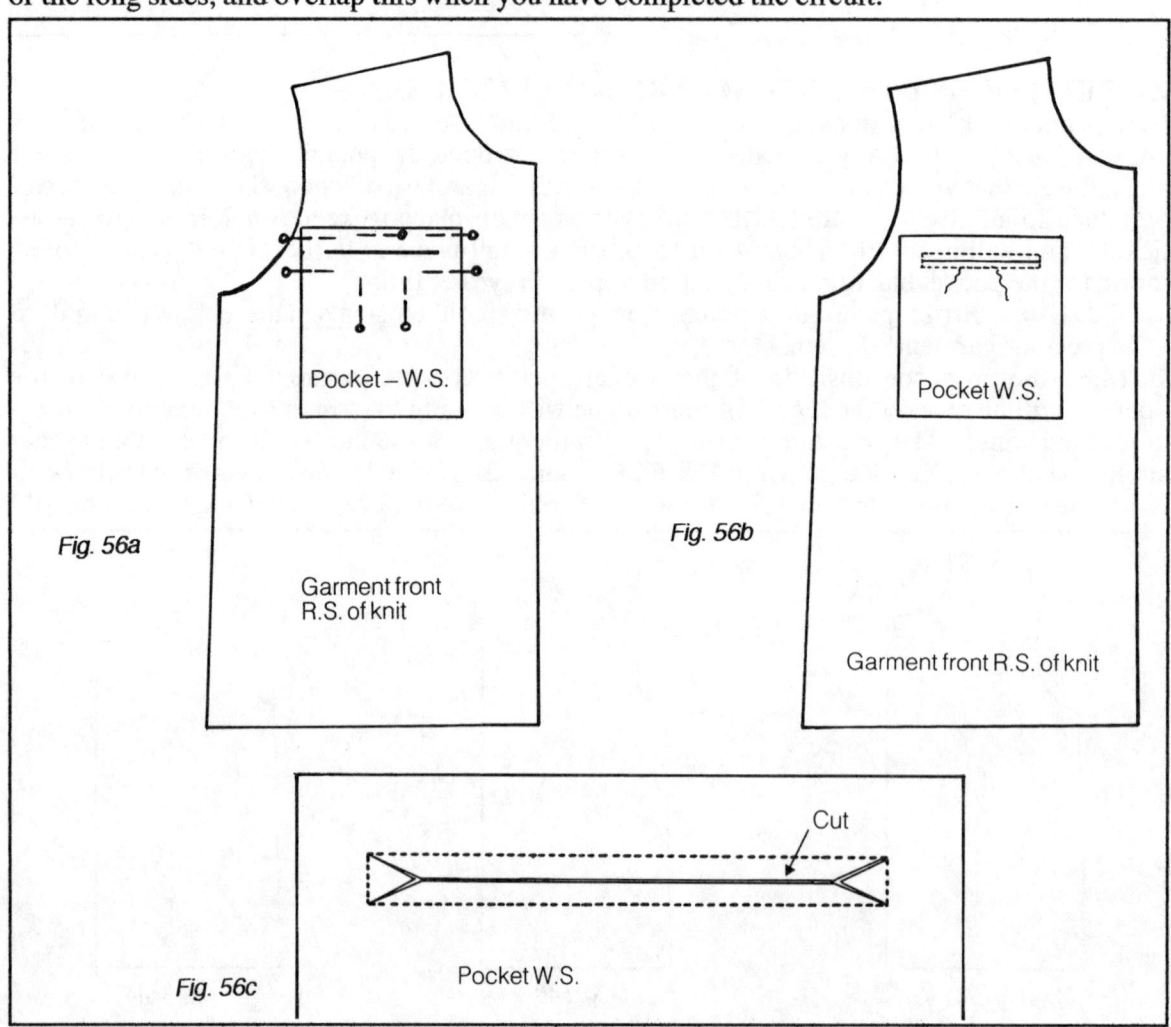

Fig. 56a

Pocket – W.S.

Garment front R.S. of knit

Fig. 56b

Pocket W.S.

Garment front R.S. of knit

Fig. 56c

Pocket W.S.

Cut

Page 59

5. Fig.56c. Cut straight up the marked line, exactly in the middle of the two long lines of stitching, and out to each corner as shown. *You must cut right up to the stitching in the corners or the pocket will not turn neatly through to the wrong side of the garment.* Be brave!

6. Fig.56d. Pull the pocket section through to the wrong side of the garment. Push out the seams from the inside so that they lie straight and parallel; press thoroughly with steam.

7. Fig.56e. From the right side of the garment, position the opening around the zip so that the edges fit quite closely against the teeth - but take care to avoid the danger of the fabric getting caught in the zip. Using a zipper foot and a medium stitch-length, machine-stitch as closely as possible to the edge of the opening

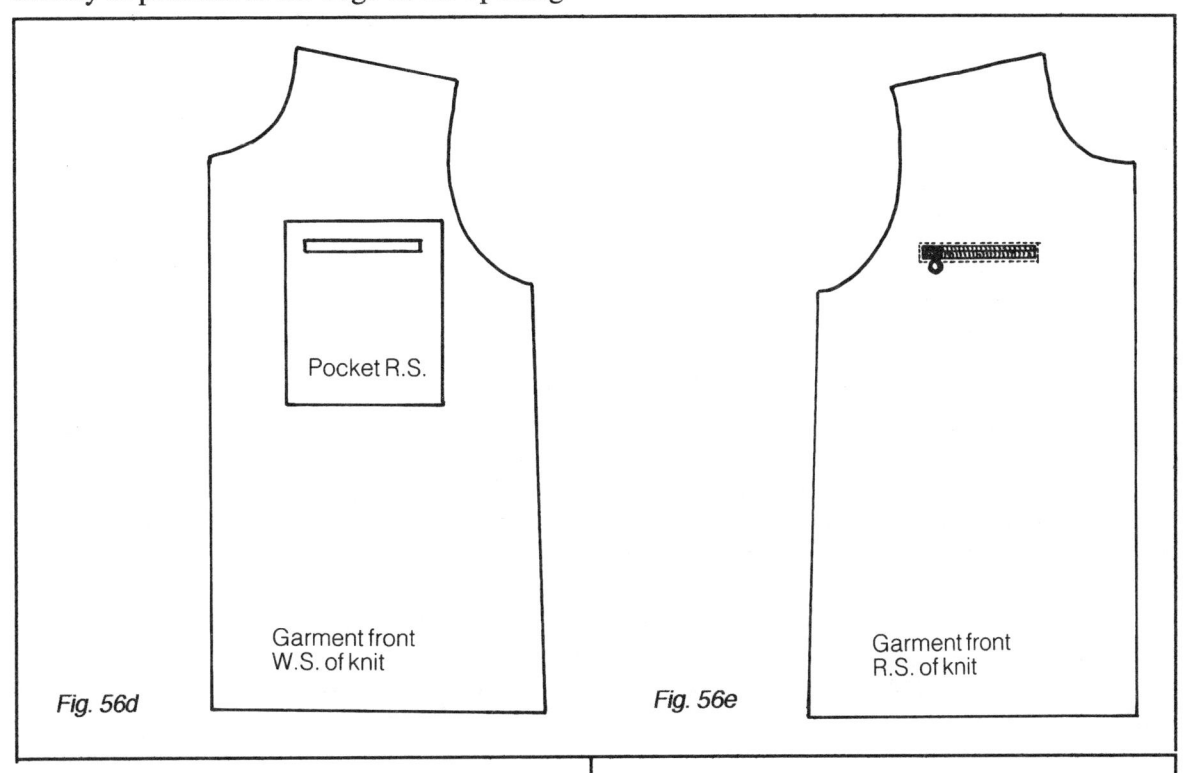

Fig. 56d

Fig. 56e

8. Fig.56f.

Place the remaining pocket section exactly over the first, right sides together, matching all the edges exactly. Pin the two pocket sections together and machine-stitch 1.2cm(1/2in) from the edge, all round.

Trim and oversew, or overlock, the two layers together.

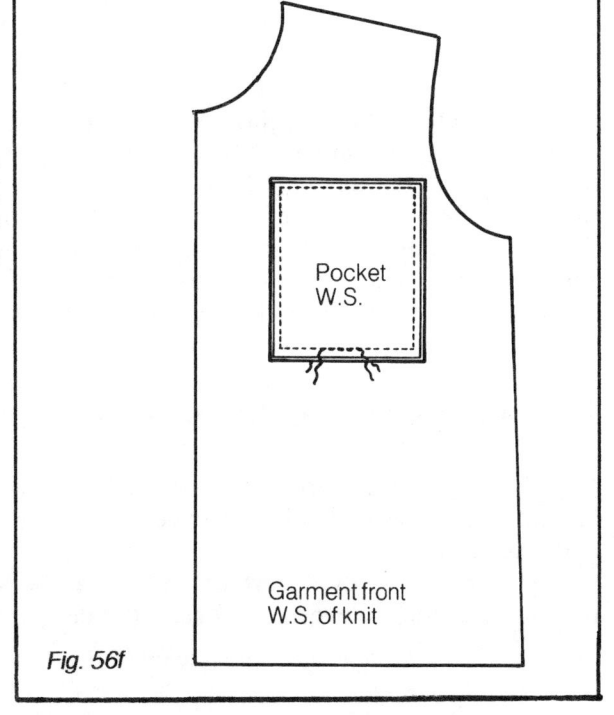

Fig. 56f

CHAPTER 9

BUTTONS and BUTTONHOLES

In order to produce a garment which looks both professionally made and expensive, great care and thought has to be given to choosing just the right buttons, because more often than not, they are the focal point. The buttonholes too, demand precision both in their placement and in their execution.

PLANNING

Choosing the size of the button
a. *If you have designed your own garment*, you will have marked in the centre front line.

Now you have to decide -
EITHER ... the width of the 'overlap', i.e. the distance between the centre-front line and the edge,
OR ... the diameter of the buttons you are going to use.

As a general rule these two should be the same: one depends upon the other. See **Fig.57.** If they are not roughly the same, the buttons will look out of proportion to the overlap width.

Always try out the effect that buttons of different size will have on a garment.

Avoid very large buttons if you are on the small side.

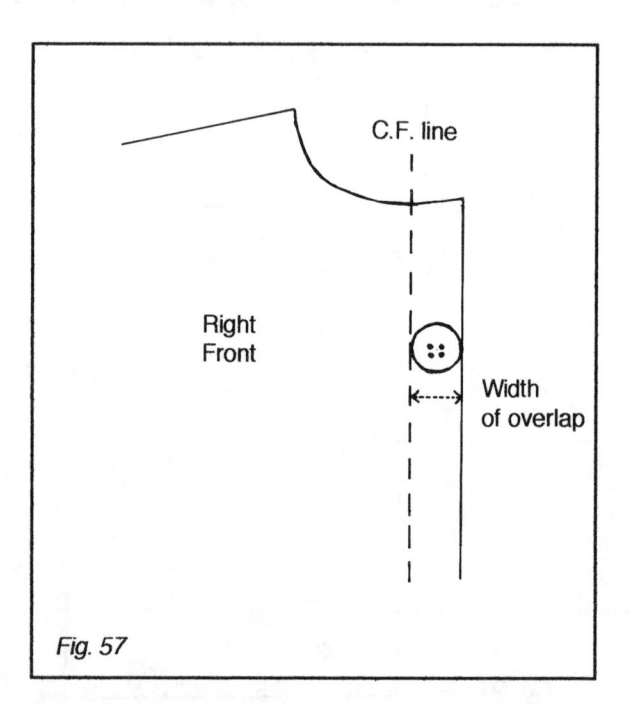

Fig. 57

b. *If you have used a dressmaking pattern*, the proposed size of the buttons will be indicated in the "Notions" section on the back of the pattern envelope; the centre-front. line will be clearly shown and the exact positions and size of the buttonholes drawn on the paper pattern. Alter the size and number of buttons if you wish, but the width of the overlap will need to be adjusted if you choose to use much smaller or much larger buttons.
Remember that if you have had to alter the body-length in the area of the buttoned fastening, this will affect the spacing of the buttonholes; in this case, providing the buttonholes are to be machine-stitched, it would be wise to postpone marking the buttonhole positions until after the first fitting, or even to abandon marking them until the garment is otherwise complete.
But you should also remember that if this is a thick, bulky garment where *bound* buttonholes are essential, then you will have to determine their new position right at the start of the construction process.

Determining the position of buttons and buttonholes

Fig.58. In the majority of clothes, *the centre-front line* determines where buttons should actually be, because that line is the exact centre of the total overlap (when one side is fastened over the other).

Where, however, garments fasten at the back, on the side or asymmetrically, the centre line of the complete overlap is, again, the deciding factor.

Fig.59. In double-breasted garments, the two lines of buttons must lie equidistant from the centre-front line.

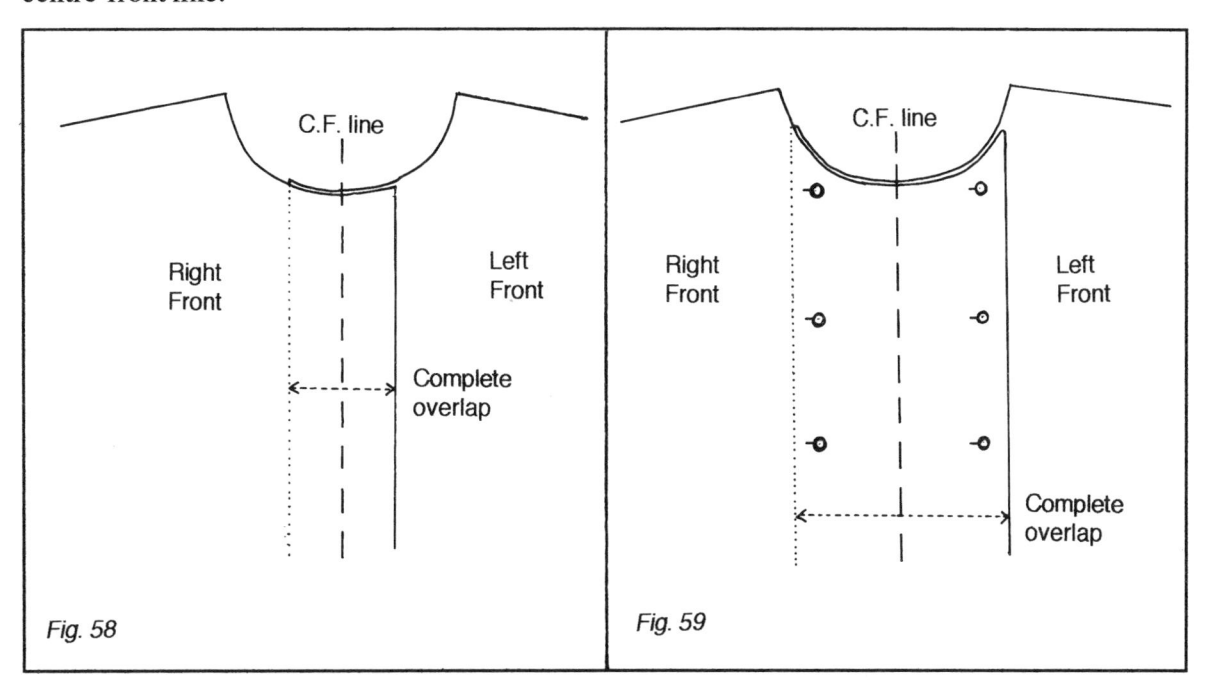

Fig. 58

Fig. 59

Note: in order to make the following instructions clearer, we will assume that the garment is fastened at the centre front.

REMEMBER TWO IMPORTANT POINTS

    1. Buttons should be positioned exactly on the centre-front line - *and then* -

    2. The position of the buttonholes is determined by the position of the buttons.

Fig.60a.

If the buttonholes are to lie in a horizontal direction, -

the line for each hole should start on the side of the centre-front line which is nearest to the edge of the overlap, leaving just enough room for the shank of the button where it is to be sewn exactly on the centre-front line.

This is usually about 3-6mm(1/8-1/4in), depending on the thickness of the knit, but may be more if it is very thick.

The line should finish sufficiently far away on the other side of the centre-front line to enable the buttons to slip through the buttonholes with ease.

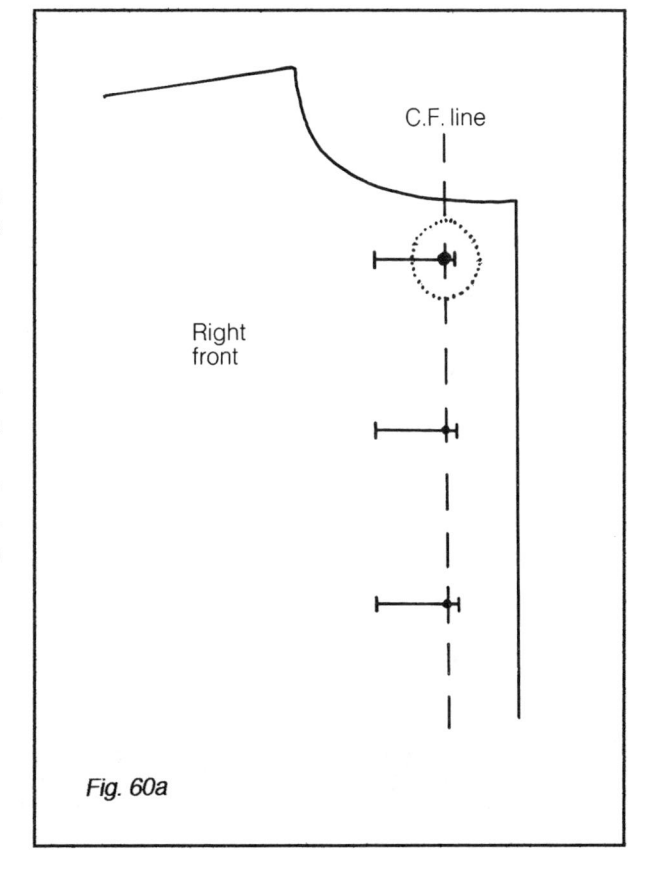

Fig. 60a

Fig. 60b.

If the buttonholes are to lie in a vertical direction -
they should be aligned precisely along the centre-front line, starting approximately 3-6mm(1/8-1/4in) above the button mark and ending sufficiently far below the button mark to enable the button to slip through the hole with ease.

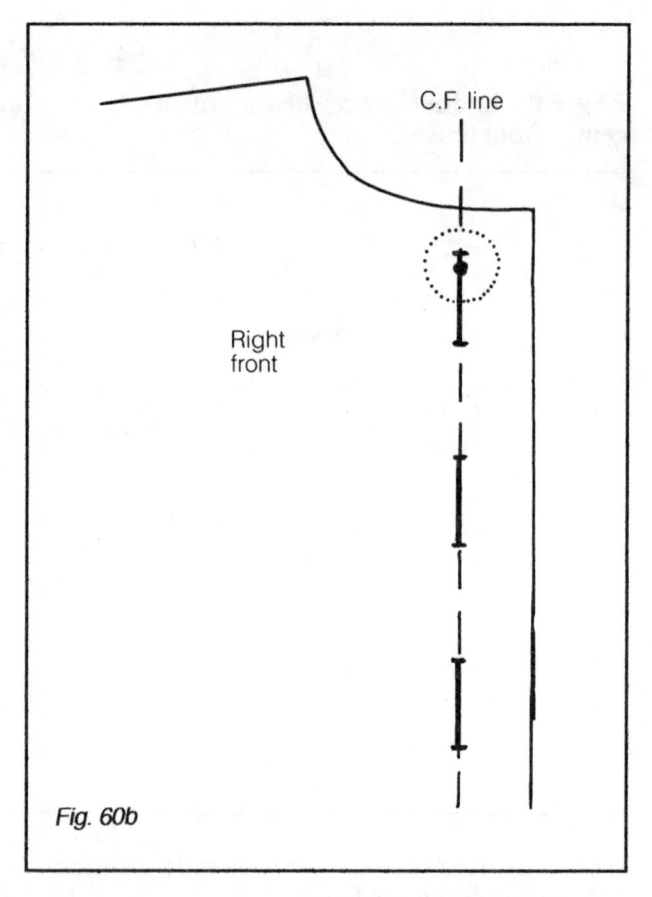

Fig. 60b

Note: if the front edge of the garment has an attached band (as in a tailored shirt) the buttonholes must be vertical so that they lie exactly in the centre of the band and parallel with its edges. If there is no attached band, the buttonholes are usually made horizontally but may be made vertically if you so wish..

Determining the distance between the buttons

1. First decide where you want the top button and mark this position with a pin; if the garment is to be buttoned right up to the top, this point is generally slightly more than half the diameter of the button, below the finished top edge.

2. Decide, and pin-mark, where the bottom button is to be; this should never be in the hem and, as a general rule, should be about one-and-a-half or two "spaces" (the distance between buttons) above the lower edge.

3. Pin-mark the positions of the remaining buttons, spacing them out evenly between the top and bottom buttons. Bear in mind that, if the garment is not to have a belt, it might be advisable to have a button at the waistline; but a button placed underneath a belt could be bulky and uncomfortable. If your figure demands it, ensure that there is a button at the fullest part of the bust.

4. Buttons placed quite close together in groups of two or three, with longer spaces between the groups, can often look very effective.

Determining the required length of the buttonhole
Measure the diameter of the button, allowing also for its thickness. For high-domed buttons, take a length of thread around the thickest part and mark it with a pen where the ends cross: then measure the thread between the marks and divide by two.

Add 3-6mm(1/8-1/4in) for ease, depending upon the thickness of the knit.

MAKING BUTTONHOLES

You may be supremely confident about making buttonholes, or the whole process may be potential heart attack material! A lot depends upon how much practice you have had, and, unfortunately, upon the quality of your sewing-machine: some make it easy and some don't. If you are considering a new sewing-machine, the buttonhole is the acid test!

Interfacing the buttonhole area

The inclusion of some kind of firm interfacing, between the main fabric and the facing, is generally vital to the production of professional-looking buttonholes. This rule applies to normal dressmaking and is generally indispensable when it comes to most cut-and-sew projects. (Possible exceptions could be where the facing is cut from a firm woven fabric or from something like petersham ribbon.) The facing will probably already be interfaced but an additional strip of some interfacing (such as one of the fusible Vilenes, fusible tailoring canvas or fusible cotton muslin) should be added to the wrong side of the garment front to cover the area in which the buttonholes will be made. This will help to control any tendency to stretch or fray when it comes to sewing and cutting the buttonhole, and will make the task a lot easier!.

TO MAKE BOUND BUTTONHOLES

Making bound buttonholes can be difficult when using knitted fabrics, but they are often advisable on coats and jackets, where the thickness of the layers creates an unsuitable situation for machined buttonholes. Well executed, they can add a wonderfully expensive-looking couture touch. I suggest that you should cut the piping strips from a finely woven fabric such as lightweight flannel or gabardine. Using your knitted fabric for this purpose is not totally impossible but can produce problems because of the sheer bulk involved.

Here is a method which works well - if you follow the instructions with absolute accuracy.

To prepare the garment by marking clearly the position of each buttonhole

1. Fig.61a.

For horizontal buttonholes:

   a. Mark the centre-front line, from top to bottom, using a fade-away marking pen or a chalk pencil.

   b. *Tack-mark line Y parallel with, and 3-6mm(1/8-1/4in) from, the centre-front line.
   *Note:** to "tack-mark", machine-stitch, using the longest stitch-length. This makes an accurate line which will not move about but which is easily removable afterwards. Test on scraps first; if the bobbin thread does not pull out easily, then loosen the tension on the needle thread. Hand-tacking is less clear and more easily moved out of position.

   c. Tack-mark line X, parallel with line Y. The distance between X and Y is the required length of the buttonhole.

   d. Tack-mark the position of each buttonhole across lines X and Y.

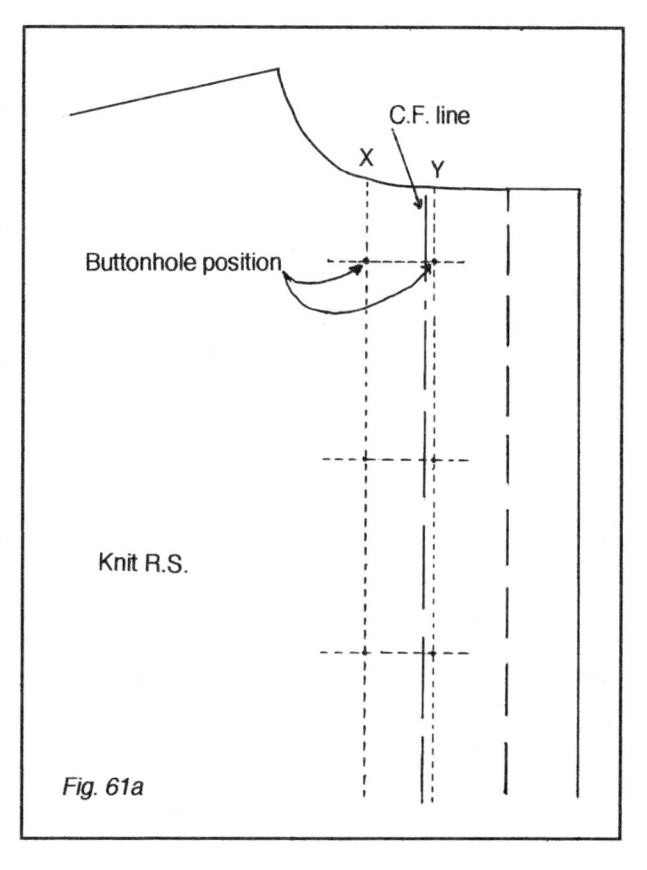

Fig. 61a

Fig.61b.

For vertical buttonholes

    a. Tack-mark the centre-front line.

    b. Tack-mark horizontal lines, across the centre-front line, to indicate the top and bottom of each hole.

2. Prepare the binding strips.
a. Cut a straight (not bias) strip of the binding fabric, as follows:
Width = usually 2.5cm(1in) but you should increase this figure if the knit is very thick.
Length - calculate this by adding 4cm(1½in) to the length of one buttonhole: then multiply the result by twice the number of buttonholes.

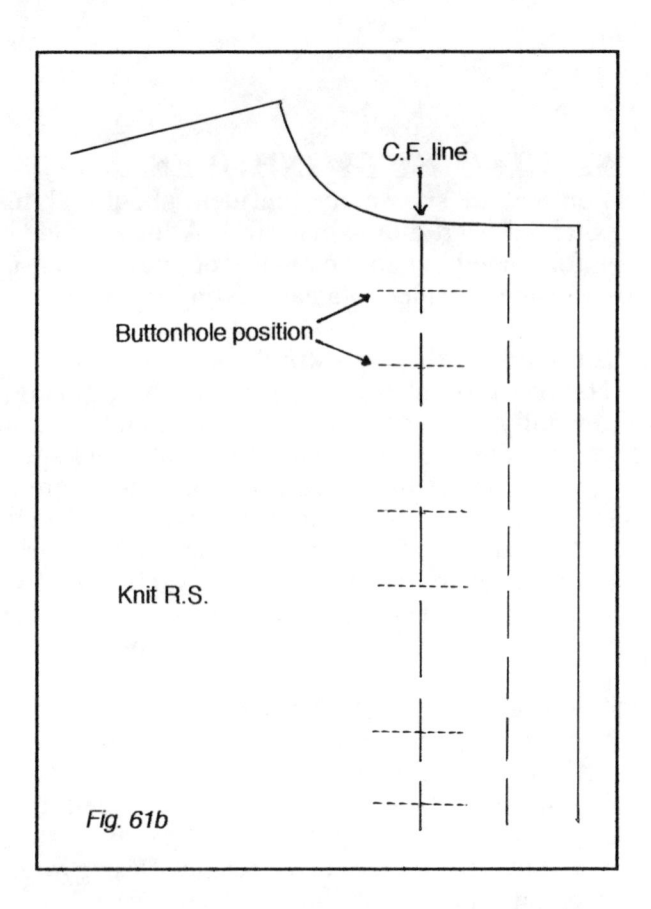

Fig. 61b

b. Cut a strip of Wundaweb to fit exactly and place it on the wrong side of the binding strip. Fold the strip exactly in half lengthwise and press with damp cloth, or steam, to fuse.

c. Cut the strip into *exactly* even lengths, two for each buttonhole; each length should be precisely 4cm(1½in) longer than the required buttonhole.

3. To apply the binding strips
Notes: a. the following instructions are for horizontal buttonholes only; adapt for vertical buttonholes if required. *b.* Keep the Facings folded out of the way until you reach Fig.62e.

Fig.62a. Place two binding strips across lines X and Y, on the right side of the garment Front, ends exactly aligned, and with the raw edges of the strips meeting on the marked buttonhole line, as shown.

    (2cm(¾in) at the ends of each strip should project beyond lines X and Y).

    Set the stitch-length to very short - about 1 on most machines. Starting halfway between X and Y, stitch *exactly* along the centre of one strip until you reach line X, *pivot exactly on this point and return along the centre of the strip until you reach line Y; pivot again and return to the starting point. Repeat on the second strip.
*To 'pivot', have the machine needle piercing the fabrics exactly on the desired spot, lift the presser-foot and turn the fabric through 180 degrees, then lower the presser-foot and continue stitching.

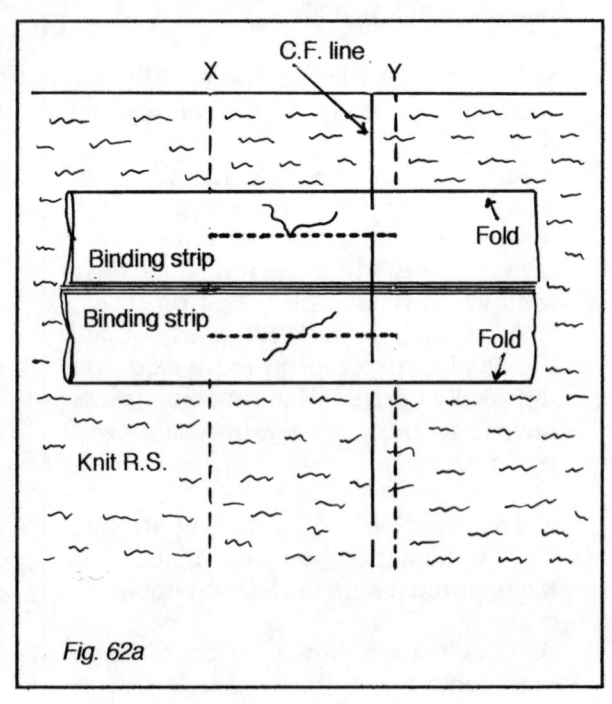

Fig. 62a

4. To complete the buttonholes

Fig.62b. Turn the garment front over so that the wrong side faces you.
Cut through the garment front fabric, as shown, exactly along the buttonhole line and out to each corner at X and Y. You must cut *right up to* the corners where the machine-stitched lines meet lines X and Y: if you don't cut far enough, the binding strips simply cannot be turned through properly and your buttonhole will look terrible!

Further warnings! Take care not to cut into the binding strips and do make sure that the triangles at each end are long enough to handle - you will need to pull on them at a later stage.

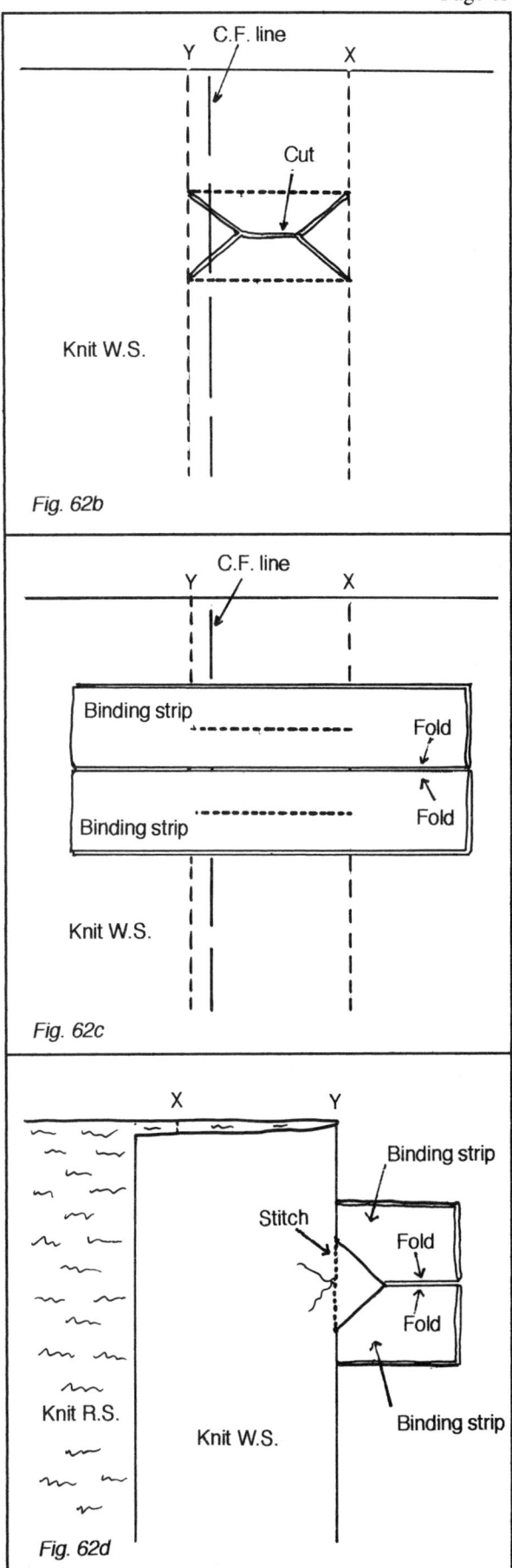

Fig.62c. Pull the binding strips through to the wrong side of the garment. Check that the binding strips are lying straight and squarely opposite each other.

Find the triangle at each end of the hole and make sure it is lying flat and straight beneath the ends of the binding strips.

It may be helpful at this stage to catch the 'lips' of the buttonhole together, with needle and thread, so that the edges just meet.

Press the buttonhole well, on both sides of the fabric.

Fig.62d. With the right side of the garment facing you, fold back the garment fabric to expose the triangular piece lying over the ends of the binding strips.

Keeping these ends level, and the triangle straight, machine stitch directly along the base of the triangle where it lies exactly on line Y. You will probably need to do this with a zipper foot on the machine as the fold (to the left of the triangle) can be very bulky. The stitching should be small and secure at the ends. Repeat on line X.

Now the rectangle which forms the buttonhole is secured on all four sides.

5. To face the buttonholes

Fig. 62e. Now fold the Facing back in place behind the buttonholes. Secure in place by pinning.

From the right side of the garment, push a large pin through each of the four corners of the buttonhole, as shown. Make sure the pins pierce the fabrics perpendicularly, not at an angle.

On the inside of the garment, on the right side of the facing, mark a dot with a cloth-marking pen or pencil, exactly where each pin emerges. With a marking pencil, join these dots with straight lines to form a rectangle. Stay-stitch (very small machine stitching) along the lines of this rectangle *through the facing only*.

Fig. 62e

Fig. 62f. Cut, as shown, through the facing, from the centre to all four corners of the rectangle. Turn under and press the cut edges of the opening in the facing, along the stay-stitching lines.

Fig. 62f

Fig. 62g. Place the opening carefully in position around the buttonhole and hem, by hand, to the machine-stitching lines on the binding strips.

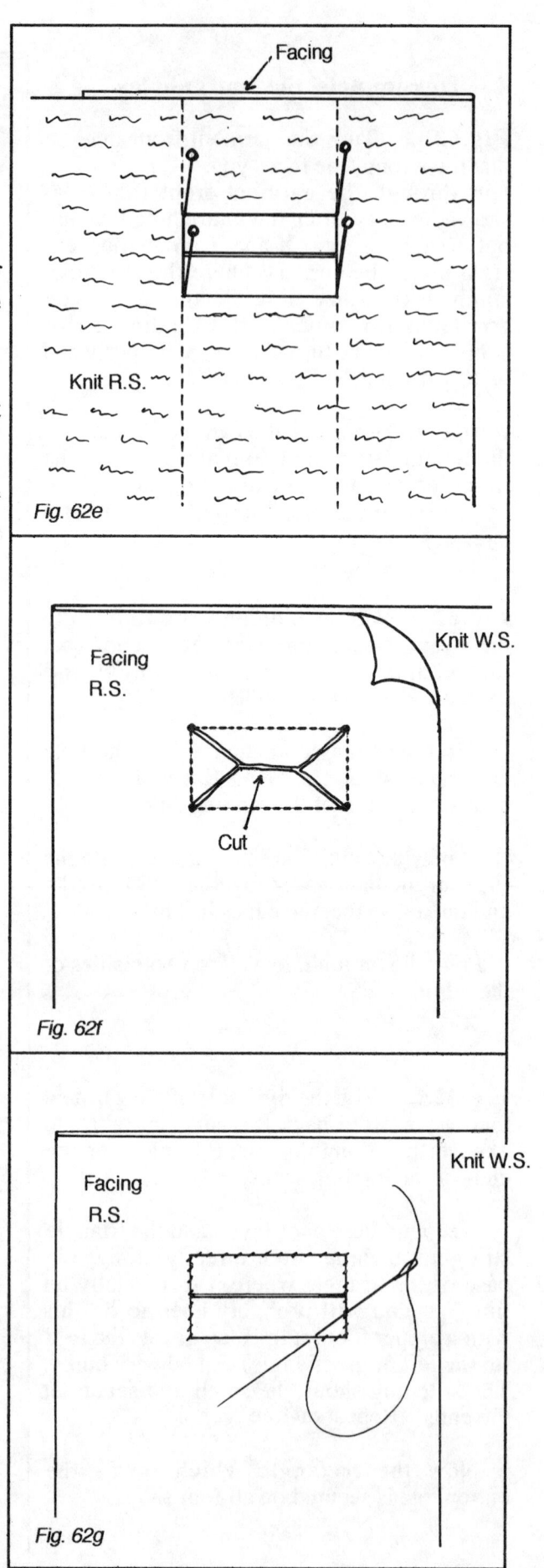

Fig. 62g

MACHINED BUTTONHOLES

Machined buttonholes are usually successful on all but very thick knits. You need to have first practised the routine thoroughly, using easily-managed, purchased, woven fabrics, in order to gain confidence. However, even when you know the routine off by heart, for cut and sew purposes you should always practise the buttonholes several times on spare pieces of your chosen knit before tackling the garment itself.

Use the following guidelines.

1. Mark the positions of the buttonholes, as in Fig.61a or 61b., carefully and exactly; using machine-tacking, a marking pen or pencil (with care) or small running stitches made with a needle and a sharply contrasting thread. Normal tacking is useless for this purpose because it can move about when under the presser-foot.

2. Read and carefully digest the buttonholing instructions, in your sewing-machine manual.

3. Fit the correct presser foot for sewing buttonholes.

4. Check on whether it is necessary to loosen the top-tension. On some machines, such as Bernina, the tension on the bobbin thread is increased instead.

5. Pin together the area around the buttonhole line, through all fabrics. Keep the pins sufficiently far away from the buttonhole line to ensure that they will not interfere with the presser foot.

6. If you are using a modern sewing-machine, the stitch-length may automatically adjust itself as required; if not, you have to adjust the stitch-length to where it should be for sewing buttonholes and then try out the stitching on a spare piece of fabric, using the same number of layers that you will have to stitch on when actually making the buttonholes. The exact position of the stitch-length lever (or dial) will vary according to the thickness and texture of the fabric. You have to get the right balance between setting the length so long that you have gaps between the stitches - and setting it so short that you risk stopping the forward-feed mechanism. Often it is better to have slight gaps and then to sew round the buttonhole twice; in fact, stitching round the line twice actually improves the look of the finished buttonhole, in most cases.

7. Use the Corded Buttonhole technique when using home-produced knitted fabrics, because it looks so very much better and is certainly stronger. An added advantage is that the cord can be pulled up to bring an accidentally stretched-out buttonhole back to its proper size. Consult your machine manual for directions and use crochet cotton for this purpose; I find that I need only black and white as the cord should be completely covered by the machine-stitching.
Usually the buttonhole presser foot incorporates some means of guiding this thicker thread so that the zigzag stitching straddles but does not pierce it.

8. If your sewing-machine does not have a corded buttonhole facility, and stretched-out buttonholes are a problem, try a line of short-length, straight-stitch machining, 6mm(1/4in) from, and all around, the buttonhole line before starting the zigzag stitching.

9. Cut the slit carefully between the two lines of stitching, using a sharp buttonhole knife (this is like a small, well-sharpened chisel) or stitch-unripper. If using the latter, cut from each end in turn towards the middle. If you try to cut straight through from one end to the other, you could have a nasty accident!

10. If some of the zigzag stitching gets cut accidentally, when slitting the hole, put the buttonhole back under the machine presser-foot again, positioning it carefully with the hole spread slightly open. Re-stitch the damaged area and sew in the thread ends carefully.

SEWING ON THE BUTTONS

Almost everyone knows how to sew on a button but it is surprising how few people know exactly *where* to sew it!

When the buttons are intended to lie in one straight line (eg. down the centre front or centre back) there is a simple foolproof method.

1. Place the two opening edges of the garment, wrong sides together, with the top and bottom ends matching exactly and the edges aligned. Have the buttonholed side on top.

2. Fig.63a. *For vertical buttonholes*, stick a pin straight through the buttonhole at a point 3mm(1/8in) below the top end of the hole. This should come out, on the button side of the garment, exactly on the centre line of the overlap.

Fig.63b. *For horizontal buttonholes*, stick a pin straight through the buttonhole at a point 3mm(1/8in) inwards from the outer end of the hole. This should come out exactly on the centre line of the overlap.

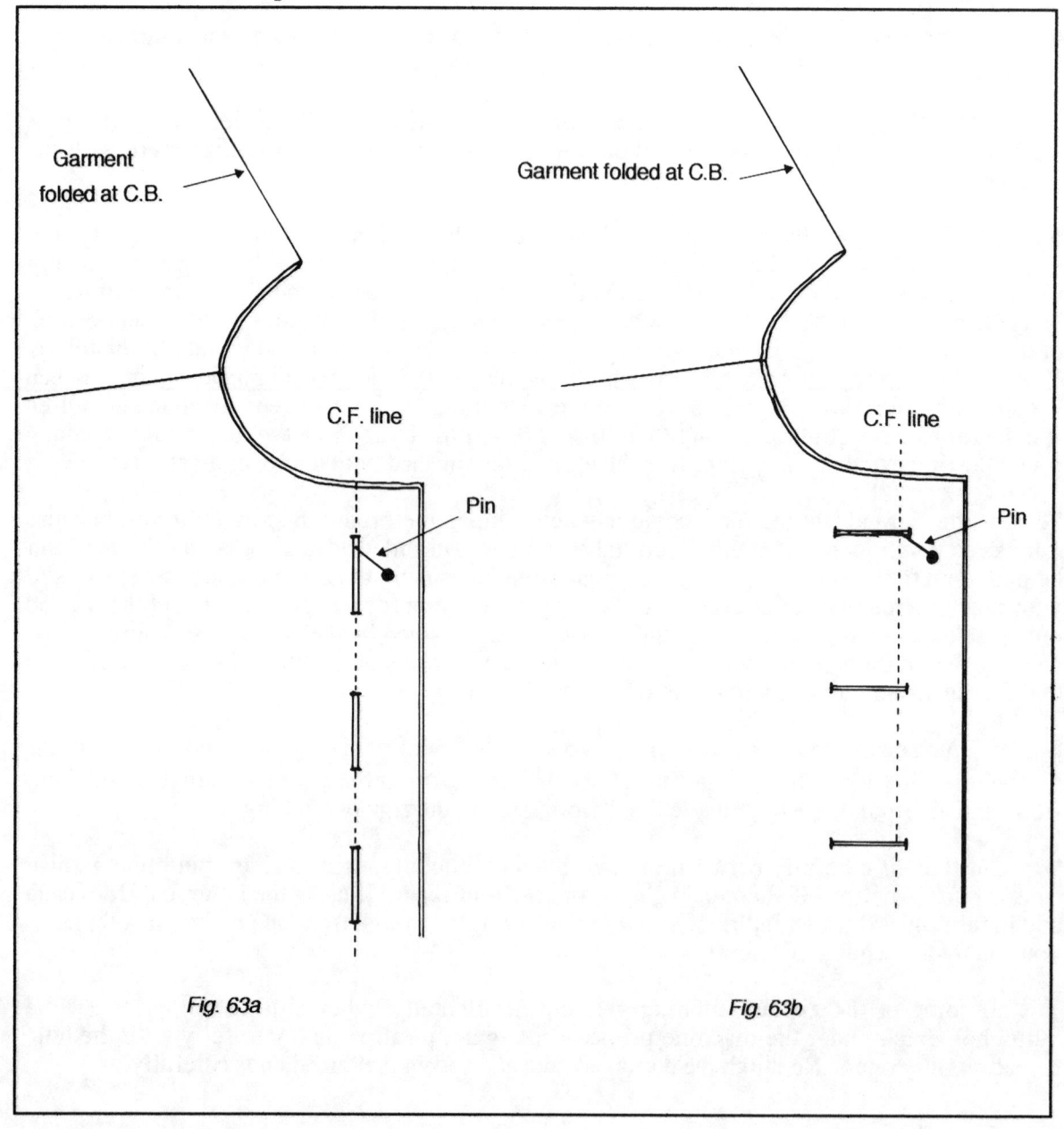

Fig. 63a *Fig. 63b*

3. Mark, with marking pen or pencil, a small dot exactly where the pin comes through, on the centre line of the overlap, on the button side.

4. Sew a button exactly on the mark. Remember to make a long enough shank to allow for the thickness of the overlapping side of the garment.

This method ensures that, in the case of vertical buttonholes, the top and bottom ends will remain level when the buttonholed side automatically slides downwards until stopped by the buttons. Similarly, in the case of horizontal buttons, the centre lines of the overlap will remain in line together when the buttonholed side is inevitably pulled sideways until stopped by the buttons.

For double-breasted or asymmetrically-buttoned garments, place the two parts together so that the centre front lines are exactly aligned; then push a pin through the upper or outer end (whichever end will be taking the strain when the garment is worn) of the buttonhole.

ADDING A COUTURE TOUCH

On coats and jackets, reinforce each button by placing another very small button on the wrong side, exactly underneath it. Both outer and inner buttons are sewn to the garment in one operation. The under button should lie directly against the fabric but the outer button should have an appropriate shank.

Fig.64. Try sewing four-holed buttons on in different ways; Where suitable, use a thicker than normal thread, perhaps in a contrasting colour related to another colour in the fabric. Eg. an emerald-green and sapphire-blue tweed knit could have matching emerald-green buttons sewn on with sapphire-blue thread.

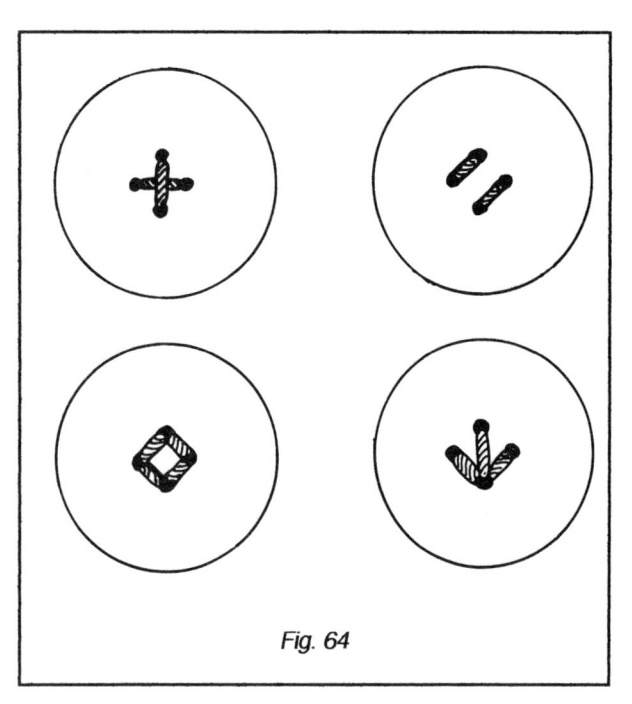

Fig. 64

MAKING YOUR OWN BUTTONS

This is sometimes a feasible alternative to searching the shops for matching ones, or sending some of your fabric away for professional button-covering. Here are just a few ideas.

1. *Purchased button-covering kits*, available from haberdashers enable you to cover metal or plastic button-forms with your own fabric (which can be knitted, woven, or even leather) providing it is not too thick and bulky.
   If you intend to use knitted fabric for this purpose you will probably need a woven lining fabric as well, to prevent the metal or plastic showing through.

2. *Dorset buttons* are made also by using curtain rings of bone or plastic. In this case, yarn is applied by buttonholing all around the ring and then filling in the centre with a network of stitches. Muriel Kent's book, "A Complete Crochet Course" (David and Charles, 1984) contains beautifully clear instructions for these buttons which are so eminently suited to all knitwear. The Womens' Institute also has a booklet on this subject.

3. Fig.65a,b,c. *Plastic or bone rings* (sold by haberdashers for curtain-making) can be covered with a circle of matching fabric, cut twice as large as the button. Make a line of tiny running-stitches all around the edge of the circle, put the ring in the middle, pull up the thread and fasten off securely at the back. Then make a line of back-stitching close to the inner edge of the ring through both layers of fabric. In this case, also, avoid thick fabrics and add a lining if necessary.

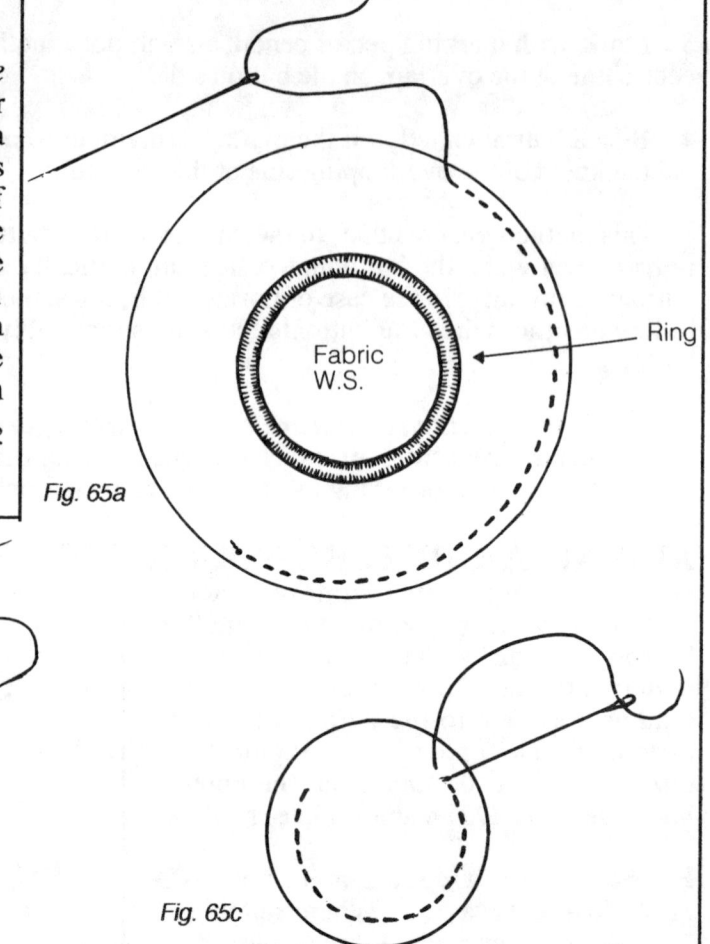

Fig. 65a

Fig. 65b

Fig. 65c

4. Chinese-ball buttons can be made from purchased cord, from neatly crocheted chain or from a length of French-knitting. Very clear instructions for these are shown in most comprehensive sewing primers. These are usually better combined with loops than with buttonholes.

5. Crocheted buttons can be made with fine yarn and a small-size hook. Aim for a circular shape which can be gathered around the edges, or shape it to make a hollow sphere. Fill with some kind of washable material such as polyester-wadding, a length of yarn, or crumpled-up fine soft fabric. Gather up the edge and fasten off securely. Fasten to the garment with a thread shank, and combine these also with loops rather than with buttonholes.

PROFESSIONALLY-MADE BUTTONS TO MATCH YOUR KNITS

See Appendix 2 for mail order details of the service provided by 'Harlequin' who will cover many different kinds of button, in a variety of sizes, (as well as belts, and other dress accessories) using your own knitted or woven fabrics. They will even make lengths of rouleau looping in your own woven fabrics - a godsend to those who make wedding dresses!

CHAPTER 10

ZIPS

There is a school of thought on the subject of cut-and-sew which declares that zips are unnecessary in clothes made of knitted fabrics simply because they are capable of stretching sufficiently without openings. However, if you are following the pattern instructions for a garment which was never intended to be made from knitted fabric (as I am, frequently!) you may find a zipped opening essential. You have to be able to get the garment on, so it all depends on how much stretch is left in the fabric - and that, in turn, depends upon what, if any, interfacing and/or lining has been used, and upon the shape and general design of the garment. In designs for which woven fabrics are recommended it is often possible to eliminate a zip by, for example, substituting elastic for tape in the waist seamline.

A word of warning; if you do incorporate a zip, *make quite certain that the knitted fabric of the garment does not have to stretch at all in order to fit the figure*. You may have sewn the zip in perfectly, but if the fabric is at all stretched, in a widthways direction, the zip will promptly 'ripple'.

Setting in a zip fastener so that it looks neat and professional is sometimes a considerable challenge to the average home dressmaker, and, when knitted fabrics are involved the hazards are multiplied; so it seems appropriate to sort out the difficulties for cut-and-sew enthusiasts.

BUYING A ZIP.

Nylon or polyester zips are lighter and more flexible than metal ones and are certainly just as strong. I also feel that they are more suited to knitted fabrics. The zip tapes should also be made from nylon or polyester as this is stronger and more stable than cotton. They are available in a reasonably wide variety of colours but a perfect match is not always possible. I strongly advise that you check carefully if tempted by the very cheap zips sometimes available on market stalls: they are not always as smooth and flat as they should be.

If you want your zip to be near-invisible, look for the one which has the smallest and flattest 'head', i.e. the part you pull. The thickness of the head can vary from 5mm to 10mm ($3/16$in - $3/8$in), and although this does not sound like a great difference, the thinner heads are considerably easier to hide away than the thicker ones.

There is a type of zip which is termed "invisible". This is sewn in by hand or with the help of a special foot which is supplied with some sewing-machines; alternatively, a special plastic foot can be obtained from at least one of the manufacturers of these invisible zips. This type of zip does disappear completely behind the seam when correctly applied but as I personally find them a little stiff and awkward to operate, I rarely use them for cut-and-sew projects.

If the zip is to be a decorative feature of the garment, consider buying one of the oversized, chunky zips, possibly in a contrasting colour. These can be obtained with fixed (closed) ends or with separating ends. Some have large ring-pulls attached. This type of zip is not intended to be hidden away behind the fabric.

Make sure your zip is long enough! Too many skirt and trouser zips get broken because the opening is not long enough to allow the garment to be slipped on with ease.

GENERAL HINTS ON ZIP INSERTION

Here are some guidelines to help you get it right.

1. Never sew in the zip until you are sure the fitting is right - otherwise you could have some tedious unpicking and re-stitching to do, with the added risk of snagging the knitted fabric. When trying on for fitting, simply pin the opening together along the two seamlines.

2. There is no need to stabilise the seam allowances before sewing in a zip because the zip tapes will eventually do that job. However, if the knit shows signs of stretching out of shape too easily, you could slip-stitch 6mm(1/4in) wide cotton tape to the seamlines first. Just be careful that this is not going to make the opening too bulky. It might be better to use a strip of paper which can be torn away afterwards.

3. Use pinning as a preliminary to stitching, placing the pins at right angles to the seamline, not parallel with it. This is a much more efficient way of holding everything in place than tacking.

4. Take great care not to stretch the knit when pinning it to the zip tapes. Don't gather it either in your efforts not to stretch it! Keep both knitted fabric and zip tapes absolutely flat together. To make this easier, do it on a table - not on your lap.

5. Unless you are very experienced, it is probably advisable to hand-sew your zips in place initially, using matching thread and the 'prick-stitch' technique described in the next paragraph. This is firmer than tacking. If you have made an error of judgment, hand-sewing is also considerably easier to unpick than small machine-stitching, especially where knitted fabrics are involved. Once you are satisfied that the zip is flat and evenly set in, you can always machine-stitch over the hand-stitching to make it more secure.

6. **Fig.66.** When hand-sewing the zip in place, use prick-stitch. This is rather like back-stitch but has less thread showing on the right side. The needle comes up from underneath the fabric and is then re-inserted only one or two threads behind where it came out; It is then carried forward, under the fabric, and re-emerges about 3mm(1/8in) to 6mm(1/4in) from the first stitch.

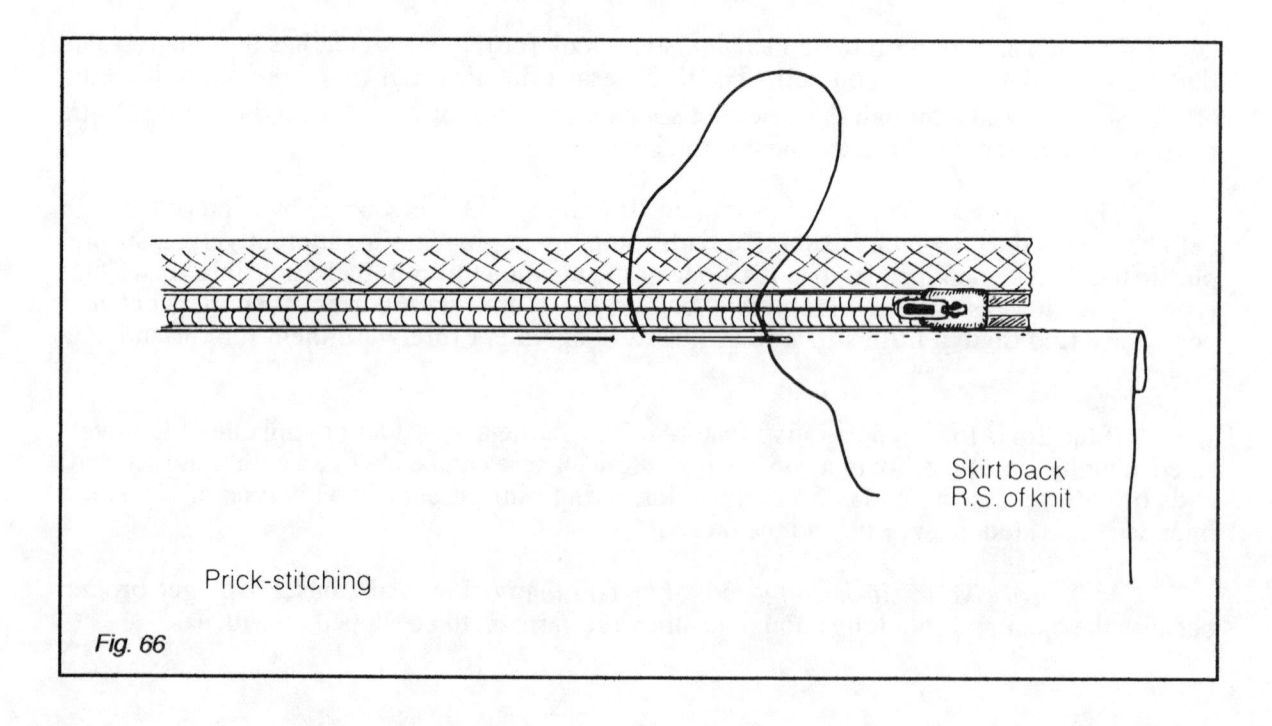

Prick-stitching

Skirt back
R.S. of knit

Fig. 66

7. When machine-stitching a zip in place, you must use a zipper foot in place of the normal presser foot on your machine. The normal presser foot guards the needle on both sides and so makes it impossible for the stitching to be really close to the zip teeth; a zipper foot leaves one side of the needle unguarded, making it possible to stitch very close to the zip teeth.

On some types of machine, the zipper foot is moved either to the left or to the right side of the needle; on others, the needle is moved either to the left or to the right side of the foot. The two types are illustrated on p.14 of "The Revised Knit, Cut and Sew: Book 1".

If you do not have a zipper foot with your machine, you should be able to buy one from a sewing-machine shop quite easily; if, however, the standard ones will not fit your machine, write to the manufacturer or try one of his agents.

8. Always move the zip slider away from the area on which you are actually working; never try to sew round it or you will have a wobble in the stitching-line. When stitching along the side of a zip, stop just before you get to the zip slider, with the needle in the fabric, raise the zipper foot, gently pull the slider past the needle until it is safely out of the way, lower the zipper foot and continue stitching.

TWO GOOD WAYS OF INSERTING ZIPS

School dressmaking lessons (in my day), and pattern instruction sheets, have taught us to sew in a zip so that the two seamlines meet exactly down the centre of the zip teeth; yet this is a method rarely used in professional garment construction: it is not easy and it practically adds a "home-made" label to the finished garment. So here are two alternative methods which I find effective in cut-and-sew work. Try them out using odd pieces of woven fabric and old zips. Once you have mastered the techniques you will be set for success with knitted fabrics.

Lapped, semi-concealed application
Use this whenever you want a zip to be placed unobtrusively in a seamline. Employ a thin light zip in a colour which matches the fabric as closely as possible.

> **Note:** *the instructions which follow are written as for the left side of a skirt; so, no matter where the zip happens to be on the garment, think of it as being on your left side and these instructions will then make sense! Zips at centre-back, on the left back hip, centre front, etc. can all be inserted in exactly the same way.*

1. Fig.67a
With the zip closed and the top end of the zip slider lying 2.5cm(1in) below the top raw edges of the skirt, check that the seam is securely sewn up to a point just above the end-stop of the zip. This will prevent strain and possible damage to the zip when the garment is put on and taken off.

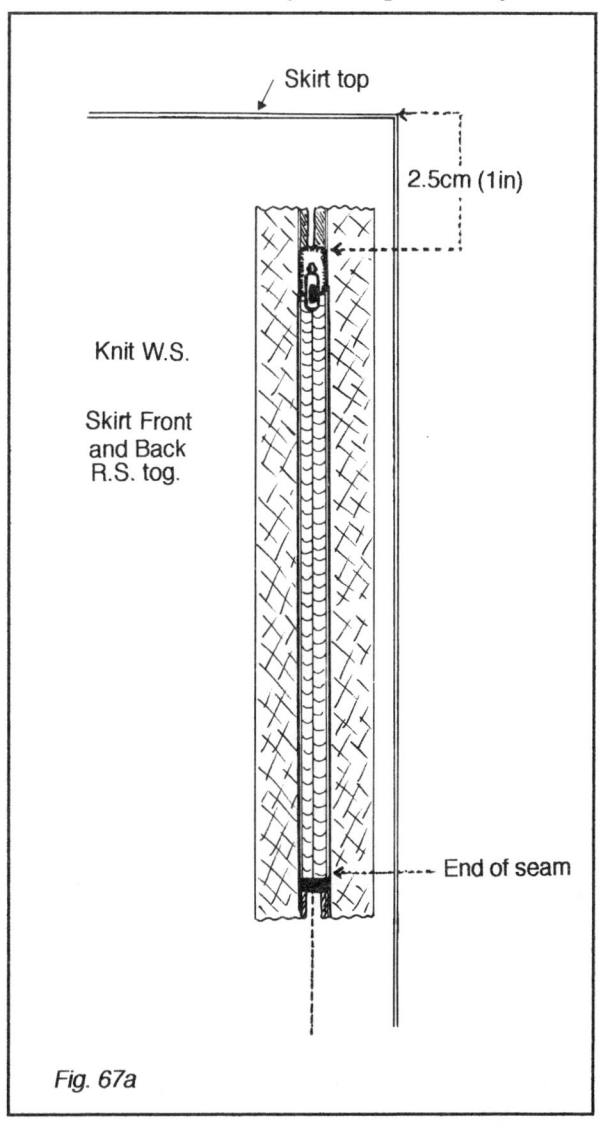

Fig. 67a

2. **Fig.67b.** On the skirt Front, turn the complete seam allowance to the wrong side. Press and/or tack in position.

On the skirt Back, tack-mark the seamline with a bright contrasting thread, finishing precisely where the sewn seam starts. This is simply to indicate exactly where the seamline lies.

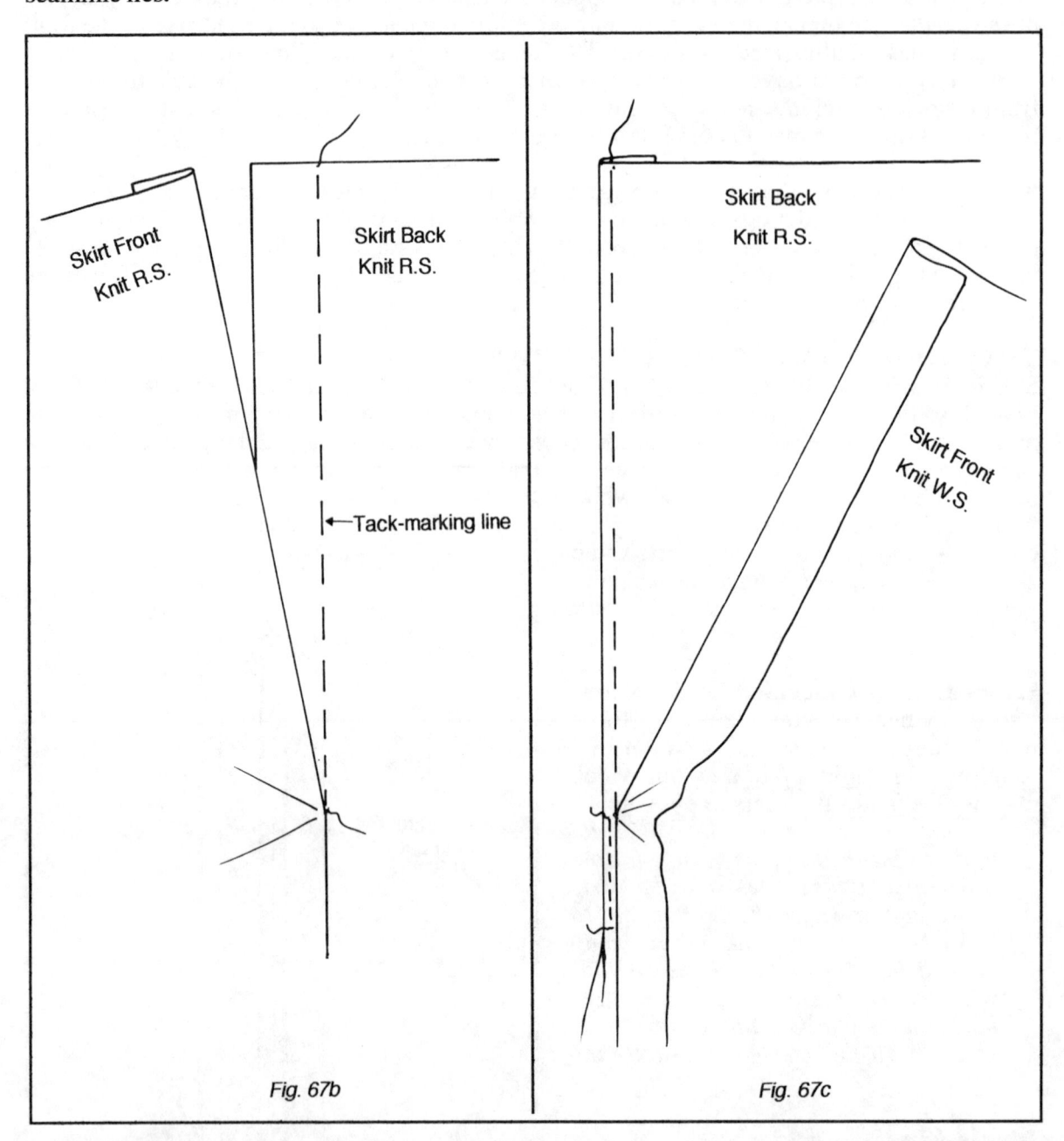

Fig. 67b

Fig. 67c

3. **Fig.67c.** On the skirt Back, fold the seam allowance to the wrong side along a line 3mm(1/8in) away from the tack-marked seamline, nearer to the edge of the seam allowance. Press and tack this fold in the seam allowance, continuing on down to about 2.5cm(1in) below the point where the sewn seam starts. Take particular care to tack, with small stitches, this 3mm(1/8in) wide fold for that last 2.5cm(1in), otherwise you can find that it has disappeared when you need it during the next stage.

(If you now lay the Front seamline exactly on the Back seamline, you will find that you have a 3mm(1/8in) wide underlap.)

4.   Fig.67d. Keeping the skirt Front out of the way, apply the folded edge of the Back seam allowance to the closed zip, keeping it very close to the zip teeth. Remember to keep a 2.5cm(1in) gap between the slider top and the top raw edges of the skirt. Pin the fabric to the zip tape, placing the pins, as shown, at right angles to the zip. Prickstitch by hand, *from one end of the zip tape to the other*, keeping close to the folded edge and the teeth. Follow this with machine-stitching if desired. All stitching must be completed on this side of the zip before starting on the other side.

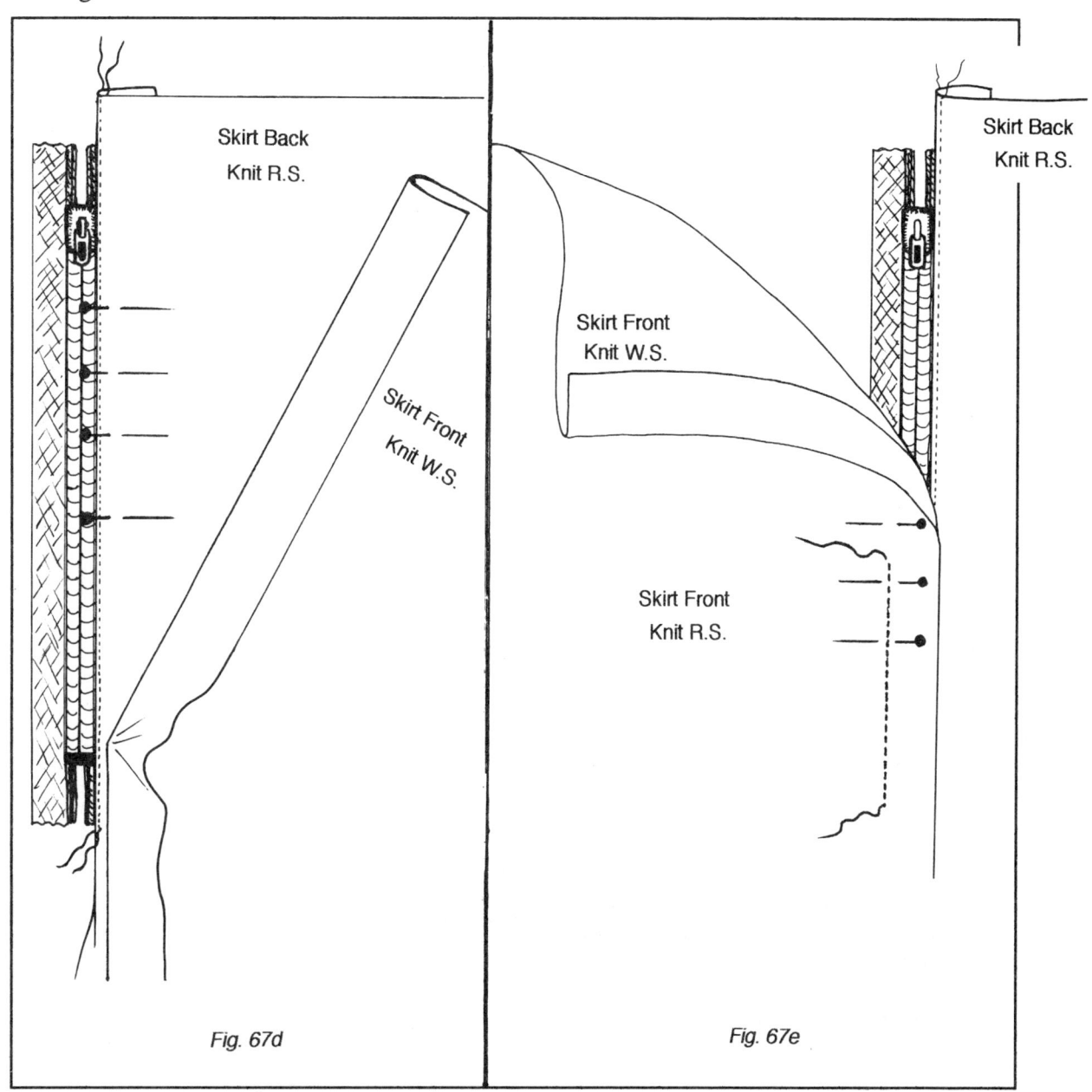

Fig. 67d

Fig. 67e

5.   Fig.67e. Position the skirt Front so that it is level with the skirt Back at the top end, and so that the folded edge of the seam allowance just covers the line of stitching made at Stage 4. (You should find that you have replaced the front and back seamlines exactly together.) Pin the fabric to the zip tape as shown, and prickstitch as before. This stitching should be near but not directly up against the zip teeth, and should be an even distance from the folded edge for the entire length of the opening - usually about 1.2cm($1/2$in) to 1.5cm($5/8$in). Stitching across the lower end is optional; it sometimes seems to make an unnecessary dent in an otherwise smooth line. Reinforce with machine stitching if there is likely to be any strain on the seam.

Visible zip application

In this case the zip teeth are completely exposed to view and can become a decorative feature of the garment. Here are two examples with directions:

Example 1: a chunky, open-ended zip, used to fasten the front-opening edges of an anorak or bomber-jacket. An example of this is the jacket illustrated on p86 in Book 1.

1. Press the seam allowance on each side of the opening towards the wrong side.

2. Lay each half of the front on its appropriate half of the zip, placing the folded seamline close in beside the teeth. Check that the ends of the opening edges will be level at top and bottom when the zip is closed. Place pins at right angles to the seamline to hold the zip in position while stitching.

3. Sew with prickstitch close to the seamline and follow with machine-stitching to make it secure.

Example 2: a zip which closes a neck opening made in a single piece of knitted fabric where no seam is involved, so the zip has to be set into a slit cut in the fabric; the slit will be faced with a piece of fine woven fabric such as pre-shrunk calico, poly/cotton poplin, linen, polyester lining, etc.

1. Fig. 68a

Cut the facing, on the straight grain, to the correct size:
    Length = the length of the zip teeth (not the zip tapes) plus 7.5cm(3in).
    Width = the width of the closed zip teeth plus 10cm(4in)
    Oversew, or overlock, three sides of the facing, as shown.

2. Draw the line of the proposed opening on the wrong side of the facing, exactly down the centre, from the top.
    To decide the length of the line, place the zip on the facing with the top of the zip slider 1.9cm(3/4in) to 2.5cm(1in) down from the top of the facing; (the distance depends on the thickness of the knit and what you intend to do at the neck edge). Measure from the top of the facing to the end-stop.

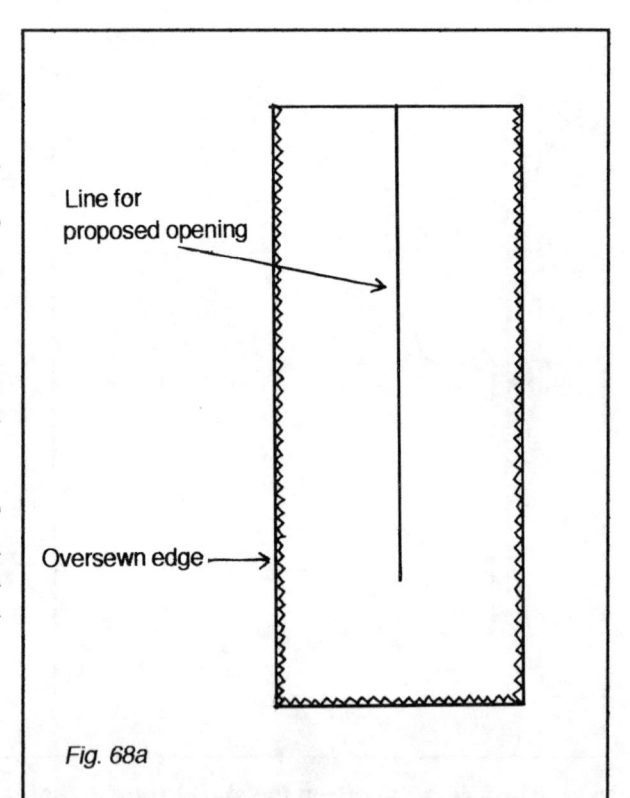

Fig. 68a

3. Fig.68b. Place the facing on the knitted fabric, right sides together, with the drawn line exactly positioned where the opening is to be. Pin in position.

4. **Fig.68c.** Machine-stitch (short stitch-length - about 1 on most machines) down one side of the drawn line, across the lower end, and up the other side. The lines should be exactly parallel, and the distance between them should be just a little wider than the width of the zip teeth.

5. Cut precisely between the two lines of stitching, from the top to a point about 9mm(3/8in) from the lower end; Then make a cut diagonally out to each corner as shown.
Note: *you must cut right up to the corners of the stitching lines* - if you shirk it you will inevitably have crinkles at the corners when you turn the facing to the wrong side! Providing your machine-stitching is sufficiently small, so that you have sewn all the fibres firmly in place, there should be no danger of fraying when you cut.

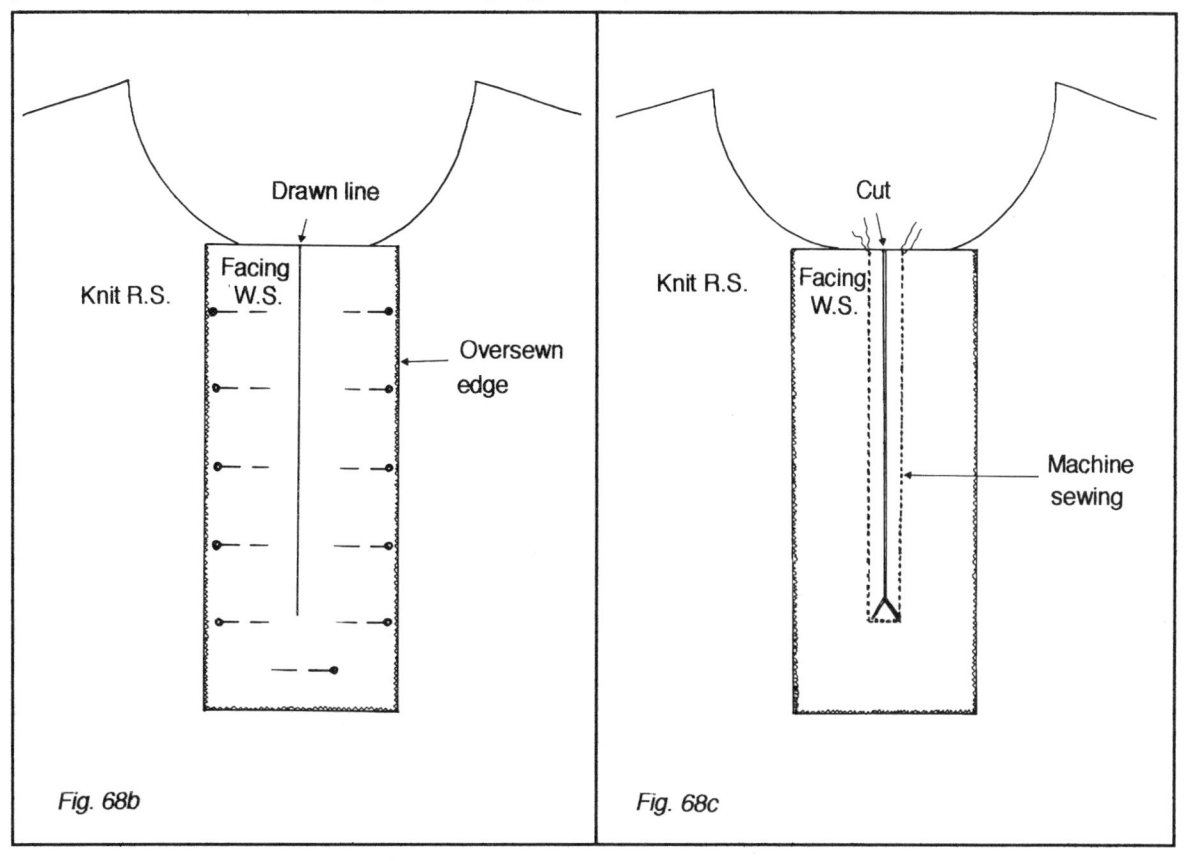

Fig. 68b

Fig. 68c

6. Turn the facing through to the wrong side of the knit and press the seamlines flat, rolling them just slightly towards the wrong side.

7. Position the slit over the closed zip, keeping the top of the zip slider in its correct position (see stage 2), and the faced edges of the slit quite close up against the zip teeth. Pin in position, prick-stitch to hold, and then machine-stitch close to the faced edges of the slit.

CHAPTER 11

SKIRTS
FITTING AND APPLYING WAISTBANDS

A skirt must not only fit well and be the right length (and this, of course, is a fashion variable) but it must also hang properly if it is to make the figure inside it look good. Remember that any skirt made from knitted fabric should have enough ease in it to ensure that the fabric is not stretched anywhere. Tightly clinging skirts are not flattering - unless you happen to be young and perfectly proportioned!

The main factor in making sure that the skirt hangs properly is correct alignment at the waistline of the body; i.e. the waist seamline on the skirt may need to be moved from its original position somewhere along its circumference to cope with figure peculiarities. No one likes to think that they are a freak, but it is surprising how many of us are not "normal"! For my own part, I have a sway (hollow) back, which means that I have to move the waist seamline down about 1.9cm(3/4in) at the centre back, on every skirt I make. Many of my students have one hip slightly larger than the other; this entails moving the waist seamline down a little above the smaller hip.

Posture comes into this too; people with large tummies tend to lean backwards, whereas those with large posteriors tend to lean forwards. Unfortunately, as we grow older, these variations from the norm become more pronounced; young people, on the whole, have fewer fitting problems. Using a dressmaker's dummy does not solve the problem, simply because the dummy is unlikely to stand precisely the way you do.

So here is a simple programme to follow which should enable you to produce perfectly fitting skirts every time.

DETERMINING THE EXACT POSITION OF THE WAISTBAND
Note: these instructions apply to fitted skirts which have an opening somewhere around the top to enable them to be slipped over the hips.

1. After the skirt pieces have been cut and the edges overlocked or oversewn in some way, any darts and all seams should be machine-tacked (or hand-tacked), leaving an opening where the zip will be. If there is no seamline at centre front or centre back, mark these lines with a tacking thread. Do not, at this stage, sew up the lining.

2. Try on the skirt. Pin the seamlines of the opening exactly together. If your choice of pattern size was correct and you carried out any necessary adjustments to the paper pattern before cutting out, the skirt should now be fitting reasonably well. If, however, it seems obviously too big, calculate how much circumference needs to be removed, divide this amount between the number of seams and take in the skirt accordingly. If the skirt is obviously too tight, let the seams out the necessary amount, but remember that you should still retain at least 1.5cm(5/8in) seam allowance on the seam where the zip will be so that you can sew it in correctly. If the zip is on a side seam, both side seams must be at least 1.5cm(5/8in) wide, or the centre Front and centre Back points will be out of place.

3. If, or when, the fitting is reasonably good, tie a length of narrow tape firmly around the waist, fastening the ends in a bow exactly over the opening where the zip will be. Pull 1.5cm(5/8in) of the skirt up under the tape so that the tape lies exactly on the present waist seamline.
   Note: the tape has probably gathered the skirt fabric in a little; this is as it should be; the skirt top should be up to 4cm(1 1/2in) bigger than your precise waist measurement, so that eventually it will be eased into the waistband rather than fitting in flat.

4. Stand in front of a long mirror and look at the seamlines and at the centre Front and centre Back lines. (To look at the centre Back line, stand with your back to the long mirror and hold a hand mirror up in front of you so that you can see the back view; be careful not to lift your arm so much that the skirt starts to lift too.) If any line or seam is hanging sideways to any degree, pull the skirt up under the tape, in the opposite direction, until the line does hang straight, at right angles to the floor. For example, if the centre front line is leaning towards the left knee, (as shown in **Fig.69a.**) the skirt will have to be lifted at the top right front to compensate (as in **Fig.69b**). A large behind will probably cause the side seams to tilt towards the back so the skirt top will have to be lifted at the centre front to compensate. A large tummy will make the side seams tilt towards the front, so the skirt will need to be lifted at the back.

Lift the skirt under the tape as necessary until all the seamlines are hanging straight.

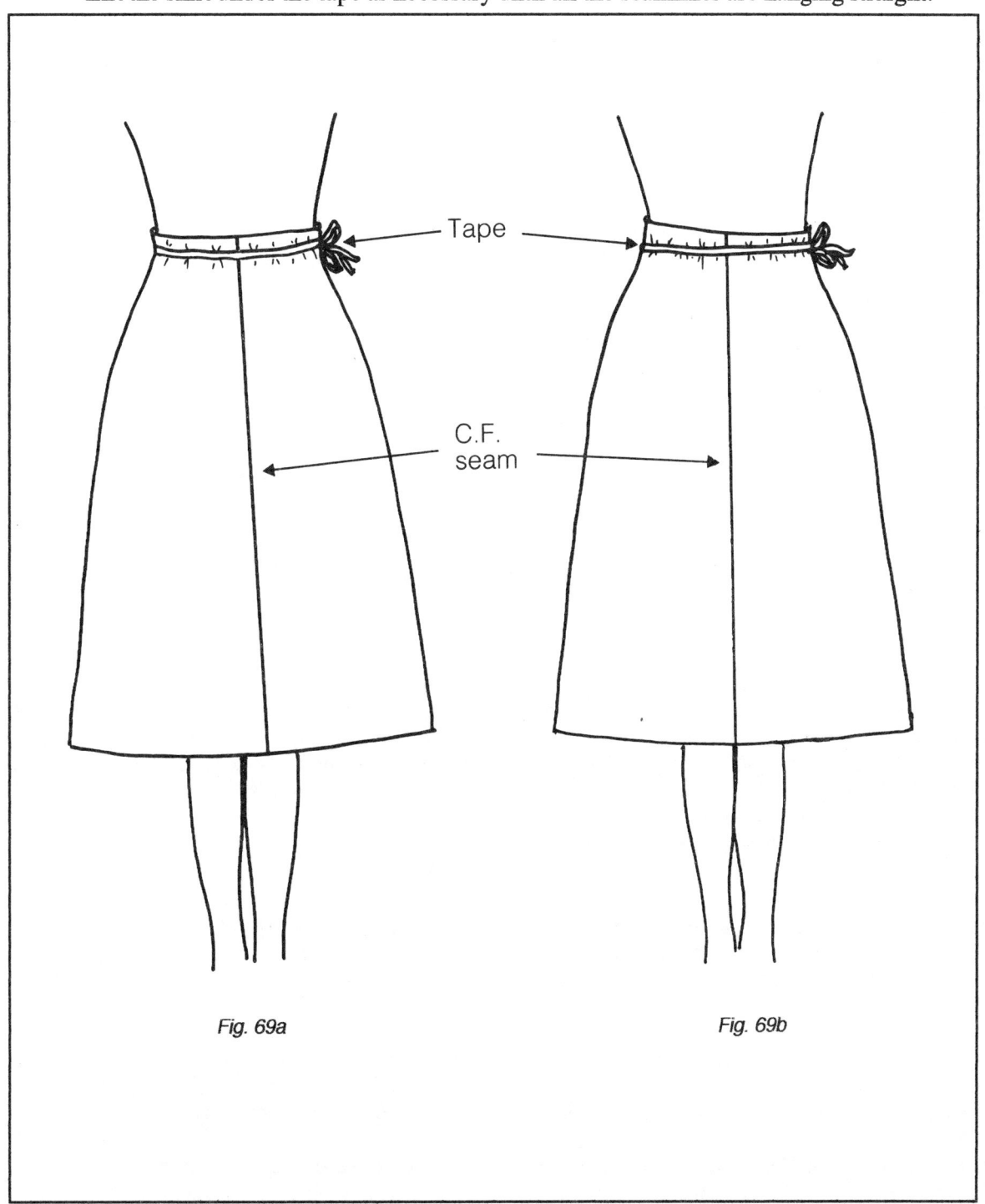

Fig. 69a   *Fig. 69b*

5. Pin the tape to the skirt all round, placing the pins parallel with the tape along its centre. Doing this for yourself can be tricky; try to get someone to help, at least with the back. If there really is no help available, you will have to manage simply by feeling and by checking in the hand mirror.

6. Untie the tape and take the skirt off - carefully, so that no pins drop out..

7. Trim off any surplus seam allowance, leaving a precise 1.5cm(5/8in) seam allowance, all round, above the centre of the tape.
Note: if you pin the piece you have removed, right side up, on to a strip of paper, and label it at the appropriate points (eg. "centre back" or "left side"), you will have a permanent record, or pattern, of the area you need to remove from every skirt you make from now onwards.

8. Make up the skirt lining, incorporating whatever alterations you made to the skirt. If you had to trim surplus fabric from the top edge of the skirt, trim exactly the same amount of fabric from the top edge of the skirt lining. *But remember* that the skirt lining will be worn inside out (i.e. the wrong side of the lining will face the wrong side of the skirt).

Now that your skirt is fitting correctly, put the zip in. (*See Chap.8*) If you did it before marking the waist seamline, you could find that it is now too high up in the seam and will have to be unpicked and re-inserted: not to be recommended with knitted fabric!

Tack the lining to the skirt, wrong sides together, all around the top. Where the darts on the skirt are pressed towards the centre, press the corresponding darts on the lining towards the sides; this avoids too much bulk at any one point.

Hem the lining to *the outer edge* of the zip tape, down both sides of the zip. If you take it too close to the zip teeth it will inevitably get caught in next time you are dressing in a hurry!

APPLYING THE WAISTBAND
Note: if your waist measurement is not exactly the same as the standard measurement for your pattern size, *the paper pattern for the waistband will be wrong. It is safer to abandon it and follow the next set of guidelines:*

1. Cut your waistband, using a strip cut straight across the knit, exactly parallel with the rows. The knit used for the skirt will be suitable providing it is not too thick or highly textured. If necessary, knit a separate strip for the waistband using a less bulky yarn and/or a flatter stitch pattern such as stocking-stitch. If the skirt happens to be part of an outfit where the collar, facings, etc. have been cut from woven fabric, you could possibly cut the waistband from this same woven fabric.
Length = your waist measurement + 10cm(4in).
Width = twice the intended depth of the waistband + 2.2cm(7/8in).

2. Interface the waistband strip, using either a fusible or a sew-in interfacing, to make it firmer and to reduce (or to eliminate) the stretch factor. What interfacing you use depends on whether or not you want the finished waistband to have a little 'give' or to be rigid. Here are some examples:

Fusible knitted nylon, cut lengthwise and covering the entire wrong side of the band; this is only suitable for narrow waistbands because it would lack the necessary firmness to stop it rolling; top-stitching would be needed as stretching could cause the two fabrics to separate.

Fusible cotton muslin, covering the entire wrong side of the band; this does eliminate all the stretch, but is not very firm. An extra layer of interfacing and some top-stitching would improve its stability.

Vilene Fold-a-Band, heavy-weight; this is fusible, non-stretch and firm; position the central line of slits along the foldline of the waistband; top-stitching is advisable to ensure that the Fold-a-Band stays permanently in place.

Belt petersham, sewn-in; eliminates all stretch and is very firm.

Loom (or 'non-roll') elastic, tacked in; when the waistband is completed the tacking stitches are removed; this is firm, has a non-roll quality and allows the waistband to "give" whilst retaining its grip. Do not top-stitch: it needs to be able to move within the knitted covering. See p83 for help with this.

3. Fig.70. With the wrong side of the waistband facing upwards (as shown), overlock or over-edge stitch the lower long edge. Mark off the upper edge of the waistband as follows, using pins or pencil marks:

A-B is the underlap: about 6.5cm(2 1/2in).

B-C should be your precise waist measurement, but allow about 1.2cm(1/2in) more for the thickness of the knit.

D is exactly halfway between B and C.

E is exactly halfway between B and D.

F is exactly halfway between D and C.

C-G is left for an overlap if required - or for letting out if you have miscalculated!

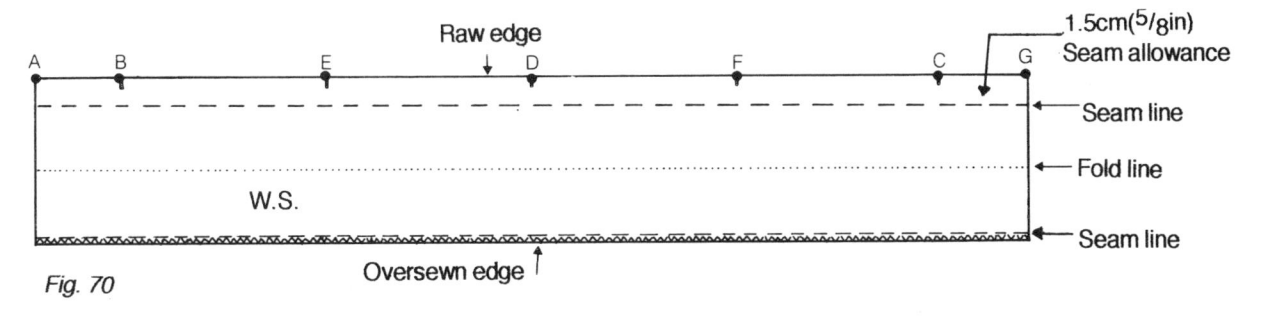

Fig. 70

4. Fig.71

Divide the top of the skirt precisely in quarters as shown, marking the points B,C,D,E and F as shown, using pins or pencil marks.

Note: do not assume that these quarter marks will be exactly where the seams occur: they might not be.

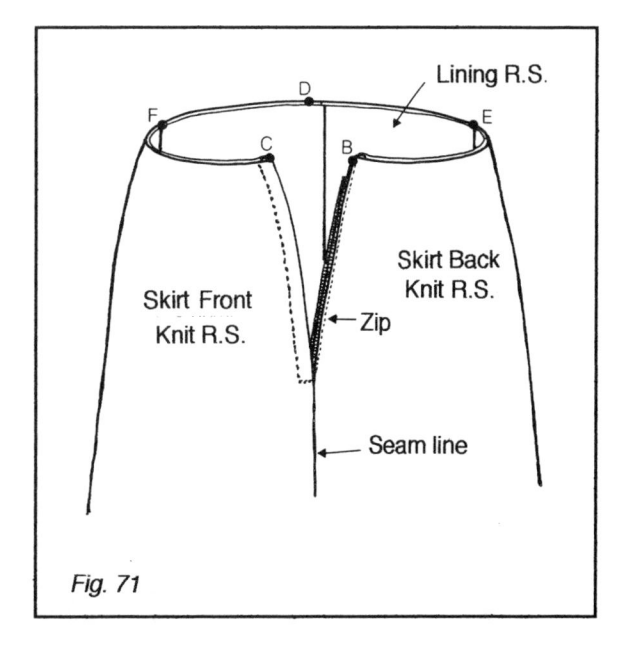

Fig. 71

5. **Fig.72a.** Place the waistband around the top of the skirt, right sides together, lining up the raw edges. Match and pin together the points, B,C,D,E and F. Pin all around the top of the skirt, using plenty of pins and placing them across the seamline as shown. Ease the skirt in to fit the waistband, as necessary, without making pleats or gathers..

6. Machine-tack along the waist seamline. Try on the skirt to check the fitting and adjust if necessary. Machine-stitch along the waist seamline again to secure.

7. **Fig.72b.** Turn the waistband over to the inside of the skirt so that the oversewn edge overlaps the machined seamline by 3mm(1/8in). Pin in place temporarily.

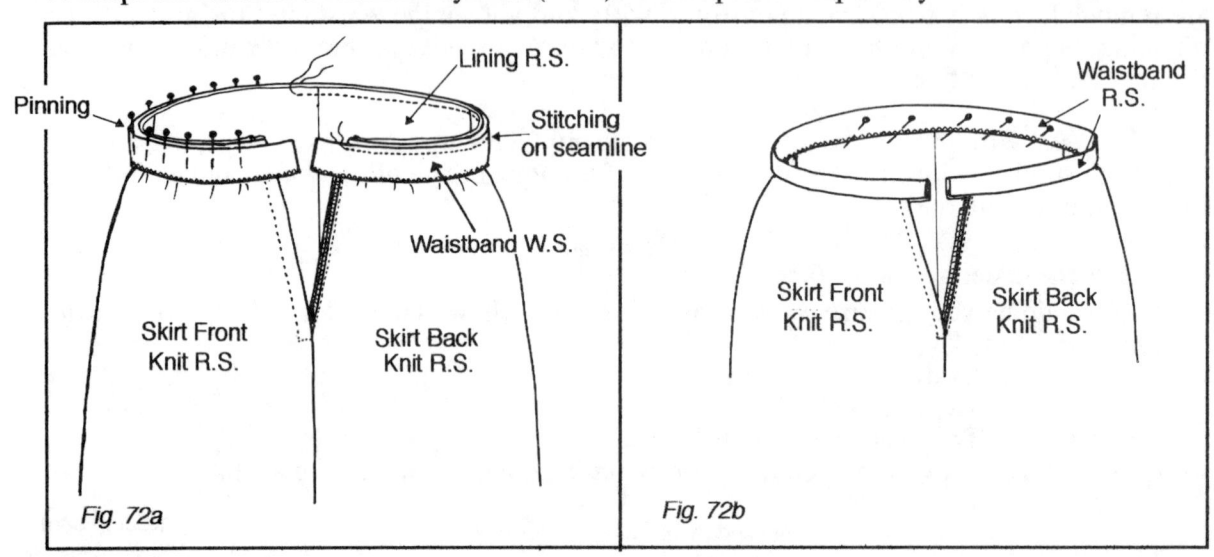

Fig. 72a

Fig. 72b

8. **Fig.73a.** Hand finish the *overlapping* end of the waistband by turning in the end and hemming. If no overlap is required, trim off the waistband so that, after hand-finishing, the end of the waistband will line up with the seamline over the zip (**Fig.73b.**). The *underlapping* end should not be turned in; simply oversew the raw edges together (**Fig.73c**).

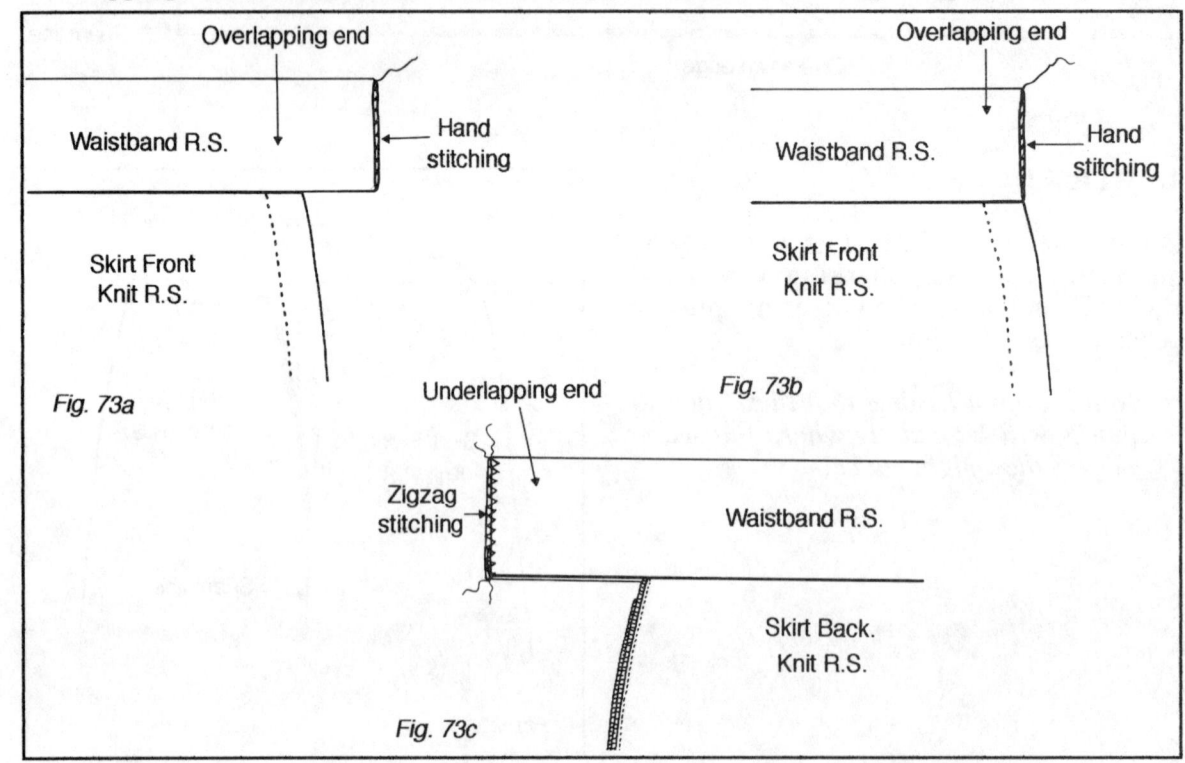

Fig. 73a

Fig. 73b

Fig. 73c

9.   **Fig.74a.** From the *right side*, place pins as shown, so that the *inside* edge of the waistband is held in place. Remove any pins left on the inside of the skirt. Still on the right side, either machine-stitch exactly in the seamline (this is called "stich-in-the-ditch"!). Alternatively, top-stitch along the edge of the waistband as shown in **Fig.74b.** Whichever way you do it, the stitching should secure the inside edge of the waistband so that it overlaps the stage 6 stitching-line by 3mm(1/8in).

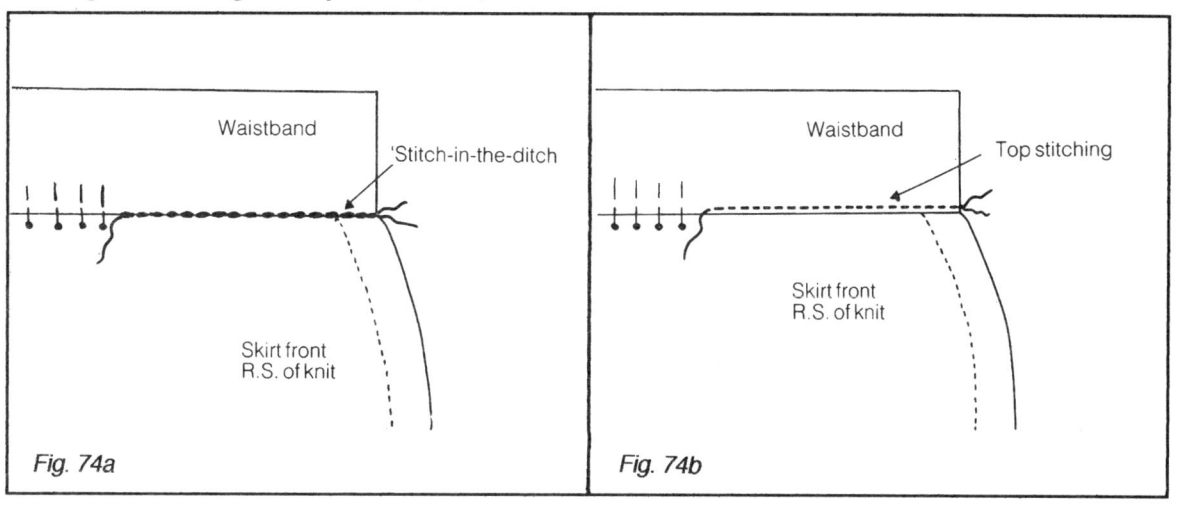

Fig. 74a   *Fig. 74b*

10.   Apply a heavy-duty hook to the underlap and a matching bar to the appropriate place on the underside of the waistband. This takes the strain of the fastening. The overlapping end can then be fastened with small invisible hooks and bars, or with hooks and buttonholed loops.

ALTERNATIVE METHODS
Many women find the conventional stiffened waistband uncomfortable; here are some suggestions for other ways of finishing the tops of fitted skirts.

1. *Curved Petersham.*
After stitching the lining inside the skirt, place the *inner edge* of the curve of the petersham so that it overlaps the top edge of the skirt by 1.2cm(1/2in); *the wrong side of the petersham faces the right side of the skirt*. Pin and then machine-stitch parallel with, and 3mm(1/8in) from, the edge of the petersham as shown in **Fig.75**. Turn the band down to the wrong side of the skirt. "Stitch-in-the-ditch" down all seamlines and darts, through all thicknesses, to hold the band in position. Do not top-stitch around the skirt top.

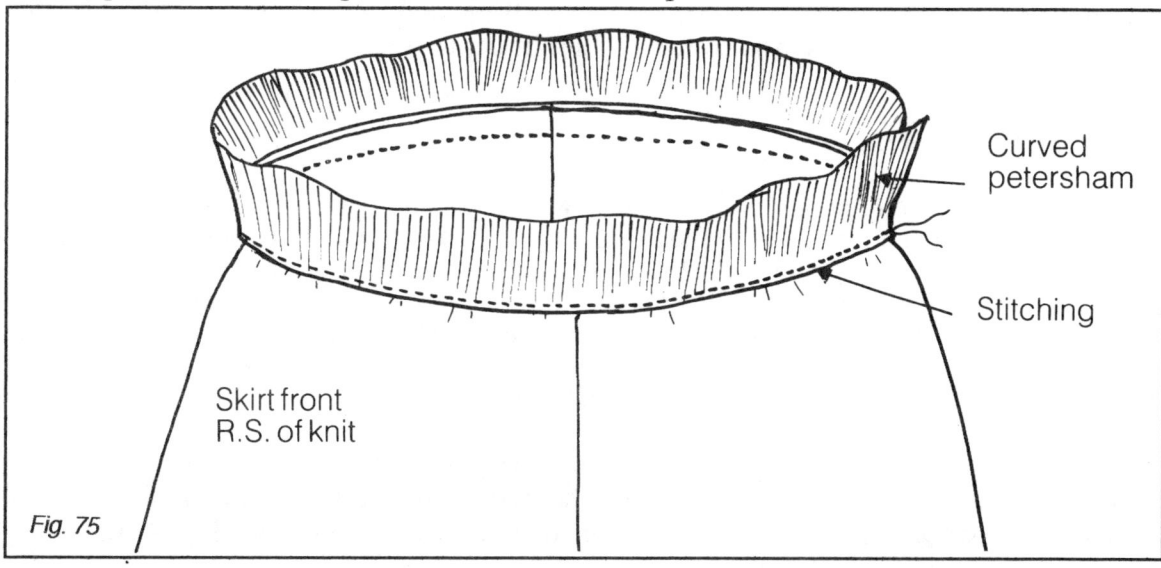

Fig. 75

2. *Loom elastic enclosed in a casing.*
Wrap a strip of the knitted fabric around the elastic, right side out, and machine-stitch the raw edges together, close to the edge of the elastic, as shown in **Fig.76a**.

Use a zipper foot as this will enable you to stitch as close as possible to the edge of the elastic without actually catching it in.

Trim the seam allowances to 1.5cm(5/8in).

Before stitching the lining inside the skirt, apply the covered waistband to the right side of the skirt top, as shown in **Fig.76b**, lining up the raw edges. Machine tack the band to the skirt, following the previous stitching line.

Place the lining on the right side of the skirt, right sides together, lining up the top raw edges; machine-stitch through all thicknesses. Turn the lining over to the wrong side This makes a neat and comfortable waistband which conveniently expands with the waistline!

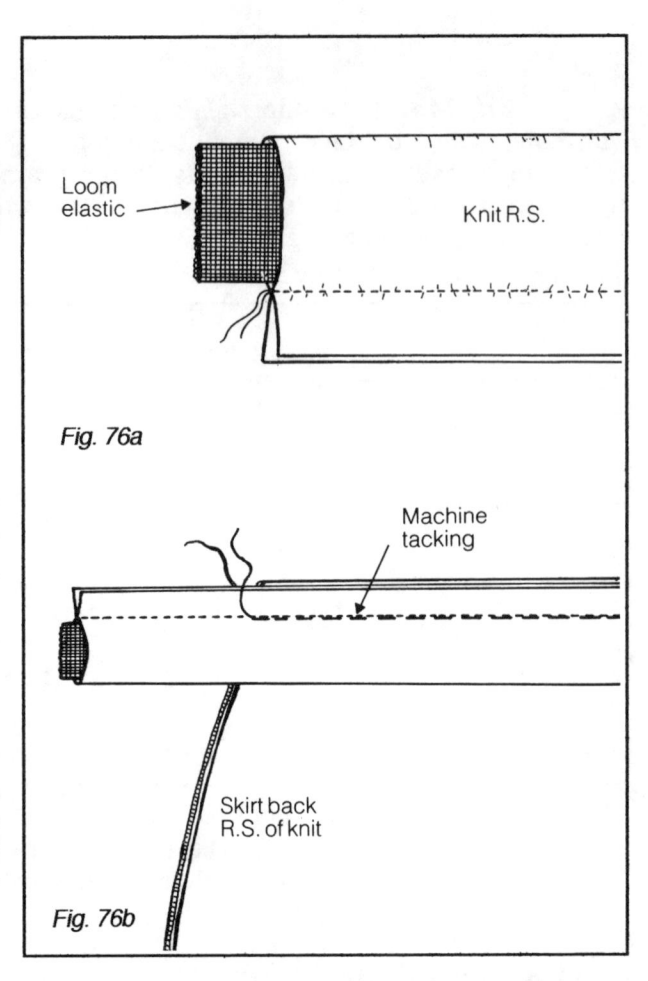

Fig. 76a

Fig. 76b

3. *Bias or straight binding*
Enclose the skirt top in a narrow binding (see Chap.12) cut (either on the bias or on the straight grain) from any fine woven fabric which matches or tones in with the knit. The length of the binding should be calculated to fit the waist snugly. This makes a comfortable finish for the skirt top, which is acceptable providing it will always be covered by a shirt or jumper.

4. *No waistband*
Sew the lining to the skirt, right sides together, all around the waist seamline; it may be necessary to add tape to the seamline to prevent it stretching out of shape. Turn the lining down to the wrong side and understitch it to the seam allowances, 3mm(1/8in) from the seamline. There will be no underlap in this case, so a small hook and eye will have to be sewn just above the top end of the zip. This works well on short-waisted figures but, like the previous method, really needs to be covered by a shirt or jumper.

Skirts without openings

It is perfectly possible to make "pull-on" skirts which have no opening at all but, of course, both the waistband and the top of the skirt must be cut large enough to slide over the hips. The waistband must then contain elastic to contract it sufficiently to fit the waist. This is perfectly feasible when using thin, fine knits, particularly on the young and slim, but is inadvisable if the knit is at all bulky and/or the figure even slightly overweight! Use loom elastic, about 2.5cm(1in) wide, enclosed in a casing (as described in Para.2 on the previous page), or use narrow elastic in several parallel casings.

Alternatively, at the cutting stage, allow 4.5cm(1 3/4in) extra fabric above the waist seamline, at the top of both the skirt and the lining; when the skirt and the lining are each made up, stitch them, right sides together, 1.5cm(5/8in) from the top raw edges as shown in **Fig.77a**.

Page 85

Turn the lining over and down on the wrong side, and press the seamline. Slip the elastic between the two fabrics and, using a zipper foot, make another line of stitching close to the edge of the elastic as shown in **Fig.77b**.

If the skirt is to have no lining, allow an extra 6.3cm(2 1/2in) of fabric above the waist seamline when cutting out. When the skirt is made up, turn 3.5cm(1 in) to the wrong side and stitch to enclose the elastic.

Very full skirts can be gathered onto a waistband which is just large enough to slide over the hips, and which is then nipped in with elastic to fit the waist. In this case, the knit needs to be very fine and soft, otherwise the skirt will be too bulky.

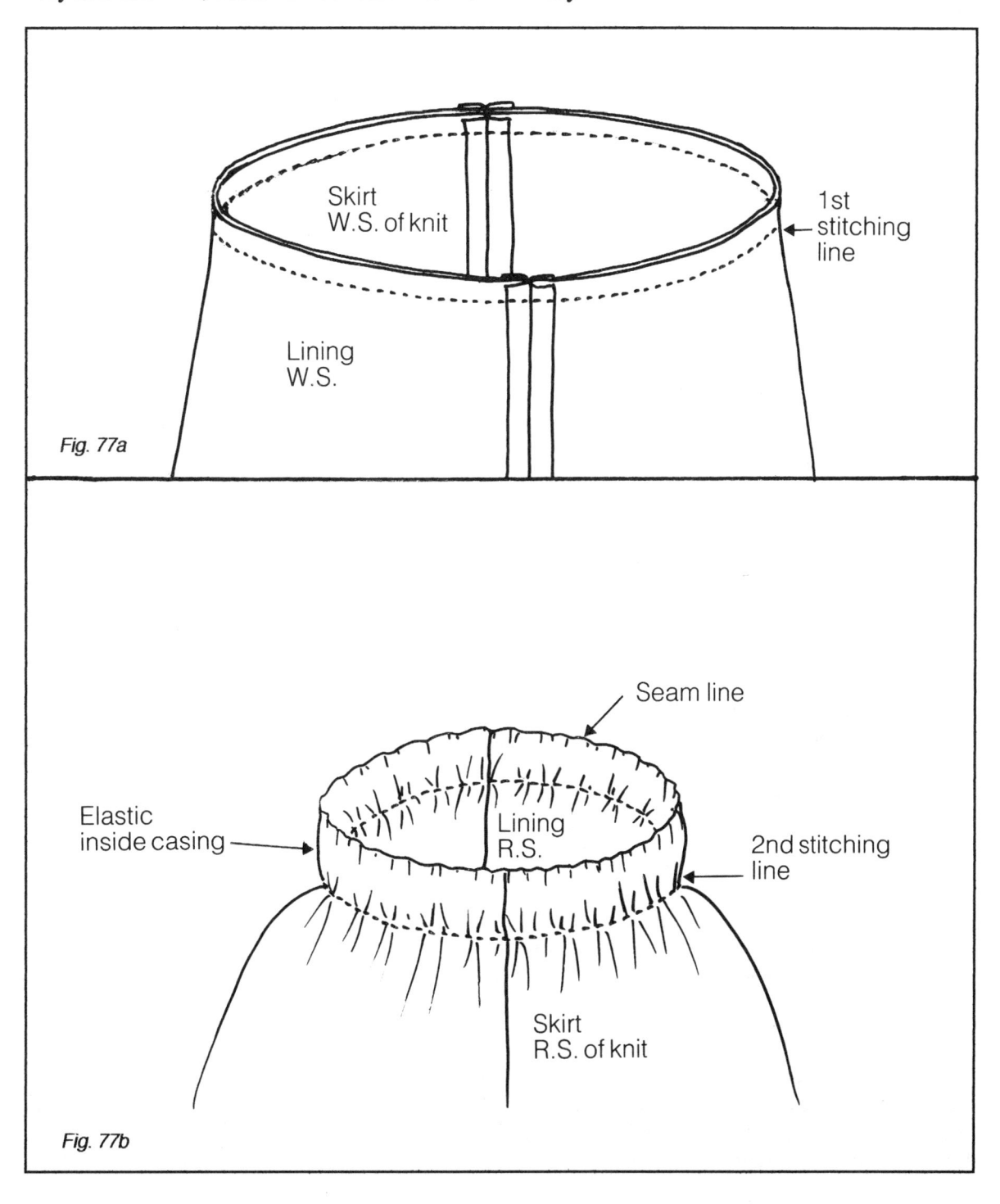

Fig. 77a

Fig. 77b

CHAPTER 12

BINDINGS

Binding is an effective way of neatening and stabilising the cut edges of the knitted fabric (where these form the edges of a garment) by enclosing it in a strip of toning or contrasting fabric.

Various types of binding are summarised on pp.64-65 of Book 1 and it seems appropriate, in this book, to enlarge on these techniques, simply because they are so useful.

BINDING WITH WOVEN FABRIC CUT ON THE BIAS GRAIN
Use striped cotton or checked gingham, as binding fabric, when experimenting with this process, especially if you have never done it before; the straight lines are helpful.

Work out how much length of binding you will require and then cut one or more strips which, when joined, will produce this length.

It is possible, of course, to buy ready-made bias-binding but the process of making your own is fairly simple, and the extra effort involved is more than compensated by having the binding made in the fabric, colour and width you personally choose.

To make the binding

1. (Fig.78a) Take a piece of the woven fabric, at least 30cm(12in) in length and preferably using the full width, from selvedge to selvedge. The larger the piece, the fewer the joins you will have to make. The four sides of the piece should, ideally, all be straight with the grain of the fabric, so that a thread can be pulled off cleanly from any cut edge. With practice though, you can learn to cut bias strips from all sorts of oddly shaped bits. It is possible, by making a large number of joins, to produce an amazingly long strip of binding from very small pieces.

2. (Fig.78b) Fold the fabric so that part of the cut edge A-B lies parallel with the selvedge A-D and the selvedge B-C is lying straight with the cut edge D-C. This sounds complicated but if you look at the diagram you will see that it is really very simple. If your folding has been sufficiently exact, the foldline will be on the true bias. It is important to be exact because you will inevitably get crinkling in the binding if your bias-cutting is not "true".

3. (Fig.78c) Cut along the foldline and then along parallel lines, approximately 3.5cm(1 3/8in) apart (possibly wider for thicker knits and fabrics) until you calculate that sufficient length will be produced when the strips are joined together.

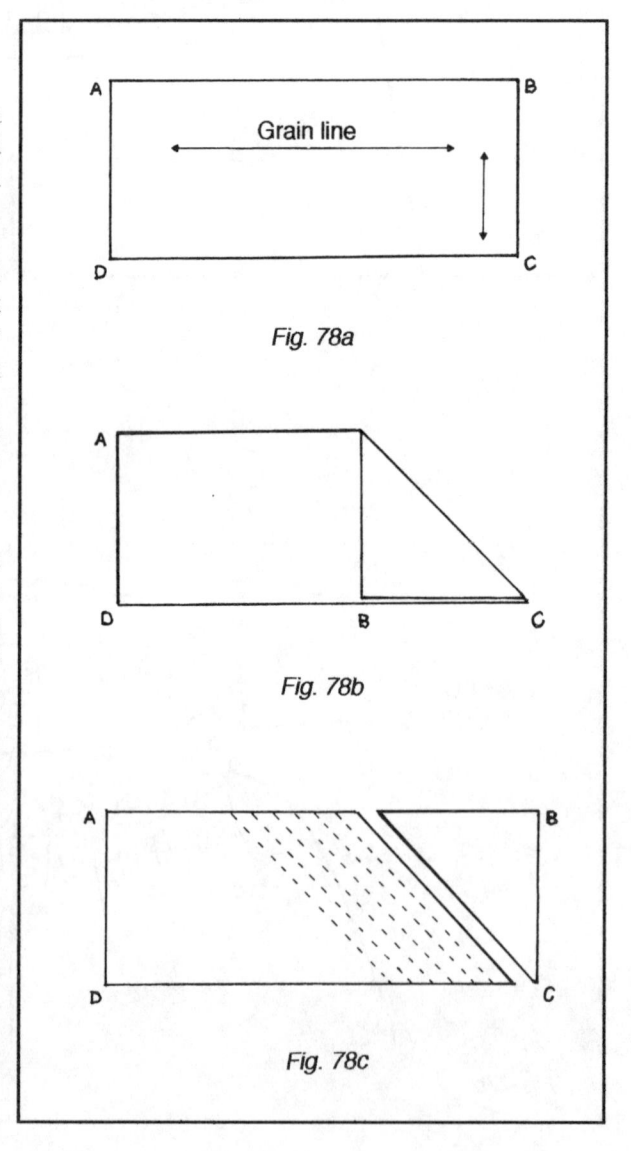

Fig. 78a

Fig. 78b

Fig. 78c

4. Check that the ends of all the strips are actually straight with the grain. Trim them so if necessary.

5. (Fig.78d) Join the strips, using a 6mm(1/4in) machined seam with the stitch-length set fairly small. Match the seamlines, not the cut edges. Pieces to be joined may be put under the machine-foot in a continuous line, as shown in **Fig.78e**, saving both thread and time.

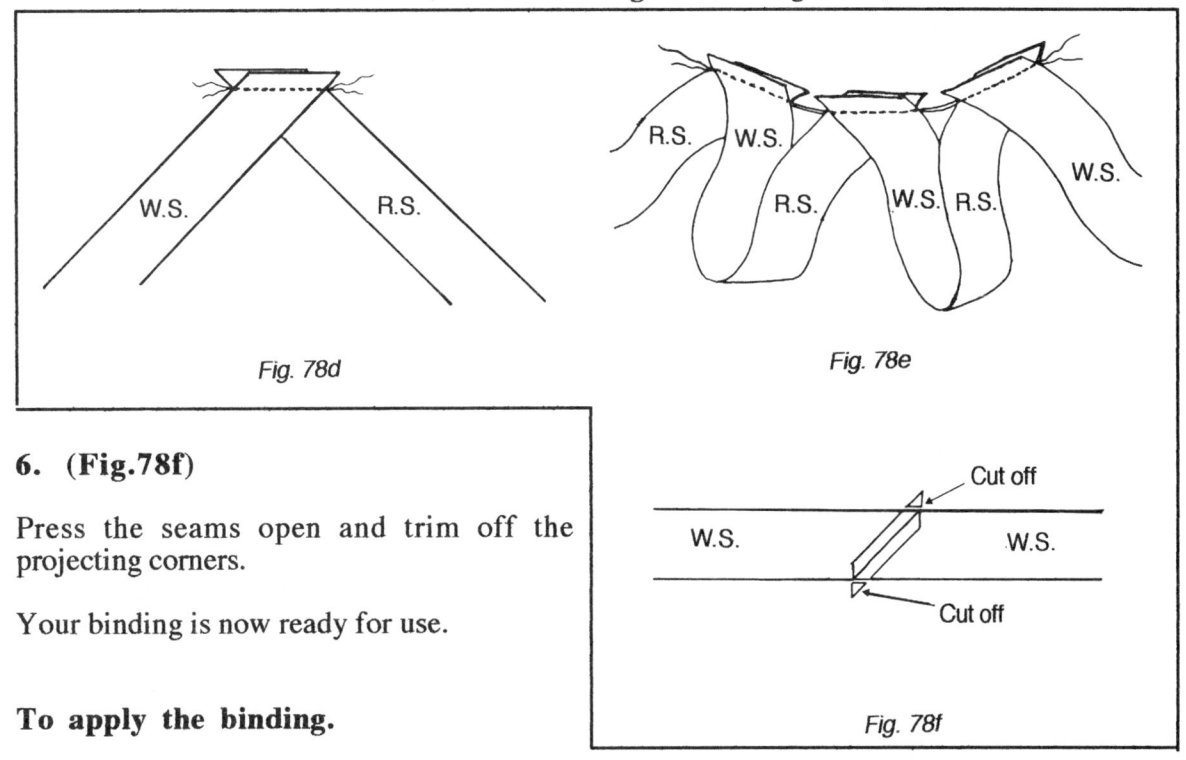

Fig. 78d

Fig. 78e

6. (Fig.78f)

Press the seams open and trim off the projecting corners.

Your binding is now ready for use.

To apply the binding.

Fig. 78f

Note: binding is best started at some point where it is least likely to be obvious. Eg. on a jacket which is to be bound all round the edge, start at the centre back of the neck: on the lower edge of a sleeve, start at the underarm seam. Turn the diagonal end of the binding strip 1cm(3/8in) to the wrong side when commencing, as shown in **Fig.79a**. When the circuit is completed, overlap this by 1cm(3/8in) as you finish and cut off the surplus binding on the same angle. The join is then diagonal and matches the other joins in the binding.

1. (Fig.79a) Place the right side of the bias strip to the wrong side of the knitted fabric, keeping the edges level. Do this on a table, keeping the work flat.
    Pin in position, placing the pins across the seamline, i.e. at right angles to it, not parallel with it.
    Take care to keep the two fabrics flat; do not stretch (or contract) either the knit or the bias strip except when a curved edge is being bound; the rule then is to stretch the bias strip on concave curves (such as necklines) and to ease the bias strip on convex curves (such as a rounded collar edge). The degree of stretching or easing depends on the degree of the curve; if you are new to this process it would be wise to do a practice piece first.

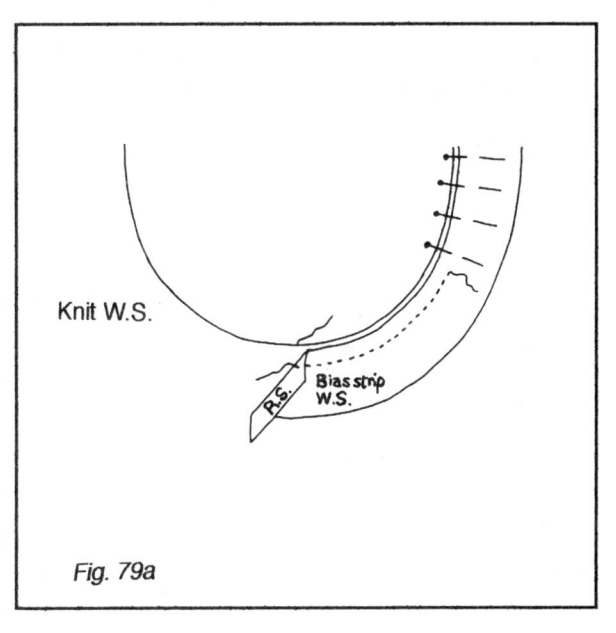

Fig. 79a

Note. Angled corners will need to be mitred. You may find it easier to "round-off" corners on your garment before applying the binding.

2. Machine-stitch, keeping the needle 9mm(3/8in) from the edges of the two fabrics and using straight-stitch set fairly small. Remove each pin in turn just as it starts to go under the presser foot of the machine.

3. (**Fig.79b**) Turn the bias strip over to the right side of the knitted fabric, fold in the raw edge and pin it down (pins at right-angles to the binding, not parallel with it) so that the edge of the binding just covers the machine-stitching line. Use plenty of pins; one every inch, at least, around curves. Take care not to pull the binding sideways so that it develops crinkles. Sensitivity is necessary here - if the binding has been cut correctly it will show you where it needs to go! Again, use plenty of pins.

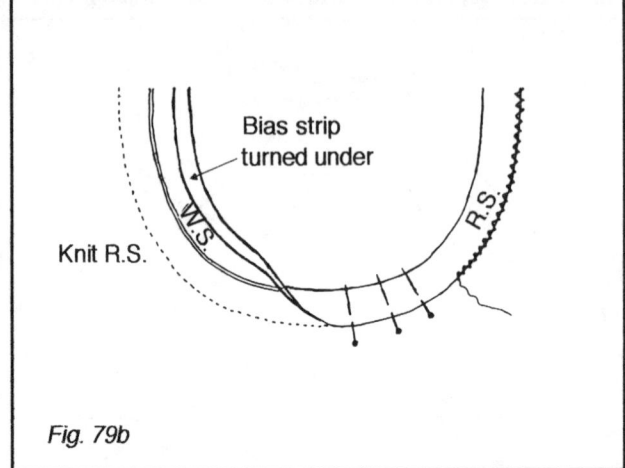

Fig. 79b

4. Machine-stitch, using either a fairly small straight-stitch very close to the folded edge of the binding, or a small, medium-width zigzag which travels on and off the folded edge.

Note: if you have problems with this, try machine-stitching the binding to the right side of the garment first: then hand hem the folded edge on to the machined line, (on the wrong side of the garment) as neatly and invisibly as possible.

BINDING WITH BIAS CUT MACHINE-KNITTED FABRIC
Bias-cut strips for binding can be cut from the main length of knitted fabric in the same way as the garment pieces are cut. As the binding needs to be fairly firm and close in texture, avoid using lace-knits, or ribbing, for this purpose.

To make the binding
Use the same method for cutting and joining as for bias-cut strips of woven fabric (p86-87). Interface if necessary, taking care to retain some degree of the stretch factor by using fusible knitted-nylon or Vilene Optima Silkysoft; both of these should be cut straight across their width in order to make the most of their stretch quality. Alternatively, use bias cut strips of very lightweight, fusible, cotton muslin.

To apply the binding
Use the same method of application as for woven bias binding. (pp87-88)

BINDING WITH WOVEN FABRIC CUT ON THE STRAIGHT GRAIN
This type of binding is useful for pocket tops, bands which will button-up, waistbands, etc., but remember that it is not really suitable for curved edges such as necklines or armholes unless you are expert at the tiny pleating involved.

To make the binding

1. Cut strips, straight with the grain, to the required width, i.e. twice the finished width of binding plus two seam allowances.

2. Join where necessary to produce the required length of binding, as shown in Figs. 78d and 78e, *but using diagonal (bias-cut) seams.*.

3. Press the seams open flat and trim off any projecting corners.
Apply in the same way as woven, bias binding (pp87-88): any corners will have to be mitred.

BINDING WITH MACHINE-KNITTED FABRIC CUT ON THE STRAIGHT GRAIN.

Straight-grain strips for binding can also be cut from the main length of knitted fabric in the same way as the garment pieces are cut. They can be cut lengthwise or across the width but great care must be taken to ensure that the strips are absolutely straight with the grain of the knitting. Remember that strips cut across the knitting will usually have more stretch than strips cut in a lengthwise direction.
     Do not attempt this method with lace or ribbing because, again, the binding fabric needs to be firm and close in texture.
     The whole piece of knit, from which you will cut the strips, can be interfaced first, if required. If you are going to be binding curved edges, take care to position the interfacing so that the stretch quality is retained.
     Use the same method for joining and applying, as for woven fabric cut on the straight grain (pp88-89).

BINDING WITH MACHINE-KNITTED BINDING
Two plus points here: you can use the same yarn that you have already used to make the main fabric of the garment (solving colour matching problems) and you have no cut edges to turn in.

To make the binding
Knit the binding on your own knitting-machine, precisely to the correct width required, so that there is no need to turn in the edges. It can be knitted either straight or on the bias. If straight, a needle can be left out in the centre in order to produce a definite foldline. Use a yarn which is perhaps finer than that used for the main fabric of the garment and keep the tension as tight as possible to give a firm texture. Make sure that the edges of the binding are firm and even. If necessary, interface the binding with a fusible interfacing, but remember that if it is to fit around curves, it must retain its stretch quality, so the interfacing must stretch also.

To apply the binding
1. Press the strip exactly in half lengthwise, keeping the edges precisely together.

2. (**Fig.80**) Pin the strip to the main fabric so that the cut edge of the garment meets the inside of the crease in the binding. Use plenty of pins (at least one per 2.5cm(1in)) placed at right angles to the edge. Keep the work flat on the table whilst doing this and check that you are neither stretching nor contracting the binding too much..

3. Hand-stitch in place with a matching thread, working on the right side and using a half back-stitch close to the edges of the binding. Check that you are catching in the edge of the binding on the wrong side.

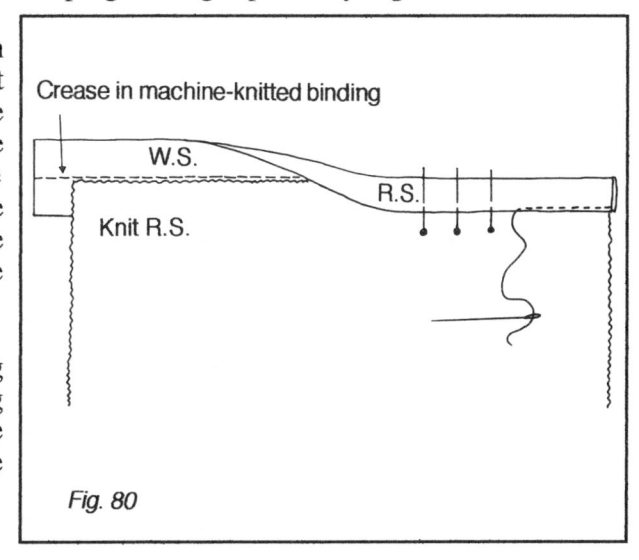

Fig. 80

4. Finish by machine-stitching close to the edge of the binding, using a fairly short stitch-length in either straight or zigzag formation.

> *Note:* If the strip has not been knitted precisely to the correct length (and this is sometimes impossible to estimate exactly) the end will have to be cut.
> Here a problem arises in that, when this cut end is turned in for finishing, it promptly stretches to become wider than the normal width of the binding.
> To solve this, thread a needle with matching thread and run it through one row of knitted stitches, across the width of the binding, about 1.25cm(2in) from the cut end, as shown in **Fig.81.**
> This thread should be fastened securely at the beginning, pulled up until the width of the binding here equals the width of the rest, and then fastened off securely again. This technique works equally well when using purchased knitted or bias-woven braids.

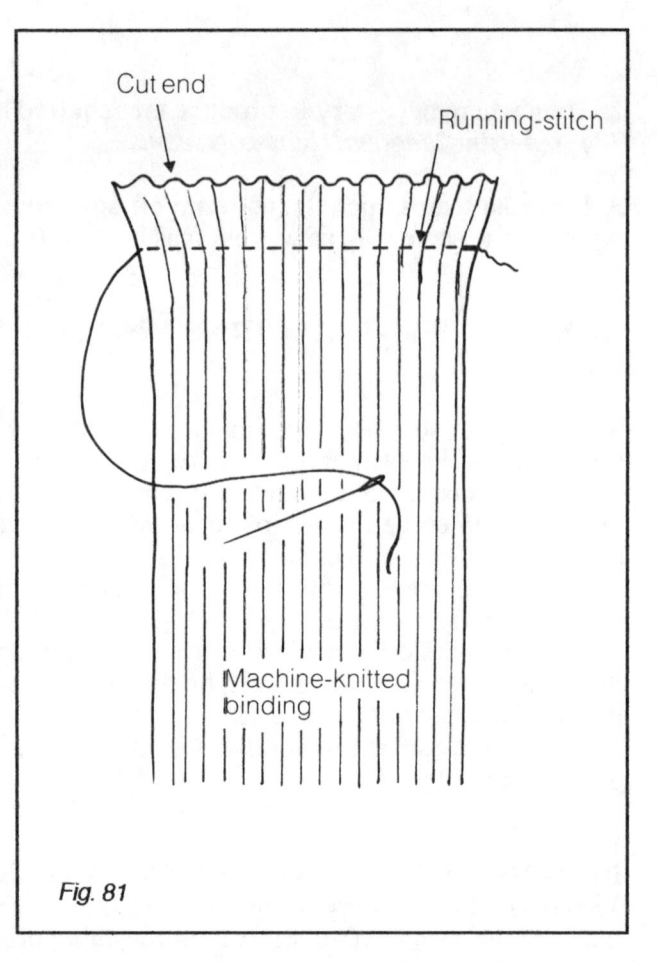

Fig. 81

BINDING WITH PURCHASED BRAID, (KNITTED OR WOVEN)
Check whether the braid you are buying is flexible or not, remembering that it needs to be flexible if it is to be applied to curved edges.
    Purchased braids are sometimes already pressed in half lengthwise; if yours happens to be flat you will have to press it yourself, taking great care to keep the edges precisely together.
    To apply, use the same method as for Binding with Machine-knitted Binding; see p89.

FURTHER SUGGESTIONS FOR BINDING
Leather or Suede: some general hints.
    1. You may be able to buy this in the form of ready-cut binding strip, or you may have to cut it yourself from a skin (use a rotary cutter and a steel or perspex rule). Avoid, in the latter case, trying to use a skin which is too heavy and which will be difficult to sew.
    2. Buy washable leather if possible; otherwise the garment will have to be dry-cleaned.
    3. As there is no danger of fraying, turned in seam allowances become unnecessary.
    4. Stick the binding in place before stitching, (using Wundaweb or a similar product), because every needle or pin which you insert will leave a mark in the leather.
    5. Use special needles for leather in your sewing-machine.
    6. See the note about using the Hongkong Binding method, on p.7 of this book.

Vinyl or other simulated leather.
This can be purchased in the form of ready-cut binding strip. Make sure that it has a fused-on backing of woven cloth so that it cannot tear or split. Alternatively, take a whole piece of unbacked vinyl and interface it by sticking some kind of thin woven fabric such as muslin to the wrong side, using Copydex or something similar (for which heat is not required); then cut strips, as for leather or suede.
    Depending on how much stretch the binding has, use it in the same way as binding which has been cut from woven fabric, either on the bias or on the straight grain.

Ribbon
Ribbon comes in a wide variety of widths and textures; it can be plain, printed or embroidered and creates wonderful possibilities when added to knits. However, because ribbon is not flexible, it should be used only for binding straight edges, unless you are prepared to sew the tiny pleats involved in persuading it to go around curves.

For binding purposes, press it exactly in half lengthwise and apply it in the same way as for Binding with Machine-knitted Binding (p89).

EXPERIMENT WITH BINDING!
Try using all sorts of fabrics, braids, ribbons, etc. on small pieces of knit - or perhaps your spare tension squares. You will be amazed at what expensive-looking effects you can achieve. Try bias-cut satin on a fine soft knit; bias-cut fine needlecord on a tweedy knit; velvet ribbon on a silky knit; gold or silver bias-cut fabric (or ribbon) on a smooth, plain-coloured knit. Consider binding a cut-and-sew jacket with bias-cut strips of the same cotton print as the dress which you will wear under it.

BINDING AS A MEANS OF SEAM FINISHING
Binding the raw edges of seam allowances is a technique used mainly in the production of unlined coats and jackets at the 'couture' level. It is extremely useful, also, as a means of making beautifully finished, unlined, cut-and-sew coats and jackets.

Hongkong Binding
This was named, I imagine, because Chinese tailors made such good use of it in the production of unlined tropical suits for taipans! Use it where only one side of the binding will be seen; for example, on the shoulder seam allowances and the vertical seam allowances; *do not use it for the seam allowances around armholes* where both sides of the seam are visible..

To make: cut 2.5cm[1in] wide bias strips of some fine woven fabric, (such as pure silk crepe-de-chine or polyester lining fabric) and join to make sufficient length (pp86-87). Choose a colour to match the knit as closely as possible. If you prefer, however, choose something which will have a dramatic effect and become a feature of the garment - think of bright scarlet satin on navy-blue knit, or narrow black/white stripes on a plain black knit.

To apply, see full directions in Book 1, pp45-46.

Binding Armhole Seams
Strips for binding the armhole of unlined garments can be cut and made in the same way as for Hongkong Binding but should be applied as shown in Figs.79a and 79b, so that the seam looks neat when viewed from either side.

Alternatively, *knit* a binding strip, either straight or on the bias grain. Make it 2.5cm(1in) wide, from yarn in a similar colour to (but perhaps finer than) that which you have used for the main part of the garment. Apply as for 'Binding with Machine-knitted Binding' (p89).

CHAPTER 13

LININGS

There are several advantages to lining a garment: it is easier to put on, it is warmer and it generally looks a whole lot better and more substantial than an unlined garment. Where cut-and-sew is concerned, the advantages are two fold: -

    (a) the lining covers all the garment construction and therefore there is absolutely no need to oversew or overlock the seam allowances:
    (b) the stretchy knitted fabric can be either partly or totally stabilised by the lining.

Fabrics for lining
Look carefully at what is available; now that good fabric shops are becoming hard to find it is worth trying the mail order firms who advertise in the dressmaking and craft magazines. Send a piece of your knit so that they can offer the best colour match.

Suitable fabrics can range from cotton sateens, through the utilitarian polyester linings available in most fabric stores, to the expensive satins and brocades such as those used in the couture houses. If you are going to put a lot of time, patience and hard work into a coat or a jacket, I really do advise that you buy good lining. For a dress or a skirt, however, you can get away with a cheaper lining because it will not be on general view.

If you are making a loosely-fitted jacket or coat, the lining can be a means of extra warmth if required: in this case consider short-pile fur fabric (from fabric shops, market stalls or the mail-order firms who specialise in toy-making supplies) or something like Viyella. Towelling fabric can be very effective inside a cotton knit but remember to pre-shrink it.

My students have often shown me garments, particularly dresses and rather full skirts, lined very effectively with finely knitted fabric made by them on their own knitting-machines.

Lining skirts which have been made by cut-and-sew methods
Skirt linings should generally be cut to the same shape as the skirt itself; only cost-cutting manufacturers make one standard skirt lining which is then put into all their skirts, whatever the shape! If there are any pleats in the design, however, fold out the pleats in the paper pattern before cutting the lining. If this makes the lining too tight to walk in comfortably, you should leave an opening at the lower end of the centre Front, centre Back or side seams when sewing these up.

If the skirt is gathered into a yoke or waistband, avoid gathering the lining as well or it will become very bulky - use darts instead, or cut an A-line shaped lining to give the same width at the hem but less fabric at the top.

In tailored skirts, the lining should fit fractionally more closely than the skirt itself, so that the knit will not be able to stretch out of shape.

The skirt lining should be stitched into the waistline seam but should otherwise hang separately.

After the hem of the skirt has been completed and pressed, trim the lower edge of the lining to an even 1.25cm(1/2in) below the finished lower edge of the skirt, all round. Turn up and press 1.25cm(1/2in) all round; then turn up and press a further 2.5cm(1in) all round. Pin in position and machine-stitch to secure.

Lining coats and jackets which have been made by cut-and-sew methods
If you have started with a paper pattern, this should include pattern pieces for the lining and instructions for assembling and sewing this lining into the garment.

If there is no lining pattern included, you will have to cut a pattern yourself, based on the pattern pieces given for the garment.

Note: the following instructions apply to a coat or jacket which has Neck and Front Facings.

1. Fig.82a. Cut the pattern for the Back Lining on the basis of the pattern for the Back of the garment but with the following adjustments:

a. lay the Back Neck Facing pattern on the Back pattern, lining up the neck edge and the centre-back line. Draw a new line for the top edge of the Back Lining, exactly 3cm(1 1/4in) above the lower edge of the Neck facing pattern, following its curve.

b. allow for a 2.5cm(1in) wide pleat all the way down the centre back line.

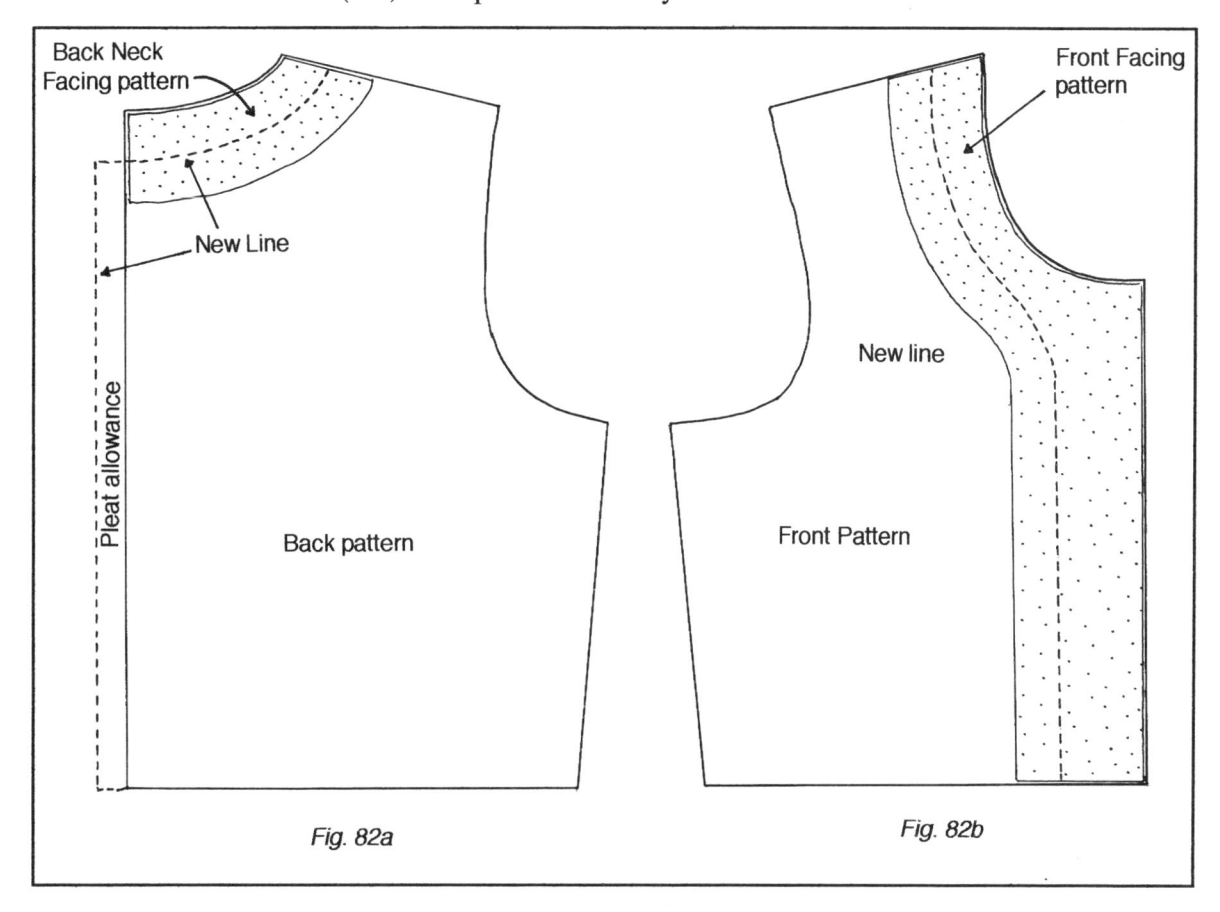

Fig. 82a

Fig. 82b

2. Fig.82b Cut the pattern for the Front Lining on the basis of the pattern for the Front of the garment but with the following adjustment.

Lay the pattern for the Front Facing on the pattern for the garment Front, lining up the shoulder line, neckline and front opening edges. Draw a new line for the edge of the Front Lining, exactly 3cm(1 1/4in) inside the edge of the Neck Facing pattern, following its curve all the way from the shoulder, down the front opening edges to the lower edge.

3. Cut the lining for the Sleeves on the Sleeve pattern given for the garment.

4. Prepare the body lining for insertion, as follows:
Note: *the assembly of the outer part of the garment, including hems, should be completed before attempting to sew in the lining.*

a. Join the Back lining piece to the Front lining pieces at shoulder and sides, and press the seams. Stitch only the top 5cm(2in) of the pleat at the centre back; press the remainder of the pleat but do not stitch it. Do not insert the sleeve linings yet.

b. Stay-stitch the curved neck edge of the lining 1.25cm(1/2in) from the cut edge (see Book 1, p22 for stay-stitching); snip the seam allowance inwards up to the stay-stitching, at intervals of 1 to 2.5cms(3/8 to 1in), depending upon the degree of curve (the more pronounced the curve, the more snips). Fold the 1.5cm(5/8in) wide seam allowance to the wrong side, all around the front and neck edges, and press.

5. Fit the lining inside the body of the garment, wrong sides together, matching and pinning together the underarm points, the shoulder seams and the lower edges. Place the folded edges of the lining (where you pressed under the seam allowances) exactly 1.5cm(5/8in) over the edge of the neck and front facings and pin in position. Keep the lining as straight as possible down the front edges, parallel with the edges of the garment - a wobbly line here will let you down badly!.
    Starting 3in(7.5cm) above where the hemline will be, catch-stitch the lining to the garment fabric all around the front and neck facing. The stitching should be quite loose and should not show on the right side. Catch-stitch the side seam allowances together, again loosely, from the underarm point to a point 3in(7.5cm) above where the hemline will be.

6. Tack the armhole seamlines of the lining to the armhole seamlines of the body of the garment, matching the shoulder seams. *If shoulder pads have been inserted*, you can fasten the two armholes together only around the underarm, up to the point where the shoulder pads start; the top portion of the lining armhole then has to be lightly slip-stitched to the underside of the shoulder pad.

7. **Fig.83.** Make up the sleeve linings and press the seams, using a seam roller. Ease-stitch the top of the sleeve lining (see pp33-34 and Fig.35), and stay-stitch around the underarm curve almost 1.5cm(5/8in) from the cut edge. Snip the underarm seam allowance up to the stay-stitching all around the underarm curve, at frequent intervals (as in Para.4b).

8. Pull up the bobbin threads at the top of the sleeve lining to ease in and shape it (p34, Fig.36). Press the seam allowance, all around the armhole of the sleeve lining, towards the wrong side.

9. Place the prepared sleeve lining inside the garment sleeve, wrong sides together, matching the shoulder seamlines, the underarm points and the armhole notches at front and back. Pin the lining in position so that it just covers the stitching which holds the armhole of the body lining to the garment armhole. Hem the sleeve lining, with very small stitches, by hand, all around the armhole.

10. Trim the lower end of the sleeve lining so that it can be turned up 1.5cm(5/8in) and hemmed to the top of the sleeve hem with a small tuck to allow for stretching.

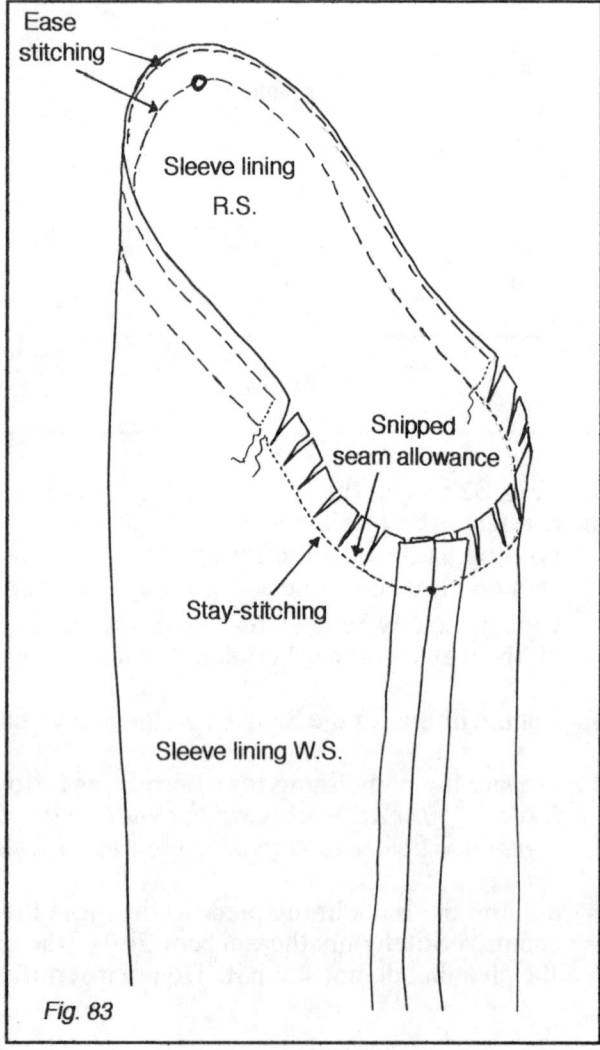

Fig. 83

11. Trim the lower edge of the body lining so that it also can then be turned up 1.5cm(5/8in) and hemmed to the top of the garment body hem with a small tuck to allow for stretching.

12. Now complete the sewing of the body lining to the facings at the lower end of the Fronts. This should fasten down the ends of the tuck in the lining hem.

For alternative ways of lining cut-and-sew garments, look at the waistcoats and jackets shown on pp.80-83 and 86 of Book 1.

LINING 'KNITWEAR' COATS AND JACKETS

Again, the additional warmth and the general improvement in the appearance of a knitted garment which has been lined makes the extra work very worthwhile. Linings can, of course, be knitted, in fine stocking-stitch fabric, to the same basic shape as the outer garment. I am assuming here, however, that you wish to line with a purchased woven fabric made from silk, polyester, wool, etc..

In this case you will have made a garment either entirely by shaping on the knitting-machine, or by using the usual knitwear methods with some cut-and-sew techniques for shaping the neckline and possibly the armholes. Either way, this has been achieved by 'knitwear' procedures and not by 'dressmaking'; therefore there is no paper pattern to help you get it right.

If you have followed a knitting pattern where diagrams are given with precise measurements for each part, then it should be a fairly simple task to draw out the shapes with a marking pen on newspaper, following those measurements.

If you plan to line a knitted coat (or jacket) for which you have no diagrams and which is perhaps already sewn together, then you have to construct a paper pattern by means of a great deal of careful folding, tracing and measuring of each part in turn.

A few helpful hints on making a preliminary paper pattern from a ready-made garment:

a. Lines, such as shoulder-lines, side seams, pocket tops, etc. are almost always *straight* and should therefore be drawn with a ruler.

b. Check that the angles are correct; not all corners are right-angled, but those that are must be true $90°$ angles.

c. Fold the Back exactly down the centre and trace off just half, marking the foldline as 'centre-Back'. (When you cut the lining fabric for the Back, the pattern will lie with the 'centre-Back' along, or parallel with, the fold of double fabric, so that the Back must then be completely symmetrical).

d. Fold the neckline in half and trace the curve carefully from centre back to shoulder seamline for the Back lining pattern. Repeat this from the Front opening edge to the shoulder seamline for the Front lining pattern.

e. Fold the sleeve in half lengthwise along the inside-arm seamline; measure from the outer end of the shoulder seam to the wrist to gauge the sleeve length.

f. When you think your paper pattern is correct, check the measurements in all directions with those of the actual garment; adjust if and where necessary.

g. Having drawn this paper pattern on newspaper; *do not cut it out yet!* You may have to make some further adjustments (see the next page) and you will certainly have to add seam allowances and hems.

But adding a lining will remove the stretch factor totally from the knit!
If the garment is already so large that it has no need to stretch *anywhere*, then a lining which has been cut to exactly the same shape and size as the knit will be satisfactory. But if that garment has to stretch, even the slightest amount, across the back when you reach forward - or has to stretch across the front when you button it up - or if the neck or wrist bands have to stretch when you put it on - *then the lining **must** be larger. You have been warned!*

To add 'ease' to the lining pattern
    a. Add a vertical pleat at centre-back. This can be a 2.5cm(1in) wide double fold, or a deeper inverted pleat and should extend all the way, from top to bottom..

    b. Depending upon how much extra stretch you need in the lining, add similar vertical pleats from the centre of the shoulder seams, at the back and/or the front.

    c. If you have very rounded shoulders you may need to make the 'dowager's hump' alteration (see pp11-12) to the lining pattern for the Back, to provide shoulder or neck darts which will then provide the extra depth and width you need.

    d. If chubby arms are a problem, make a vertical pleat from the centre top of the sleeve lining all the way down to the wrist.

    e. Where the knitted coat is required to stretch (for example at the neck, wrist, hip-band, etc.) the lining fabric will need to be wider so that it can be eased in to fit and will then stretch *with* the knit. If the armhole fits snugly you should add to the sleeve lining, to give more height and more width at the top of the arm.

    f. *Now check it all.* Measure the entire bust circumference of the pattern i.e. twice the distance from armhole to centre-back, plus twice the distance from armhole to centre-front. Check the result with your own measured bust circumference; there should, ideally, be at least 10cm(4in) to spare.
    Check the sleeve circumference at upper arm and at the elbow - take your own measurements here with the elbow bent.
    Check the length carefully - if the knit is inclined to drop when hanging vertically you should add extra length to the lining pattern.

Adding seam allowances, hems and grainlines to the lining pattern
Note: I would advise that you add 2.5cm(1in) seam allowances to all seamlines and hems; this may seem over generous but does mean that you have a little extra space to let out if the lined coat proves to be constricting when worn.

a. Draw in the cutting lines, incorporating the seam and hem allowances.

b. Draw in the straight-grain lines as follows:
    Back - straight down the centre-back foldline
    Front - parallel with the front opening edge
    Sleeve - straight down the centre-fold

Finally -cut out the paper pattern for the lining and use it to cut the lining fabric.

Page 97

CHAPTER 14

PATCHWORK and QUILTING

This is a "fun" chapter; a way of adding a little touch of luxury and individuality to your cut-and-sew clothes. Although I would suggest that you perfect your basic techniques first (simply because I believe firmly that professional-looking fit and finish is more important than decoration), by all means go on from there, experimenting, playing, inventing, and using your imagination to produce clothes which are entirely your own.

**HOW TO MAKE A PATCHWORK QUILTED JACKET
FROM SCRAPS OF KNIT**
Creating a garment, such as a sleeveless vest or a short coat, entirely from left over pieces of knitted fabric, can be satisfying and fun. This is probably one of the many answers to those folk who complain that cut-and-sew is wasteful! If you have insufficient left-over pieces of knitted fabric, undoubtedly you have some odds and ends of yarn stored away, too small to be knitted up into garments but enough to make narrow strips or squares, which can then be cut up for patchwork.

The jacket drawn in **Fig.84** was simply an exercise in this field. It has aroused much interest when shown and because so many knitters have asked how it was constructed, I decided that it deserved a place in this book. You should certainly not aim to copy it slavishly - use any simple jacket pattern that flatters your own shape and then cut and arrange the patchwork pieces in any way you wish.

Fig. 84

Planning the jacket

1. Choose a dress-making pattern for the jacket. Keep it as simple as possible: a back, (seamed down the middle) two fronts and two sleeves. These pattern pieces will be used for the patchwork, for the polyester wadding which forms the interfacing, and for the lining. In the illustration, these are the only pattern pieces used but, of course you can choose to add a collar, neck band, pockets, etc. as you please

2. Get all your pieces together, whether in the form of knitted fabric or of yarn still unused. Sort out colours which look right together, which complement each other and which will suit the wearer. This is very much a matter of personal taste and only you can know what effect you really want: it could be quiet and subdued in toning shades of one or two colours with neutrals; it could be bright and rather shocking in all sorts of contrasting hues - a veritable "Joseph's coat of many colours"; or it could be somewhere between these two extremes. You could, of course, decide that some of the 'patches' might be cut from woven fabrics such as satin, velvet, tweed, brocade, etc.

3. Decide on whether you want all your pieces in the same type of yarn and texture, or whether perhaps you might like to mix them. Remember that you can always back the thinner ones with a fusible interfacing to make them firmer where necessary. In my jacket, the pieces were in a variety of stitch patterns but all in synthetic yarns such as acrylic/nylon mixtures and bright acrylics; however, a mixture of textures such as fluffy with flat or rough with smooth, could be even more attractive.

4. Make sure that all the pieces you are going to use are thoroughly washed and pressed before they are cut to shape so that any alteration in size or texture takes place now and not later. Refer to pp.29-30 in Book 1 for instructions on washing and pressing.

5. Interface all those pieces of fabric which need to be made firmer or less transparent. Refer to Book 1, p.33, for help with this. Because these pieces are relatively small (compared, say, with a whole coat front), it is reasonably safe to interface a whole piece of knit before cutting it into patchwork pieces. In my jacket I used Vilene Ultrasoft Lightweight for the pieces which needed to be made a little stiffer, and fusible knitted nylon for those which were too open and transparent. Vilene Optima Silkysoft and finely woven, fusible cotton muslin would also be very suitable.

A warning note here: beware of using too many heavy yarns and textures, and overdoing the interfacing, or you could end up with a very weighty garment.!

6. Decide upon the shape and approximate size of the pieces you are going to join together. I used strips of knitted fabric which varied in width from 4cm(1½ in) to 10cm(4in) and were however long they happened to be when I found them. You could cut a large number of squares or rectangles instead. Look at any good book on patchwork for ideas (see Appendix 1), but keep it fairly simple if this is your first attempt.

How many strips, squares or rectangles you are going to need is rather a matter of guesswork at this stage, but I think it is probably advisable to aim initially at a fairly short sleeveless coat which you can then extend in length, or to which you can add sleeves later on, if you find you have plenty of spare pieces. If you find that you have insufficient pieces of knitting (or yarn ends to be knitted up) you could add some woven fabric here and there, and this could give extra interest to the overall effect.

Check carefully what the effect will be at the shoulder and side seams when the front is sewn to the back.

Cutting and joining the jacket pieces

1. Cut the pieces with sharp scissors, and be exact, to avoid trouble when joining them. If you cut long strips, as I did for the jacket shown in Fig.84, they can vary in width but each strip should be even in width down its entire length. (I aimed at a symmetrical pattern so I took care to cut all the strips of one colour to the same width.) Squares must all be precisely the same size. Cut straight with the grain, following a row *widthwise*, or one stitch *lengthwise*.

2. Join the pieces. Decide on what your seam allowance is to be and stick to that rigidly throughout; 1.2cm(½in) is normally sufficient.

Joining is simple if you use squares: just ensure that the ends of the seam match exactly every time. Pin across, at right angles to the seamline, *on* the seamline, to hold the two pieces firmly together while you stitch. Remove each pin as it reaches the presser foot.

If you use long strips, it can be difficult to ensure that one strip does not end up tighter than its immediate neighbour, making curved seams instead of straight ones! To avoid the problem, hold the two strips to be joined between two fingers and let them hang down; pin the strips together, near the end of the shorter one, just as they hang together (see **Fig.85**). Add more pins to hold both lengths evenly.

Machine the seams using straight-stitch. Press each seam out flat after stitching it.

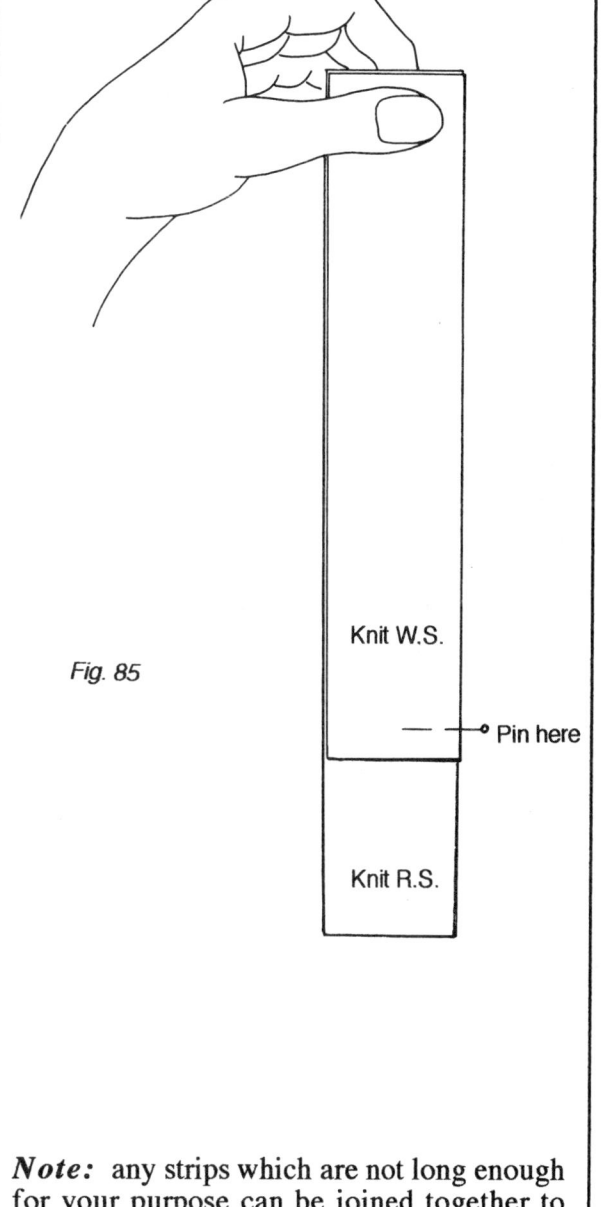

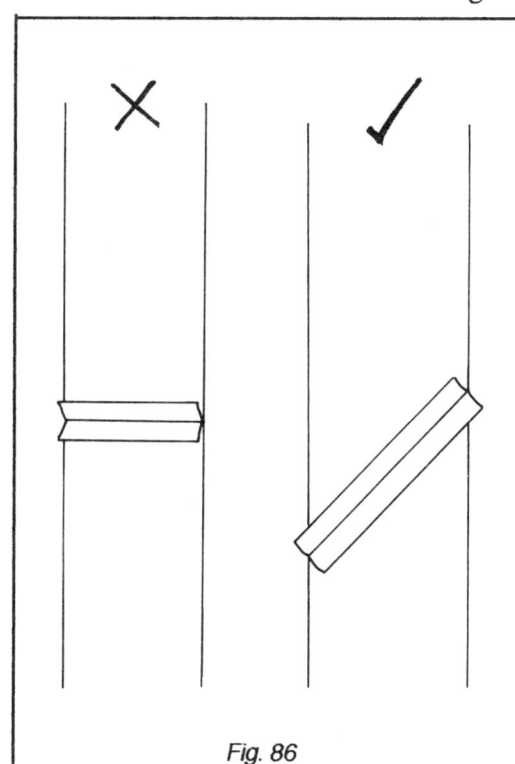

Fig. 85

Note: any strips which are not long enough for your purpose can be joined together to make longer ones.

Make the joins diagonally (on the bias) rather than on the straight. See **Fig.86**.

Fig. 86

3. Join enough pieces to cover the entire area of each pattern piece, *with 3.7cm(1½in) to spare all round.* **Fig.87** shows some possible examples of this.

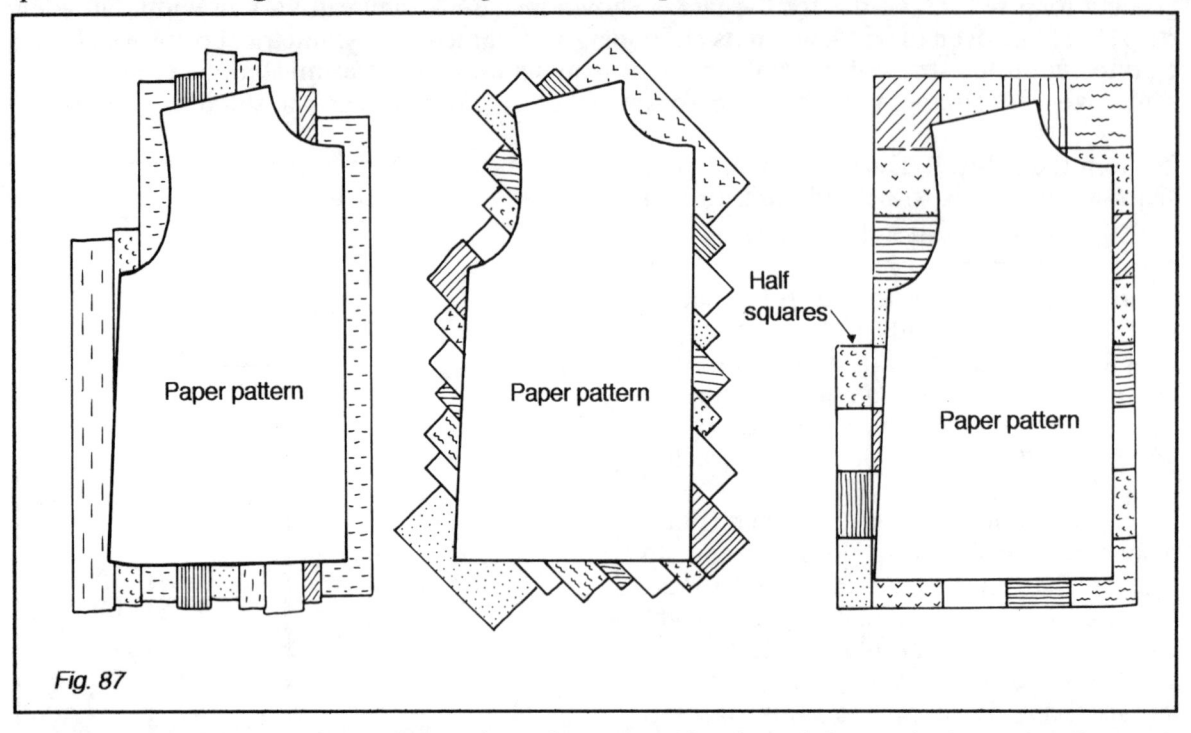

Fig. 87

For my jacket, I placed the straight strips using a combination of the vertical and the diagonal.
Fig.88a. I cut both Front *and* Back pattern pieces into two sections along a ruled line X-Y.
Fig.88b. A 1.25cm(½in) seam allowance was added to each pattern piece at X and Y.
Fig.88c. The pattern sections were placed on the patchwork which was then trimmed along the seam allowances at X-Y. The seam was then stitched and pressed open flat.

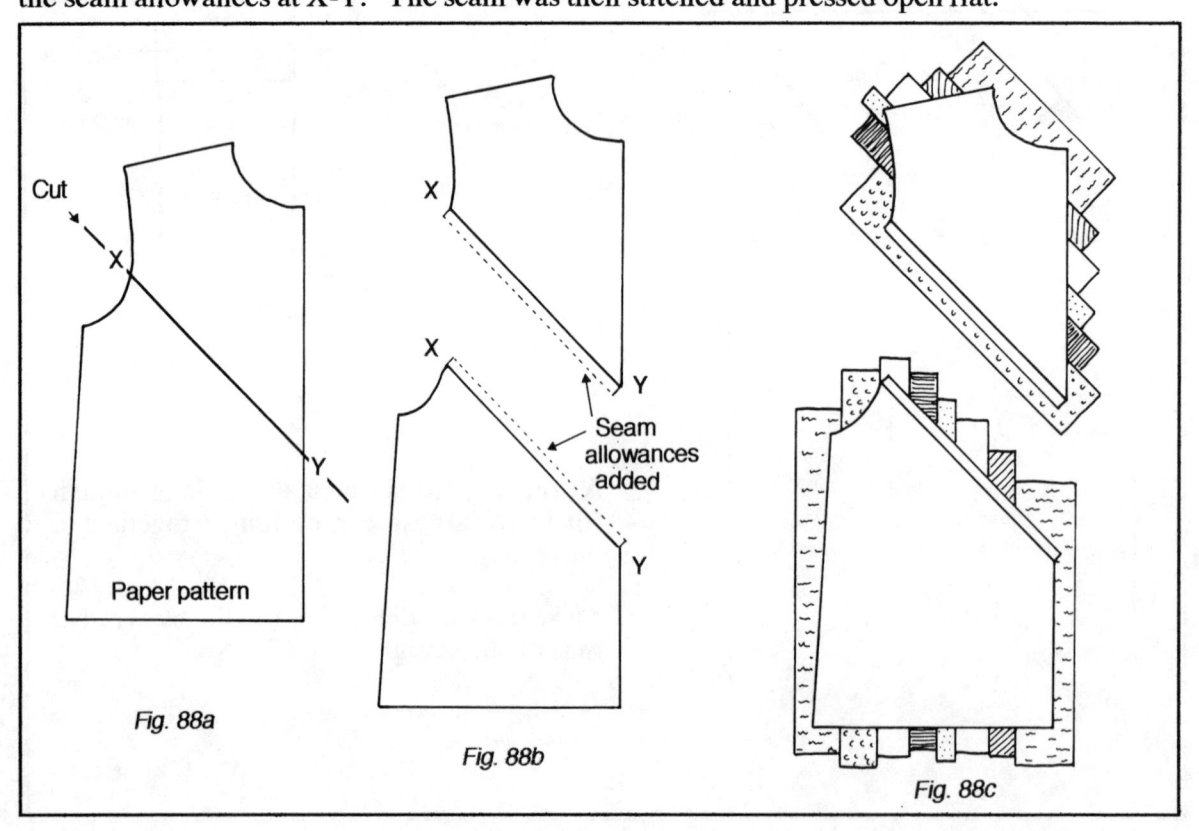

Fig. 88a

Fig. 88b

Fig. 88c

4. Place the pattern pieces on the polyester wadding; pin in place and cut allowing a 3.7cm(1½in) seam allowance all around each pattern piece.

5. Place each patchwork garment piece on its corresponding polyester wadding piece, wrong sides together. The new Vilene 280 Volume Fleece is excellent for this purpose. Pin the two layers together all around the edge, and machine-stitch 9mm(⅜in) from the edge all round, using a fairly long straight-stitch. If you are not confident about doing this successfully, then tack first by hand, but take the occasional back-stitch to prevent the layers slipping when you machine. It is important to keep both layers flat together.

Quilting the jacket pieces
Quilt each separate garment piece by machining through the two layers; I did this by first following the seamlines already there and then adding more lines of stitching in each stripe. However, there are many variations on this theme. Have a spare piece of knit, with polyester wadding attached, and do some experimenting.

Helpful tips on machine quilting:
If your quilting lines are intended to cross the seamlines, rather than simply following them, you will need some help in keeping the lines parallel.

1. Mark the *first* line with a ruler and a well-sharpened piece of tailor's chalk; then machine-stitch along this chalked line.

2. Use *a quilting bar*, positioned on the line you have just stitched, to enable you to keep the next line exactly parallel with the first. **See Book 1, p15** for an illustration which shows how this works. If the box of spare parts, which came with your machine, does not include a quilting bar, write to the manufacturer (or call on one of his agents) to see if you can get one; also make sure that he supplies (or you already have) a presser foot which is adapted to take a quilting bar. Otherwise, dots made with a chalk-pencil or a fade-away marker, giving you points to aim at the needle, are helpful .

3. When stitching, watch the previous stitching-line and keep it moving directly in line with the quilting bar - do *not* watch the needle!
Keep the tension on both needle and bobbin threads fairly easy (but not so easy that you have loops in the stitching!); if the tension is too tight, the quilting could reduce the size of the garment pieces, quite considerably.

4. To ensure that the two layers feed through evenly, and to avoid puckering on the top layer, *pin across* your proposed sewing-line through both thicknesses. Pin at roughly every 4cm(1½in) down the length of the line. A 'walking foot' is also helpful.
Help the process by using finger pressure to stretch the fabrics slightly sideways, on both sides of the presser foot, as you sew.

Assembling the jacket
1. When all the garment pieces have been quilted, pin the paper pattern back on each piece in turn and cut to the correct shape and size. Leaving that extra allowance all round was simply a safety precaution against the slight reduction in size which occurs during quilting.

2. Sew the seams at shoulders and sides. Trim away any surplus wadding within the seam allowances to reduce bulk. Check the fitting.

3. Press the seams open flat, *very lightly!* Remember that the polyester wadding can be irretrievably flattened by the heat of the iron, so you must use a seam roller (See Book 1, p8) to enable you to press only the seam itself and not the surrounding fabrics.

4. Make up the sleeves and stitch them in.

5. Cut the lining pieces for the jacket, using the same paper pattern and whatever fabric you choose for the purpose. (The back can be cut in one piece, on the fold of the fabric.) Seam these together and press the shoulder, side and sleeve seams open flat.

6. If you intend to use shoulder-pads, attach these now to the inside of the quilted jacket. (See Chapter 7 for help with this)

7. Place the lining inside the quilted jacket, wrong sides together, and pin the two exactly together as follows. Use plenty of pins placed at right angles to the edges.
   a. Start at the back of the neck and match the shoulder seamlines. You may find that the back neck edge of the lining appears smaller than that of the quilted knit jacket; this is because the jacket has already stretched at this point; simply make the jacket fit the lining by easing it a little.
   b. Pin the lining to the jacket at under-arm and top-arm points. Catch these points with hand-stitching, as invisibly as possible.
   c. Pin the lining to the jacket down each front edge.
   d. Pin the side seams of the lining to the side seams of the jacket.
   e. Pin the lower edges of lining and jacket together: take care to get these level, trimming if necessary; put the jacket on a dummy or a coat-hanger at this stage, so that you can see exactly where they meet.
   f. Pin the lower edges of the lining sleeves to the lower edges of the jacket sleeves, making sure that they are exactly the same length.

8. Machine-tack the jacket to the lining along all the outer edges; keep the stitching close to the edges and remove each pin in turn as the presser foot reaches it.

9. Bind the garment edges. See Chapter 12 for information on choice of bindings and methods of application.

I have described here the way in which I constructed the jacket shown on p97 but there are many other ideas you could pursue along similar lines. At a machine-knitting convention which I once visited, I came across the work of Mady Gerrard, a Hungarian-born designer who had worked in Britain, Canada and the U.S.A., and who then had a designer workshop in Bath. Many of her beautiful jackets were made entirely from square patches, set diagonally, cut from all kinds of knits intermixed with leather, suede, satin and tweed, and banded with knitted ribbing.

Do try 'log-cabin' patchwork as a cut-and-sew exercise; it can make very effective cushion covers. In this case, a small square of knit is applied to the centre of a much larger square of woven fabric; (traditionally, calico is used) then narrow strips of knit, in varying tones, are applied to the edges of this small square, following each side in turn, until the square of woven fabric is completely covered. Dark tones are used on two adjacent sides of the square and lighter tones on the other two. Completed squares are then sewn together in varying combinations to produce many different effects. Consult any good book on patchwork for detailed instructions on this process (see appendix). Wadding and quilting can be added as desired. A complete garment made in log-cabin patchwork might well be too heavy but a few squares used as trimming on an otherwise plain knit, could be very effective.

CHAPTER 15

APPLIQUÉ ON KNITTED FABRICS

Any kind of motif can be appliquéd to knitted fabrics, but do try making your own motifs rather than buying them because they really are quite simple.

Consider using **scraps of woven fabrics** such as cotton gingham, silk satin or needlecord, or small offcuts in **leather or suede.**

Simple shapes can be used, such as stylised flowers, leaves, trees and balloons; a young child's colouring book will provide lots of help and inspiration for these! Geometric shapes - circles, curved lines, interlocked squares, etc. can be very effective and are easy to draw with the aid of templates and rulers. It all depends on what effect you want and the shape of the garment on which you are working.

Being able to draw well is helpful but not in the least essential: you can trace outlines from pictures in newspapers, magazines, books, birthday cards, etc.: you can even pick up fallen leaves and trace around them. Almost everybody "doodles" when talking on the telephone and these unplanned, unpredictable scribbles are sometimes very attractive when translated into fabric, colour and texture.

Retailers of furnishing textiles occasionally sell off their out-dated manufacturers' samples and these are often a rich source of **printed motifs**, such as sprays of flowers, birds or figures.

Lace can be very effective on knits; I recently made an evening dress and jacket, in French crepe yarn knitted in plain black stocking-stitch, embellished most successfully with strips of fine black net, heavily embroidered with turquoise metallic thread, bought from the lace department of a local store. The black net became totally invisible when sewn on the black knit and so it appeared that I had spent hours and hours executing some highly skilled hand embroidery!

All of these can be enhanced with **beads, hand or machine embroidery** and **fabric paints.**

Given a reasonably good-tempered sewing-machine and good lighting, the techniques are not difficult, *but, as with every other aspect of cut-and-sew, do allow time for experimenting and practising before applying these techniques to a garment.*

Here are some guidelines for a trial run.

To appliqué a simple leaf shape
1. Cut a small piece of woven fabric, about 10cm(4in) square. Use cotton poplin, calico, gingham, etc. while practising - you can go on to velvet or gold lamé later!

2. Find a piece of knit, roughly 15cm(6in) square: perhaps an old tension swatch will do, but remember that it should be reasonably smooth in texture, knitted on a reasonably firm tension, and it should have been washed and steam-pressed.

3. Fig.89a. Draw (or trace) the leaf shape on the right side of the woven fabric, using a sharp pencil or a cloth-marking pen. Keep the lines thin and well-defined and, for this exercise, simple.

4. Fig.89b. Cut out the leaf shape, leaving about 6mm(¹/₄in) of fabric outside the drawn line.

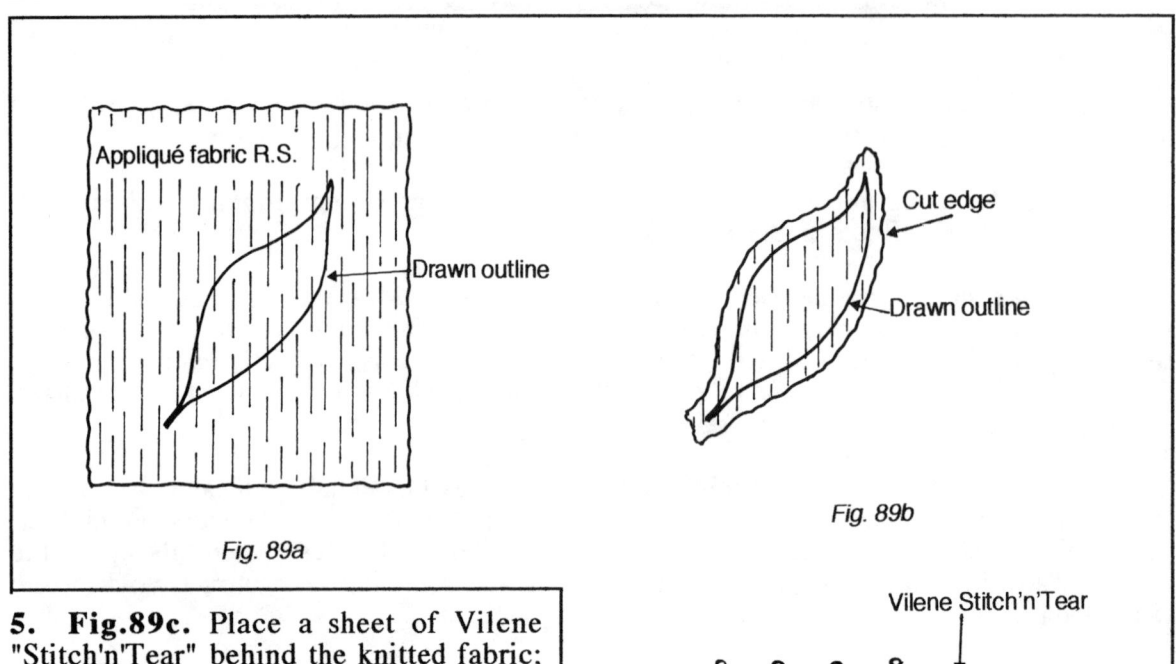

Fig. 89a

Fig. 89b

5. Fig.89c. Place a sheet of Vilene "Stitch'n'Tear" behind the knitted fabric; pin or tack the two layers together, around the area where the leaf will be placed.

Note: Vilene "Stitch'n'Tear" is available from most haberdashery shops and departments who stock Vilene products; it is wonderfully successful in providing a temporary means of stabilising the fabrics and thus preventing stretching and distortion. If you cannot find it and want to get on with the exercise, use typing paper instead; you will just have to take care to avoid tearing it too soon.

6. Place the leaf shape on the knitted fabric and pin in position. I find pinning more effective and safer than tacking, but you can use needle and thread, with a small running stitch, if you prefer.

It is possible to stick the leaf in position, using Wundaweb, but I find that this sometimes stiffens the appliqué too much.

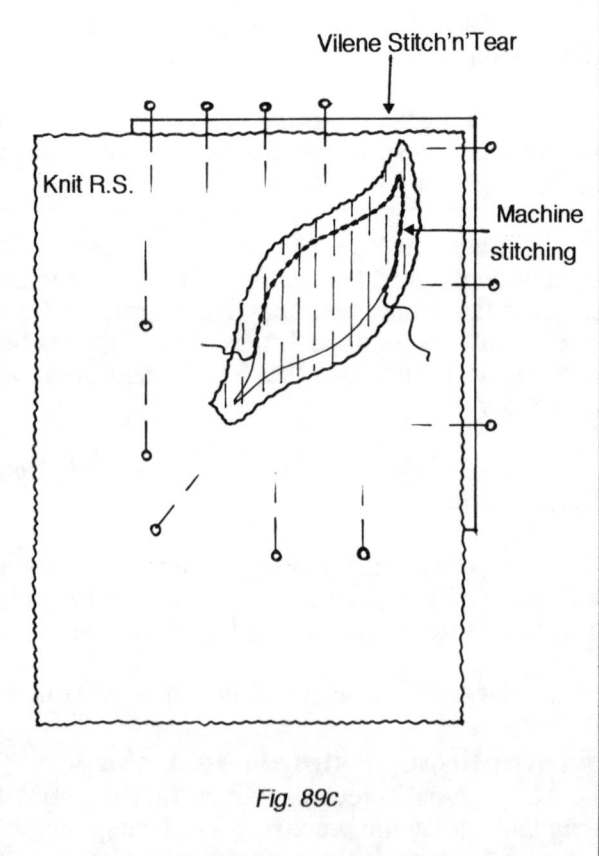

Fig. 89c

7. Now prepare your sewing-machine. For a more lustrous look, use proper machine-embroidery thread through the needle rather than your normal polyester sewing-thread. This is obtainable from most good haberdashery departments, although you may have to ask for it. Use the presser foot intended for embroidery, rather than the normal presser foot with which you stitch seams. Check that your needle is undamaged and that it is the right size for the weight of the fabrics - if it is too heavy it will not stitch well, if too light it could snap.

8. Fig.89c. again. Machine-stitch, following the drawn outline of the leaf, using straight-stitch set on a very small stitch-length: about 1 on most machines. When you get to the point of the leaf, set the needle in the fabric, lift the presser foot, turn the fabric, lower the foot again and continue down the other side of the leaf. Continue stitching until you overlap the point where you started.

9. Trim off the surplus woven fabric outside the stitching line, as close as you can get to it. The best way to do this is to hold the scissors flat, i.e. horizontally, not vertically.

10. Set the machine to do a satin-stitch, i.e. a zigzag stitch with the stitch-length set short enough to eliminate gaps between the threads; this is just what you do when sewing a buttonhole, so your normal buttonhole setting (on the stitch-length control) would probably be right. Adjust the stitch-width until it is sufficiently wide to cover easily both the cut edge of the leaf and the straight-stitch line.

11. Fig.89d. Starting on one side of the leaf, satin-stitch all around. For curved shapes, turn the fabric gently as you stitch. When you reach the point of the leaf, you have two alternatives:

either gradually reduce the zigzag width until you taper off into a straight stitch a little beyond the end of the leaf point, turn the fabric, and gradually increase the width so that it is back to its original setting when you reach the leaf point again -

or - keep the zigzag setting constant: when you reach the point of the leaf, stop with the needle on the outside of the line, pivot on the needle, turning the fabric until the second side of the leaf is lined up, and continue stitching. This makes a more blunt end to the leaf.

Note: the general principle when turning any corner is that you turn the fabric, using the needle as a pivot, with the needle positioned in the fabric and *always on the outside of the corner you are turning.* If you turn with the needle on the inside of the corner, you will leave a gap in the stitching.

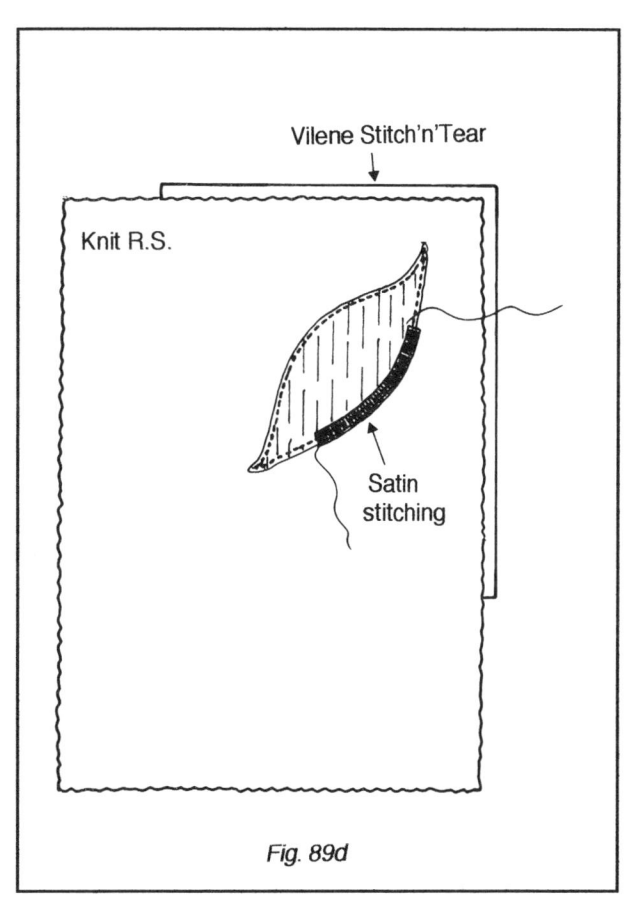

Fig. 89d

You now have lots of possibilities; you can machine-stitch lines on the leaf to simulate veining, and you can add stalks by using the same satin stitch on lines drawn directly on to the knitted fabric; you can apply more leaves (or berries, apples, clouds, birds, initials, whatever); you could even add beads, for extra lustre, sewing them on by hand with a very fine needle, or adorn with fabric paints.

12. When you have finished the appliqué, tear away all the Stitch'n'Tear from the back of the knitted fabric.

Having successfully applied your little leaf to a spare piece of knit, now go ahead and try something more ambitious!

The fabrics used for the appliqué can be varied widely to contrast with each other and with the background knit. Try velvet, needlecord, suede-cloth, satin and fabrics woven with metallic threads. Some of these may be difficult to handle because they fray badly but never hesitate to try them out. If necessary they can be stabilised a little by ironing a very lightweight, fusible interfacing, such as optima Silkysoft, to the wrong side before cutting; but beware of making the motif too stiff. If you are in the United States try small scraps of Ultrasuede; this is totally non-frayable, looks exactly like real suede, comes in glorious colours and washes like a dream. Use also, your left-over scraps of knitted fabric, varying and contrasting the stitch-patterns and textures.

Machine Embroidery
This is an area which I have not explored fully but having, occasionally, extended my applied leaves by adding satin-stitched stalks and straight-stitched veins, I can see no reason why it should present any extra problems providing that the Vilene Stitch'n'Tear is firmly in place at the back of the knit and used in the same way as for appliqué; the instructions, given inside the packet, suggest the use of an embroidery hoop: I have to confess that I have not so far tried this method but I think the knit would probably stretch badly and thus distort the finished work.

At a machine-knitting seminar in Nashville, Tennessee, I met a lady who wore a stunning, white knitted jacket upon which she had very successfuly executed some beautiful open-work embroidery - an idea I have yet to try. One day, when I have finished all this writing - !

CHAPTER 16

HOW TO MAKE
A SIMPLE CUT-AND-SEW TAILORED SKIRT

Fig. 90. Here is a way for knitters who also sew to make a smartly tailored, perfectly fitting, cut-and-sew skirt without the expense and trouble of buying a pattern.

TO MEASURE AND KNIT THE FABRIC
1. Stand in front of a mirror, wearing only underwear and measure (honestly!) what appears to be the widest part of the figure below the waist. In most cases this will be the hip circumference but in some cases it could be the stomach.

2. Write down that measurement, *add* 5cm(2in) for 'ease' and then *divide the result* by 3.

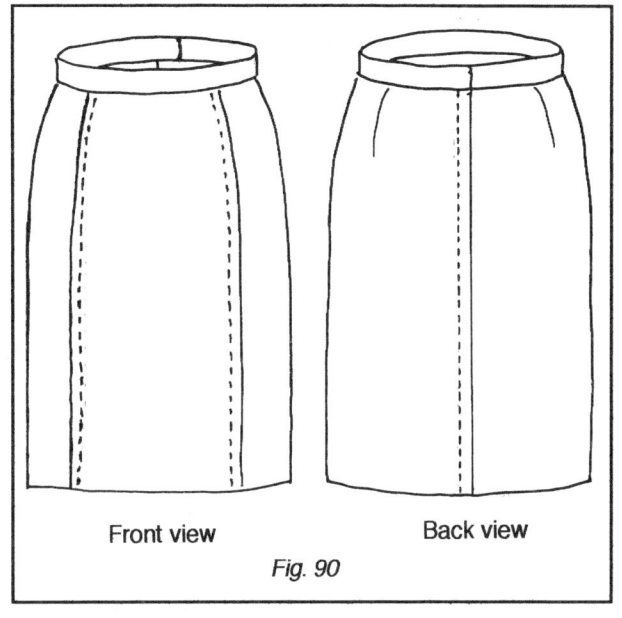

Front view   Back view
Fig. 90

3. Write down that figure and *add* two seam allowances (usually 1.5cm(5/8in) each).
This will be the WIDTH of each of the three pieces you will knit - and it is generally a convenient width to knit on your knitting-machine.

4. Decide on the finished length of the skirt by measuring one you already have, down the centre back. Write it down - and *add* -   1.5cm(5/8in) seam allowance for the top
plus   5-6.5cm(2-21/2in) for the hem
plus   5cm(2in) as a margin of error

5   Write down the result of all that.
This will be the LENGTH of each of the three pieces you will knit.

6. Now go through the usual routine (see Chapter 5, Book 1) of choosing a suitable yarn, tension, texture, colour and stitch pattern; make a tension swatch, wash and steam-press it (or just steam if you prefer - see p.7). Measure the width and length of the swatch when cool: then calculate how many needles you will need to employ to knit the width you wrote down at Stage 3 and how many rows you will need to achieve the length you wrote down at Stage 5.

7. Knit the three lengths. Wash, dry and press. Leave to cool and contract.

You will also need the following items
Sufficient lining fabric to cut three pieces measuring the same as the width you calculated at Stage 3 - and the length you calculated at Stage 5 but minus the hem allowance.
Sufficient non-roll elastic or *curved petersham* to make a waistband to fit.
A nylon or polyester zip, lightweight, 20cm(8in) long.
Matching polyester sewing thread.
Corset Hook and Eye, 1 pair.   Standard Hooks and Bars, size 2, 2 pairs.

Depending upon the content and texture of the knit, you may need sufficient fusible knitted nylon interfacing to strengthen it - in which case, lining fabric will probably be unnecessary.

TO MAKE THE SKIRT

1. If the knit requires interfacing, cut and fuse it now to the wrong side of each section. (See Book 1, p16, and this book, p6, for help with this.)

2. Fig.91. Join two of the lengths together and sew in the zip, following the directions given on pp73-75 for 'Lapped Semi-Concealed Application'. With the right side of the fabrics facing you, continue to lap the Left side of the skirt Back over the Right side, from below the zip, all the way down to the lower edge. The machined top-stitching line can then be continued down the remainder of the seam.

3. Join the third section to the first two, to complete the circle. Curve the seams inwards at the top to give the effect of darts there. Also make one dart (see Chapter 3) at each side and two more over the back hips. Collectively, these darts should reduce the circumference of the skirt top to that of your waist plus 5cm(2in).

4. When the fitting is correct, make lapped and top-stitched seams (see Book 1, p.51), lapping the Front section over the two Back sections.

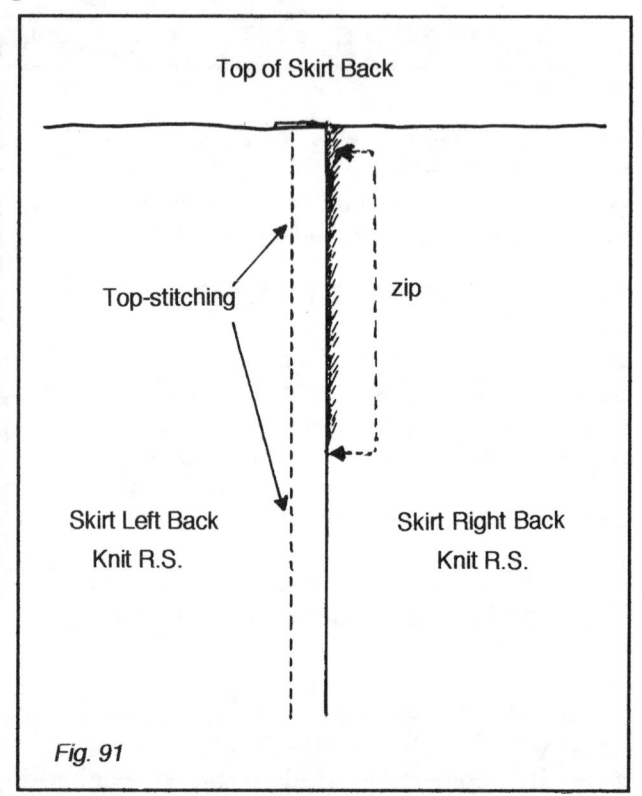

Fig. 91

5. Assemble the lining to fit and place it inside the knitted skirt, wrong sides together. Tack the lining to the knit all around the top and hem it by hand around the zip tapes. Re-check the fitting, remembering that the waist should be 5cm(2in) too big at this stage.

6. Adjust if necessary and mark the correct waistline; then and make and attach the waistband as shown in Chapter 11, easing the skirt in to fit the waistband..

7. Sew the corset hook to the outside of the waistband, at the end of the underlap. Sew the corset eye to the inside of the waistband so that the hook will hold the band snugly into the waistline with the centre-back seamlines meeting exactly.
The corset hook and eye should take all the strain.

8. Attach the Size 2 hooks and bars to hold the overlapping end of the waistband down on the underlapping side. Alternatively, use buttonholed thread loops instead of the bars. There should be no strain on this fastening.

9. Now for the hem! Put on the skirt and get a friend to use a hem-marker to mark a level line all round. See Book 1, p.10, for this and Book 1, pp.65-67 for help with making and sewing the hem. Depending on the texture of your knit, and also the skirt length, you may find that stabilising the hem with lightweight Vilene Fold-a-Band makes it a little too stiff. Consider using a bias-cut strip of fine fusible muslin, or fusible knitted nylon, instead.

10. Wear your skirt with pride!

APPENDIX 1

RECOMMENDED READING

In addition to those books already listed in Book 1 -

"Pressing Matters" by **Erica Thomson**. A machine-knitter's guide to Pressing and Finishing. This controversial subject thoroughly analysed and explained.
Available from Erica Thomson, 77 Institute Rd., Kings Heath, Birmingham B14 7EY.

"Treasury of Machine Knitting Stitches" by **John Allen**, to inspire you to make beautiful fabrics. Published by David and Charles. Available in hard-back and paper-back.

"Cut and Sew for the Machine Knitter" and **"Appliqué for Machine Knitters"** both by **Meg Tillotson**, 6 Court Close, Horfield, Bristol. BS7 0XH.

The Singer Sewing Reference Library Books - particularly the following titles:
"Sewing with Knits" - *"Sewing with an Overlock"* - *"Creative Sewing Ideas"*,
"Sewing Specialty Fabrics" - *"Quilting by Machine"* - *"Decorative Machine Stitching"*
"Sewing Update".
The last-named contains a section entitled "Knit, Cut and Sew" by Susan Guagliumi!
All the SSRL books are beautifully illustrated and are published by Cy DeCosse in Minnesota, U.S.A. They are usually available in the United Kingdom from The Home Workshop Ltd., 1 Hollybush Lane, Burghfield Common, Reading, Berks. RG7 3EL. Tel. 0374-833958.

"The A-Z of the Sewing-Machine", by **Maxine Henry**, published by Batsford

"Power Sewing" and **"More Power Sewing"**, and other books by **Sandra Betzina.**
(ISBN numbers 0-9615614-0-8 and 1-880630-02-8). For Sewing Techniques, Fitting Problems, Pattern adaptation, etc., etc. An absolute mine of information on almost every aspect of clothes-making, well illustrated and explained with good humour and great common sense. Available from the Home Workshop Ltd., as above; also from Rochester Sewing School, Medway Adult Education Centre, Eastgate, Rochester, Kent. ME1 1EW. Tel. 0634-845359.

"The Serger Idea Book" - another **Palmer/Pletsch** book about Overlockers in a larger, more detailed format than "Sewing with Sergers" and "Creative Serging", with plenty of colour photography. Published in Portland, Oregon but available in the U.K. from John Lewis, Oxford St., London W1A 1EX. Tel. 071-629-7711.

"Patchwork: from Beginner to Expert" by **Jenny Bullen**, published by Batsford.
"Machine Quilted Jackets, Vests and Coats", **Nancy Moore**, published by Batsford.
"Machine Quilting and Padded Work", **Anne Hulbert**, published by Batsford.

CUT AND SEW PATTERNS. Two very different designers who are using Cut and Sew methods and are now selling their designs. Write for further information.
In England, **Dominique Nightingale of Brookville Designs**, 39 Quilter Road, Felixstowe, Suffolk. IP11 7JL.
In the U.S.A., **Janet Pace,** PO Box 528, Searcy, AR 72143-0528.

APPENDIX 2

SUPPLIERS

In addition to those already listed in Book 1

VARIOUS FUSIBLE INTERFACINGS.
Abakhan Fabrics, Llanerch-Y-Mor, Coast Road, Mostyn, Clwyd. Tel. 0745-560312. Branches also at Liverpool (051-207-4029), Manchester (061-839-3229) and Birkenhead (051-652-5195)
Bachers Ltd., of 58 High Street, Manchester M4 1EA. Tel. 061-834-0828 or 061-8325260. The stock varies from time to time but this can be a valuable source as Mr. Bacher buys from the garment manufacturers.
Craftswoman Fabrics, 1st. Floor, Unit 1, Kilroot Business Park, Carrickfergus. BT38. Northern Ireland.
Fine Fabrics of Magdalene Lane, Taunton. TA1 1SE. They also have a Training and Meeting Room and run excellent sewing courses, taught by real professionals in their field.

THREADS
Empress Mills Ltd., Empress St., Colne, Lancs. BB8 9HU. Threads for overlocking, dressmaking, hand and machine embroidery, hand and machine quilting, and all kinds of craft work. For free information pack telephone 0282-863181.
Kinross (Supplies), 33b Bridle Rd., Pinner, HA5 2SP. Overlocking and sewing-machine threads. Will match your fabrics. Send 9"x4" s.a.e. for list.

BEAUTIFUL AND UNUSUAL "COUTURE" BUTTONS
Button Treasures, 4 Charterhouse Buildings, Goswell Rd., London EC1M 7AN. Tel.071-608-3745 for details of a fully illustrated catalogue

MISCELLANEOUS EQUIPMENT
The Fiskars Rotary Cutter. Available from branches of John Lewis. If in difficulty contact Fiskars Ltd., Brocastle Ave., Bridgend, Mid. Glam. S31 3YN for stockist list.
"Steam-It" Portable Steamer. Ideal for steaming knitwear, and also for knitted fabrics whenever 'killing' them is not the required effect. Details from Kamalini Trentham, Machine Knitting and Design Centre, High Cross House, Aldenham, Watford, Herts. WD2 8BN. Tel. 0923-859242.
Tailor's Ham Kit. Make your own with the aid of this kit and some clean dry sawdust (not supplied with the kit). Available from Pam Turbett, Liss, Hants.. Tel. 0730-893654 for current price.

INDEX

Adjustments,
    to bust darts, 8-9
    to skirt waistline, 79
Appliqué
    on knits, 103-106
    fabrics for, 103
    to apply a 'leaf', 103-105
Armhole seamline, 31-36
    styles, 31-33
    to neaten, 36
    to bind, 91

Bias binding
    to apply, 86-87
    to cut, 86
    to join, 87
    to make, 86-87
Binding
    armhole seamlines, 91
    as seam finishing, 91
    experimenting with, 91
    Hongkong, 91
    strips for buttonholes, 64-65
    with knitted strip, 91
    with leather or suede, 7, 90
    with machine knitted fabric, 88, 89-90
    with purchased braid, 90
    with ribbon, 91
    with woven fabric, 86-89
Book 1 'Update', 5-7
Braid, purchased, for binding, 90
Bust darts
    creating, 10-11
    to enlarge, 8-9
    to sew, 15
Buttonholes
    bound, 63-66
    distance between, 62
    horizontal, 61
    length of, 62
    machined, 67
    marking position of, 63-64
    vertical, 62
Buttons
    covering kits for, 69
    Dorset, 69
    made from rings, 70
    planning size and position, 60-63
    professionally made, 70
    to make, 69-70
    to sew on, 68-69
Buying
    interfacings, 6
    piping cord, 16
    rotary cutters, 5
    shoulder pads, 44
    zips, 71

Concave shaped darts, 13-14
Convex shaped darts, 13-14
Collars, 20-28
    attaching, 23-24
    cutting, 21
    fitting problems, 20
    'funnel', 24
    making up, 21-23
    planning, 20
    re-styling, 21
    sewing, 21-24
    stabilising, 20
    tailored, 23
Covering-kits for buttons, 69
Covering shoulder pads, 45-46
Cuffs, 40-43
    buttoned, 40-42
    elasticated, 43
    other types, 43
Cut and Sew necklines, 30
Cut and Sew skirt
    lining for, 92
    to make, 107-108
Cutting
    collars, 21
    neck facings, 28-30
    patch pockets, 51
    patterns for linings, 92-93, 95-96
    pockets for side seams, 54-55
    waistbands, 80

Darts
    concave, convex shaped, 13
    how to sew, 13-15
    pressing, 15
Decorative zips, 71, 76-77
Dorset buttons, 69
'Dowager's Hump'
    adjusting patterns for, 11-12

Ease, added to linings, 96
Ease-stitching sleeve head, 34
Elastic
    in cuffs, 43
    in waistbands, 84

Fabrics
    for covering piping cord, 16
    for lining, 92
Faced necklines, 28-30
Faced neck opening for zip, 76-77
Faced openings
    in sleeves, 37-38
    in neckline, zipped, 76-77
Facing bound buttonholes, 66
Fitting problems
    with collars, 20
    with skirts, 79
    with sleeve heads, 31-33
Fold-a-Band, in pockets, 51-52
'Funnel' collars, 24-27
Fusible interfacings, 6

Home-made
    shoulder pads, 47-48
    buttons, 69-70
Hongkong binding
    as edge binding, 7
    as seam finish, 91

Inserting
    sleeves, 35-36
    zips, 72-73
Inset pockets, 50
Interchangeable shoulder pads, 47
Interfacings
    in collars, 21
    in patchwork piecing, 98
    in waistbands
    new, 6
Invisible zips, 71

Jacket, patchwork, quilted, 97-102
    to assemble, 101-102
    to cut, 99-101
    to plan, 98
    to quilt, 101
Jetted pockets, 50

'Knitwear' coats and jackets,
    to line, 95-96

Lapped zip insertion, 73-75
Large bust, pattern adjustment for, 8-11
Leather or suede as binding, 7, 90
Length of sleeve, to check, 36
Lining, 92-96
    cut and sew coats and jackets, 92-95
    cut and sew skirts, 92
    cutting patterns for, 92-93, 95-96
    fabrics for, 92
    'knitwear', 95-96
    patch pockets, 51-52

Log cabin patchwork, 102
Loom elastic in waistbands, 84

Machine embroidery, 106
Machined buttonholes, 67
Machined quilting, 101
Machine-knitted fabric as binding, 88, 89-90
Marking with correcting fluid, 5

Neatening armhole seamline, 36
Necklines, 20-30
    faced, 28-30
    T-shirt, 28
Neck openings, zipped, 76-77

Openings in sleeves, 36-40
    bound, 39-40
    faced, 37-38

Pad-stitching, 27-28
'Pam's Ham' (Tailor's Ham kit), 5, 110
Passap Steam-iron system, 5
Patch pockets, to make and apply, 50-54
Patchwork
    cutting and joining, 99-100
    interfacing knit pieces, 98
    jacket from scraps, 97-102
    planning, 98
    quilting on, 101
Pattern alterations
    for large bust, 8-11
    for rounded shoulders, 11-12
Pattern markings on collars, 22, 27
Pentel Micro-correct pen, 5
Piping
    around continuous edge, 19
    around corners, 18
    suitable fabrics for, 16
    to apply, 17-19
Piping cord,
    buying, 16
    sizes, 16
    to cover, 17
Planning,
    a patchwork jacket,
    collars, 20
    size and position of buttons, 60-63
    'Update', 6, 7
Pockets, 49-59
    applying, 53-57
    checking position of, 49
    general points, 49-50
    inset, 50

jetted, 50
    patch, 50-54
    side seam, 54-57
    welt, 50
    zipped, 57-59
Preparing the fabric, 7
Pressing
    darts, 15
    the fabric, 7
    Prick-stitch, 72
Purchased braid for binding, 90

Quilted patchwork jacket, 97-102
Quilting bar, 101
Quilting, machined, 101

Raglan sleeves, pads for, 46
Re-styling collar patterns, 21
Ribbon as binding, 91
Roll-line in tailored collars, 27-28
Rotary cutters, 5
Rounded shoulders, pattern alterations for, 11-12

Satin-stitch, 105
Seam finishing, with binding, 91
Set-in sleeves, 31-32
    pads for, 44-45
    covering pads for, 45-46
Sewing in shoulder pads, 46-47
Sewing in zips, 72-77
Sewing on buttons, 68-69
Shoulder pads, 44-48
    buying, 44-45
    covering, 45-46
    for see-through fabrics, 47
    home-made, 47-48
    interchangeable, 47
Side-seam pockets, 54-57
Skirt
    Cut and Sew, 107
    with no waistband, 84
    without openings, 84-85
Skirt waistbands,
    to measure, fit and apply, 78-85
Skirt waistline, to adjust, 79
Sleeve-head, to prepare, 35
Sleeve-head pads (Vilene), 6
Sleeve
    armhole seamline, 31-36
    armhole styles, 31-33
    checking length of, 36
    cuffs, 40-43
    inserting into armhole, 35-36
    openings, 36-40
    preparing sleeve-head, 35
    supporting top of, 48

Stabilising
    by use of interfacing fabrics, 6
    by using edge tape, 6
    collars, 20

Stay-stitching neck seamline, 24
Steaming knitted fabric, 7
'Steam-It' steaming system, 7, 110
Suede as binding, 7

Tailored collars, 23
    interfacing and shaping, 27
Tailor's Ham Kit, 5, 110
Tension swatch, 6
T-shirt neckline, 28
Typists correcting fluid, 5

Updating 'Book 1', 5-6

Vilene
    Edge tape, 6
    fusible interfacings, 6
    Sleeve heads, 6
    Stitch'n'Tear, use in appliqué, 104-105
Visible zip insertion, 76-77

Waistbands
    curved petersham, 83
    determining position of, 78-80
    elastic, 84
    overlap, underlap, 82
    to apply, 80-83
    to cut, 80
    to finish ends of, 82
    to fit, 78
    to interface, 80-81
    to mark, 81
Waist seamline, to adjust, 78-80
Welt pockets, 50
Woven fabrics, binding with, 86-89
Wundaweb, use in bound buttonholes, 64

Zipped openings, 76-77
Zipped pockets, 57-59
Zips
    in faced openings, 76-77
    lapped application, 73-75
    to buy, 71
    to sew in, 72-77
    visible application, 76-77